Forever Farang

FOREVER FARANG

Ashley Krepps

Contents

Dedication

THANK you, Rotary International, for making this experience possible. A special thanks to my Youth Exchange Officers, Dave and Bill, who worked so hard to make sure that I would be prepared for my exchange year. Thanks to my host parents for allowing me into their lives and treating me like a part of their family. To Mom and Dad, thank you for being incredibly supportive and open-minded toward an amazing opportunity that has changed my life forever.

Dedication

แสดงความขอบคุณ Rotary ที่ให้สาลี่ได้มีโอกาสไปอยู่ที่นครพนม
และขอแสดงความขอบคุณในน้ำใจไมตรีต่อครอบครัวที่นครพนมด้วยค่ะ
ที่ให้ความรักและคำแนะนำให้แก่สาลี่ และได้สอนให้สาลี่พูดและเขียนภาษาไทย
ให้สาลี่ได้ประสบการณ์ดีๆที่น่าประทับใจมากๆ   สาลี่คิดถึงทุกๆท่านมากๆค่ะ
ถ้ามีโอกาสเราคงจะได้พบกันอีกน่ะค่ะ

1

THE BEGINNING OF AN ADVENTURE

⁙

THIS morning was the start of an ordinary day at Ottawa Township High School. My good friend, Veronica, turned to me in homeroom, "Ashley, there's a meeting that I want to go to during first hour. Will you go with me?"

"What's it about?"

"It's about being a foreign exchange student. Some people from the Rotary club are speaking. It's something I think I really want to do. You remember how much fun we had on our trip to France last year. Wouldn't it be terrific to travel for a whole year?" Veronica and I were close, having been in French class together for four years, as well as visiting France with our teacher during spring break.

I had a test in my first period class for which I had not adequately prepared, so it took me all of thirty seconds to decide to accompany her. There were only a half dozen other students there, most of whom we knew. The speaker discussed the program briefly, showed some pictures of past exchange students, and told some stories about their experiences. I have always loved to travel and try new things, so I was hooked. The Rotary members gave us paperwork to fill out—including essays to complete—and set up a follow-up meeting for us and our parents.

At the beginning of my senior year of high school, I couldn't imagine that I would become a "super senior," repeating the academic year and being abroad on a student visa or that I would be spending that year in a country I had only heard about from history and geography classes. I was a fairly good student throughout high school, getting As and Bs in most of my classes, but I felt like I was still a kid, nonetheless.

We moved on to the interview process, which was held the next week. The interviews, conducted in the evening by two local Rotary clubs, were held in the office of a local architect who also was a Rotarian. I was nervous as I awaited my turn to be called. The students were interviewed first—Veronica, Derek, Jessica, and I—then the parents were asked to join midway through their child's interview to answer a few questions. Derek and Jessica both had family members who were active in Ottawa Noon Rotary club. During the first meeting, we learned that the Ottawa Noon and the Marseilles Rotary clubs would each choose just one student. I had a fifty-percent chance.

I was nervous in the waiting area. When it was my turn to be interviewed, I was told to sit at the head of the conference room table. There were five other people in the room. Four were at the table, two seated on each side. There was, also, a mean-looking guy sitting in the back corner of the room. I had met two of the men at earlier meetings, and I believe they are Rotarians. Carlee, a year ahead of me in school and a former exchange student to Brazil, was sitting at the table on my far right. After a few preliminary questions, the man sitting to my near right asked me to name my greatest personal weakness. I wracked my brain to think of an answer as quickly as possible but also come up with one that wouldn't make me look like a poor candidate for an exchange program. Everyone was staring silently at me; finally, I said something about being a poor impromptu speaker when not given adequate time to prepare. The man to my far left commented about my being politically correct, then everyone laughed, and I felt a little more at ease. For the rest of the interview, I was asked a series of hypothetical questions: "What would you do if you were served an unfamiliar dish, such as dog?" "What would you do if you came home to find your maid going through your luggage?" I answered them all honestly and tried to elaborate as much as was needed.

The interview was over in 20 minutes, and I did what any high school girl would do; I immediately called my closest friend in the program and talked through every detail of our interviews. Veronica and I discussed our answers to the similar questions we were given and then focused on each interviewer's reaction. We were both reassured by Carlee's presence but were taken aback by the unfamiliar "mean-looking guy in the corner," as we referred to him from then on. That man hardly ever looked up from his notebook, asked only a few pointed questions, and never smiled.

My eighteenth birthday was a week or so later. As I was getting ready for the homecoming dance I was planning to attend that evening, I received a phone call from a Rotarian, who introduced himself as Bill, informing me that I had been chosen to be sponsored by the Marseilles Rotary club and that Jessica was chosen by the Ottawa Noon Rotary club. After briefing me on the next steps I needed to take, he asked me if I had any questions. My only question was concerning Veronica and Derek. I knew Veronica wanted this a lot more than I did, and I didn't see how I could accept, knowing that I bumped her out of the slot. He told me not to worry, that they had both interviewed well, and that the Rotary clubs were trying to do something for them, but he couldn't make any promises. Eventually, Ottawa Noon Rotary sponsored Derek as well, and the Streator Rotary club sponsored Veronica. I thanked him, yelled the news to my mom, and then speed-dialed my best friend, who was really excited for me and asked me how my parents felt. Then I realized that I needed to hang up and call my dad.

At our next meeting, we received a list of hosting countries and were asked to rank them, 1 through 40, in the order of our preference. We were informed that most students are sent to one of their top 10 choices, but they needed 40 anyway. The sheet also specified that some countries, mostly European, would not take any student who was, at the start of the exchange year, older than 18 and a half. Veronica and I were both very upset because we initially believed that we would only be able to choose from six countries. As it turned out, there were only about 10 countries that we could not go to. Choosing my countries was the hardest decision I had to make; I wanted to go everywhere, preferably to a country whose citizens did not speak English as their first language. My top three choices were India, Japan, and Iceland.

After completing the application, I was told that I would be interviewed at the district level, which was held at a hospital in Sterling, Illinois. This would be a less stressful interview because I already had a sponsoring Rotary club. In fact, it was a good experience. While there, I met Dave, District 6420 Youth Exchange Officer (YEO), as well as all of the inbound exchange students from District 6420. Probably because I was so nervous, I really don't remember a lot about the interview.

One question that I was asked was, "You could be going to a country where you will be old enough to drink alcohol. What will you say if you are offered a drink?"

I felt strongly about this issue and said (rather forcefully), "I know that it is illegal for people who are my age to drink. But many still drink. The fact that I do not drink has nothing to do with legalities."

The lady smiled and slowly said, "Or . . . you could say . . . that drinking is against the rules . . . of Rotary Youth Exchange?"

I returned the smile and said, "That, too!" Everyone laughed.

I was actually going to be a foreign exchange student! I never imagined an opportunity like this could happen to me. I never thought of myself as leading a very exciting life. I live in a small residential development in Ottawa, Illinois. Ottawa has a population of about 18,000 people and is located about 80 miles southwest of Chicago. I live at home with my parents and my dog, Ladybug. My brother, Collin, who is five years older than me, lives in Catonsville, Maryland, close to the city of Baltimore.

I have not always lived in Illinois. Soon after I was born, my parents moved from our home in Tallahassee, Florida, to Ottawa, Illinois, due to my dad's promotion within his company. My dad works as an Administrative Manager for US Silica Company, a facility that mines and processes industrial silica, and my mom owns and operates a local children's daycare center.

My parents are originally from Pennsylvania, and both of them have a lot of relatives in the eastern part of the USA, which is why I chose to attend college there. Because this was my senior year of high school, I was in the final college selection process—then this whirlwind experience started.

The following two months went by slowly. Everyone I knew seemed to have heard that I was going on exchange, but they couldn't seem to understand that I did not know where I was going. After being accepted as an outbound exchange student, I began attending the Marseilles Rotary club meetings. There I met Bill, my YEO, who was both excited for me and anxious to help in any way necessary. After my first lunch meeting, I drove back to school and ran straight to Veronica. "You will never guess who my YEO is! Remember in the interview that mean-looking guy in the corner?" First impressions are often misleading because I now know that Bill is one of the nicest people I've ever met. He and the other Marseilles Rotarians would do so much for me until I would leave for the exchange year and in the months following my return. I then informed Veronica about everything that Bill and I had talked about at the meeting, and I promised her that I would ask Bill if she could attend a Marseilles Rotary meeting sometime. During the next nine months, I attended as many Rotary club meetings as possible. I came to know all of the members of my sponsoring club because the Marseilles Rotary does not have a large number of members. In addition, I was invited to attend Ottawa Sunrise Rotary, which is also small, and discovered that I knew several of its members. Ottawa Noon Rotary is larger, and, although everyone seemed to know me, I didn't get to know all of them as well as I wanted. Of the three clubs that I came to know, Ottawa Noon definitely had the best food!

Finally, just after the New Year's holiday, my mom called me at my brother's house in Maryland, whom I was visiting, and told me that I needed to call Dave to find out my country. I quickly hung up and anxiously returned Dave's call. Instead of ending my anticipation quickly, he made me guess where I thought I was going and hinted at it by asking if I liked elephants. After incorrectly guessing, he made me wait no longer and told me my country: Thailand! After thanking him, I quickly called Mom back and asked her two questions: "How exciting is that?" and, "Where is Thailand, anyway?" Shortly thereafter, I learned that Veronica, to whom I give credit for getting me interested in the exchange program, would be spending her year in Taiwan. She would return to America a year later speaking Chinese.

I was assigned to Nakhon Phanom, located in northeastern Thailand. Meaning "City of Mountains," the name was given to the city by King Rama I in the eighteenth century, although it has been a city for several thousand years. Nakhon Phanom has a population of less than 35,000 and is situated on the banks of the Mekong River, bordering Laos. I would likely be the only exchange student assigned there because the city is not that large, forcing me to learn the Thai language more quickly.

Once school resumed after Christmas break, I was still bubbling over with the excitement of going abroad. My parents were trying to find someone who spoke Thai to help me start to learn the language, and Bill was asking around as well. They found someone in Marseilles! That was a surprise because Marseilles has a population of less than 5,000. Oni (pronounced ON-ee) had recently arrived in America and was working in a Thai restaurant. I would meet with her weekly until my departure.

I was telling everyone about my assigned country because even my friends who knew that I was going on exchange still did not know that I would be going to Thailand. One day, one of my teachers was talking about graduation day coming soon and stated that we should be thinking about our futures. "What are your plans after graduation?" he asked the class. I raised my hand and said, "I'm going to be a foreign exchange student. I will be spending the next year in Thailand." He responded with one word: "What?" He was totally blown away. I was so proud.

District Informational Meeting

During the second weekend in March, District 6420 conducted an informational session for all outbound students and their parents. I was really looking forward to this meeting. During this weekend, we would get to meet everyone else from the district that was going on youth exchange, as well as meet all of the current inbound students. I hoped there was an inbound student from Thailand.

Dave conducted most of the meeting, with many guest speakers for various topics. It was all really good information, helping to ease a lot of the fears and concerns of the parents. I learned some exchange program terminology that would become a part of my vocabulary.

Outbound　　Students who are going to leave their home countries to go on youth exchange.

Inbound　　Students who are on exchange in a foreign country.

Rebound　　Students who have returned to their home countries from youth exchange.

Yo-yo　　Students going on a second year of youth exchange.

We were also given our navy blue Rotary blazers at this meeting. I had already been given a number of pins to decorate it, and I had been busy making personal pins to exchange with the other students. One of the students I met at this meeting was Sadapod, an inbound from Thailand. It was fun practicing the little bit of the Thai language I had studied.

The meeting started on Friday evening, beginning with a presentation by the travel agency selected by Rotary. After that, we tried on our blazers. I had already made up my mind that I would try to return home with my blazer completely covered with memories.

Dave really emphasized the importance of the rules of international youth exchange. They were known to outbound students as the four Ds:

No Drinking;
No Driving;
No Dating;
No Drugs.

There is also an unwritten fifth D, "No Disfigurement", refer-ring to tattoos, body piercing, hair coloring, and other forms of altered personal appearance. Breaking any of these four Ds would result in punishment provided by the hosting Rotary club in the host country. Some countries' Rotary clubs strictly enforce these rules; others, not so much. For example, drinking alcoholic bever-ages could be cause for being sent home in some cases, while, in other countries, drinking is socially accepted. I didn't drink or do drugs anyway, so I intended to make the most of this year without breaking the rules.

This was my first encounter with other outbound students and with some of the inbound exchange students, as well. I had met several inbounds at my district interview. There were a lot of one-hour and two-hour meeting sessions, and most of the informa-tion went over my head, but my parents were feverishly writing everything down. One session was about culture shock and reverse culture shock. At the time, I didn't really understand just how much this would affect me. All in all, this was very good training, and, at the end, we were given a challenge. We were to introduce ourselves at the Rotary District Conference in April—in our target language! I was really glad that we had found a Thai tutor.

Rotary District (6420) Conference, Rockford, Illinois

This was a very boring day. We spent the entire day in a hotel lounge, while the Rotarians were in various meetings. We prac-ticed for a flag ceremony that we would perform at the banquet on Saturday evening. There were some interesting presentations by a few of the inbound students, and it was a lot of fun hanging out with them.

My introduction in Thai went okay. I was more nervous about

speaking in English because no one would be able to know if my Thai was correct. District 6420 had about 20 outbound exchange students, and we all did well on the introductions. I had written out my speech just in case, but I had it memorized. Will, an outbound to Germany, had written a lengthy introduction. No one in the audience was quite prepared for it. As he read on and on in German, a few murmurs could be heard in the room. As the murmurs became louder and louder, Will stopped reading his speech, looked up, and announced, "Look, I spent a lot of time preparing this, and I'm going to read it!" The room broke into laughter and applause. He obviously left the next outbound with a hard act to follow.

I was now really looking forward to the Central States conference in mid-July, held on the campus of Calvin College in Grand Rapids, Michigan. It is a three-day meeting for all outbound, inbound, and rebound students of the many districts within the Central States region. Some yo-yos would be there, as well.

On May 14th, I received the following e-mail from Prapart Sudhipongpracha:

To: Inbound Exchange Student Ashley Krepps, District 6420: USA-- Illinois

Dear Ashley,

(Please reply to this e-mail so that we know you have received it. Thanks!)

Welcome to the Rotary District 3340 Youth Exchange Program, and congratulations on being accepted for this wonderful opportunity. I know you must be excited and nervous about your upcoming year in Thailand, and anxious to know what your host country and city will be and everything else about your exchange. So let me provide you with some information.

My name is Prapart Sudhipongpracha, friends in Rotary Youth Exchange call me as Peter but you may call me as Prapart when you are in Thailand. I am the Youth Exchange Chairman for District 3340, which is located on the northeastern part of Thailand and eastern sea coast area. The major cities in the Northeast are Korat (Nakhon Ratchasima), Khon Kaen, Udon Thani and Ubon Ratchathani. The major cities in the Eastern Sea Coast are: Chon Buri, Pattaya, Rayong and Chantha Buri.

The Northeast of Thailand, commonly referred to as I-san (pronounced E-san), is made up of nineteen provinces: Amnat Charoen, Buri Ram,

Chaiyaphum, Kalasin, Khon Kaen, Loei, Maha Sarakham, Mukdahan, Nakhon Ratchasima (Korat or Khorat), Nakhon Phanom, Nong Bua Lamphu, Nong Khai, Roi Et, Sakon Nakhon, Si Sa Ket, Surin Ubon Ratchathani, Udon Thani and Yasothon.

The word I-san denotes prosperity and vastness, which is appropriate considering that the Northeast covers a total area of more than 170,000 sq.kms., or roughly one-third of the entire country. It borders on Laos and Cambodia to the east. The Northeast's ancient traditions and customs are still reflected in fairs and festivals found nowhere else in the country. These included the colorful Bun Bang Fai (rocket festival), the Candle Procession and the Was Castle Festival.

Thailand's Eastern sea coast, from Chon Buri, Si Racha, Pattaya, Rayong, Chantha Buri on the way to Trat is among the most attractive and complete seaside destinations. Nature has endowed the area with waterfalls and mountains, beaches and islands, and man has added some facilities and conveniences to make it a truly beautiful and enjoyable destination area. The Eastern coastal region is also rich in archaeological and historical terms.

Our climate is tropical with average temperature of 28 C or 82.4 F. The lowest, in December and January, is around 25 C or 77 F and the highest, in April, is 39 C or 102.2 F.

You have been placed in **Muang Nakhon Phanom City, Nakhon Phanom Province** on the **Northeast** and will be hosted by the **Rotary Club of Khong River-Nakhon Phanom.** Would you please ensure having Insurance cover as required by Rotary International. If you need assistance, talk to your Rotary Youth Exchange Chairman in your District. The Guarantee Form, School Acceptance and documents that you need for your visa application have been sent to your District Chairman.

We require our students to arrive **between August 1 thru 5, if it's possible**. You will be greeted by host family, counselor and district committee members on your arrival to BKK. It is also important that we receive word of your travel schedule as soon as it is known. Please wear your Rotary Blazer, you won't be the only student traveling at this time of year. Use common sense while traveling. Problems do arise while traveling, be prepared to deal with them. When in doubt, spend the night in the airport. Please mark your bags with the name and address of your first host family. If your bags get lost, you won't want them to be sent back home. Once you have arrived, our Inbound Coordinator will be responsible for you. You are one of a class of more than *FORTY (40)* students, approximately, from many countries/districts whom arrive Thailand on 1- 5 August 2006 like you but at that time there are *FIVE (5)* inbound students from the southern-hemisphere countries whom arrived Thailand since January 2006.

Me and Inbound Chairman will be briefing you and your host family at your host city after your arrival to Thailand 4-6 weeks.

I have something very important to share with you. Recently, our District 3340 Youth Exchange program was named the **Outstanding Rotary Youth Exchange District in Thailand** for the year 2006. This is a great honor for us, and also a wonderful opportunity for you and all of our other inbound students to help us maintain our standard of excellence for many years to come. If you provide a good experience for your host family, your host club, and your school, then they will want to continue to participate in Rotary Youth Exchange next year and the year after that, and our program will continue to be one that others will respect. So that is your challenge. I'm sure you can succeed.

The better your knowledge of Thailand when you arrive, the more successful you are likely to be. Spend whatever time you can, between now and your departure, learning as much of our culture and tradition as possible. It will help you greatly from the moment you arrive. If you have any questions, I would encourage you to ask me.

You are about to embark on a wonderful journey, an adventure of a lifetime, and we are happy to be part of that. I look forward to meeting you in a few months time and officially welcoming you to Rotary District 3340.

(Please remember to reply to this e-mail so that we know you have received it. Thanks!)

Warmly,

Prapart "Peter" Sudhipongpracha, PDG, Major Donor
Co-Chair and Overseas Correspondent
District 3340 Rotary Youth Exchange Programme
Thaweephon Restaurant
376-380 Phromaraj Road
Muang Ubon City
Ubon Ratchathani Province 34000
THAILAND

Then on July 4th, I received the following e-mail from Prapart Sudhipongpracha about my arrival:

Dear the Newies,

Your travel itineraries will be forwarded to your host families. I guaranteed that you will be seen by your host families on your arrival to the BKK at your schedule. There will be also the District 3340 committee members waiting for you at the airport! **EXCEPT for ONES** who have not sent me the itineraries!

Below is the updated schedule as of today: (Any incorrect please inform).

Prapart "Peter" Sudhipongpracha, PDG, Major Donor
Chairman and Overseas Correspondent
District 3340 Rotary Youth Exchange Programme
Thaweephon Restaurant
376-380 Phromaraj RoadMuang Ubon City
Ubon Ratchathani Province 34000
THAILAND

I immediately noticed that the names on Prapart's list were alphabetized by first name. Although this was a minor difference from U.S. practices, it was just one of many differences that I would encounter in Thailand. I had a lot to look forward to.

2

FINAL PREPARATIONS

❦

Central States Youth Exchange Conference, Grand Rapids, Michigan (July 13-16, 2006)

IMAGINE 3,000 people coming together on a college campus for an exciting weekend, all having the same focus. We wore color-coded wristbands and name tags with our country printed in large letters. A green wristband meant "outbound," blue meant "inbound," and red meant "rebound." I could quickly glance at the wristband and then the name tag and determine, "Ah, outbound to Switzerland," or "Inbound from India." It was really easy to start a conversation with someone.

The Central States Conference includes 17 Rotary districts in Wisconsin, Illinois, Indiana, Michigan, North Dakota, part of Minnesota, and southern Ontario, Canada. We had small meetings for those with specific countries or subject matter and general sessions that filled the auditorium to overflowing.

A psychologist gave a presentation at one of the meetings on culture shock and reverse culture shock. I recognized some of the subject matter in the presentation from a similar session in Rock Falls back in March. Still I couldn't imagine what culture shock would feel like.

One of the speakers read, *The Road Not Taken,* by Robert Frost. I remembered studying this poem in my high school literature class, but it had no special meaning at the time. Now, because I had chosen to follow a road less traveled, I found new meaning in the lines. We watched portions of a recorded speech by a former Rotary President, in which he said, "If all the world's boys and girls participated in a youth exchange program, there would be no war." I knew this coming year would have a tremendous effect on my life.

One of the meetings was focused on Thailand. The meeting included all Thai inbound students, as well as us outbounds and the rebounds. We were able to ask questions and hear of the experiences of the students who had just returned from Thailand. We learned how to *wai* and the proper way to pray to Buddha from the Thai inbounds. *Wai*ing is done by placing ones hands together in a prayer-like fashion and bowing. The correct way to *wai* is to bow until the nose touches the thumbs. The rebound students were very excited about their experiences, but it was clear that most had broken the "D" rules many times. I sat next to Jennifer, who was from a small town in west central Illinois. We chatted a bit, neither of us knowing that we would become really close during the coming year. I asked if her parents were here. She said that her dad was but not her mom. She went on to say that her parents were having some difficulties and that her mom had moved out of their house.

Although I didn't learn about it until later, my dad and Jennifer's dad were also sitting next to each other. As they were introducing themselves and talking, Jennifer's dad stated that he and his wife were divorcing. At the time it was no big deal to me. Later, I would see how this situation and clear lack of communication by her family would negatively affect Jennifer.

I also met Kelly, Jeff, Samantha, and Jason. Kelly was only 16 and had just finished her sophomore year of high school in Grand Rapids, Michigan, but seemed more mature than her years. Jason, from Chatham, Illinois, was my age and was a yo-yo, having gone on Rotary Youth Exchange to the Czech Republic a few years earlier. Samantha and Jeff were both from Canada. We would become almost like a family in the coming year.

Grand Rapids was great but was over so quickly. All in all, it was very informative and a lot of fun. I met a lot of people and made a ton of new friends. District 6420 had prepared us well for the upcoming exchange year, and the Central States conference was a great way to top it off. Just think, I would be returning to the Grand Rapids conference next year as a rebound. I got excited just thinking about it. Great experience, great preparation. I was ready! It was hard to believe that in just two more weeks I would be on my way to Thailand.

THE ROAD NOT TAKEN

By Robert Frost

Two roads diverged in a yellow wood,
And sorry I could not travel both
And be one traveler, long I stood
And looked down one as far as I could
To where it bent in the undergrowth;

Then took the other, just as fair,
And having perhaps the better claim,
Because it was grassy and wanted wear;
Though as for that the passing there
Had worn them really about the same,

And both that morning equally lay
In leaves no step had trodden black.
Oh, I kept the first for another day!
Yet knowing how way leads on to way,
I doubted if I should ever come back.

I shall be telling this with a sigh
Somewhere ages and ages hence:
Two roads diverged in a wood, and I-
I took the one less traveled by,
And that has made all the difference.

August 2, 2006

I had two suitcases and a carry-on to pack my entire life into. I designated the smaller of the two suitcases for gifts only, thinking that upon my return I would have an entire empty suitcase to fill with souvenirs and presents for people at home. My larger suitcase lay empty in the living room with the "bare minimum" of my life scattered all over the floor, waiting to be packed. The worst two words any exchange student could hear when trying to shove his or her entire life into every open crack of a suitcase: "weight limit." Around 2:00 a.m., I went to bed.

3

FINALLY ON MY WAY

August 3, 2006

WE got up before 8:00 a.m. because my dad was nervous about leaving on time. We left our house at about 8:30 and headed for Chicago's O'Hare Airport. Despite the anxiety, we arrived in plenty of time. The waiting was hard because I wanted to get going. Before long, I spotted a blue blazer. Another exchange student on the same flight! We quickly became reacquainted with Kelly and her parents. Then Jennifer appeared, and then Jason. In all, there were about 10 students from Central States who were going to various countries in Asia, so I knew it was going to be a fun trip.

The flight was incredibly long. I think I was too excited because I couldn't sleep at all; I watched five movies to help pass the time. Still, the 13 hours from Chicago to Seoul, South Korea, was a long time to sit.

The layover in South Korea was a lot of fun. I got to know the other foreign exchange students better, and we met up with about 10 more from other parts of the world who would join us on the flight from Seoul to Bangkok. During our layover, there was some sort of parade. Korean men walked down the right side of the main walkway in long cloaks and hats. Two men in the front were beating drums. They walked all the way down the corridor and then turned around and went back. No one in our group had a clue what was going on. We also saw a man on stilts, dressed as a clown, walking through the terminal. I never would have imagined that the layover would be so eventful.

The service on Korean Airlines was great. On one of the flights, we were served seaweed soup. It was really good! I don't see why it isn't served in the states. Seaweed-flavored potato chips, I found out later, are also quite tasty.

When our flight arrived at the Bangkok airport, I realized that it had been more than 24 hours since we left Chicago, and I had slept for only about one hour. When we landed, everyone was excited about getting off the plane and meeting their host families. Jennifer got really air sick on this flight, so I stayed behind with her while everyone else ran ahead. Getting through customs was really confusing, but the airport employees helped by pointing us in the right direction. Because Jennifer was not feeling well, we were really late to baggage claim, but Prapart, who is the Youth Exchange Officer for our Rotary district in Thailand, was okay with it. He gave Jennifer some "nose crack," an exchange student nickname for an inhalant medicine containing eucalyptus oil, menthol, camphor, and borneol. This liquid medicine seems to be a cure-all for Thais. Surprisingly enough, it works quite well. Jennifer seemed to feel better immediately.

P'Nan, my eldest host sister, who works and resides in Bangkok, and P'Kip, a good friend of P'Nan, who was introduced to me as my host brother, met me with a sign that read, "Ashely." Even though she slightly misspelled my name, I immediately learned that P'Nan is fluent in English, which would help me a lot. They gave me a present, which I opened later. It was a notebook and colored pens to be used to begin documenting my experience. They were very excited to meet me and rushed me out of the airport. The drive to P'Nan's apartment was quick. It wasn't that she lived close to the airport, but that P'Kip drove so fast. I had heard that people in Thailand drive crazily, but I never expected it to be that crazy. At one point, I glanced at the speedometer and saw that we were going 140 kph, which is faster than 87 mph, and we were on a very winding road.

P'Nan's apartment was similar to an American one bedroom/

one bathroom apartment, but there were a few differences that I noticed immediately. In the corner of the living room, there was a shrine with a small Buddha statue that had food and water sitting in front of it. The room was a decent size and had a TV against one wall and posters on the others. Instead of a bathtub in the lavatory, the showerhead was above an empty bathroom floor sloped toward a drain. There was a Western style toilet in the bathroom, but toilet paper was replaced by a short hose with a spray nozzle for personal cleaning. The kitchen was in a nook outside the bathroom and consisted of a mini-fridge, microwave, and sink. P'Nan explained to me that I would be staying at her apartment in Bangkok for a few days before traveling to Nakhon Phanom, where I would be residing for the remainder of my exchange.

After spending the past 24 hours traveling, I was very anxious to get to sleep, as were my host siblings who had to stay up until 3:00 a.m. to get me. P'Nan asked me if I minded if P'Kip slept in her room with us, which I did not. P'Kip then started rolling out a thick blanket on the floor at the foot of our bed. P'Nan's bed was a double bed mattress that was placed on the floor. She had a bunch of small pillows atop the light sheet and comforter on the bed, which she began arranging into a line down the middle of the bed in an effort to divide the bed into two sections.

I got settled in and was almost asleep when I realized that I had forgotten to make my mandatory call home to let my parents know that I had arrived safely. We spent about 20 minutes trying to figure out how to call long distance because P'Nan said that a code was needed in order to make the call. Because I didn't have a clue about the "code," we just called Prapart and asked him how to do it. He said it was a "code area." Aha! As it turned out, the "code" P'Nan wanted was my area code. This would be the first of many miscommunication stories.

In the Thai language, there are two words to distinguish between the relative ages of siblings. *P'* means an older sibling and *Neung* means a younger sibling. Since Nan is older than I, it is proper for me to refer to her as P'Nan, translating to, "my older sister, Nan." Similarly, when I arrived in my hometown of Nakhon

Phanom, I learned that I had a younger sister, Noo, whom I would call NeungNoo.

Thai people are very open and welcoming individuals. They become "family" with their close friends and distant relatives. Most children use the prefix P' for any older kid that they feel close to or look up to. Many of my friends at school who were in lower grades would refer to me as P'Salee, as the Thai nickname given to me was Salee (pronounced sa-LEE). Just as some sounds in Asian languages are difficult for Westerners to pronounce, Asians would also struggle with, and mispronounce, many American names. Solution? Simply rename the students. Salee was the nickname given to me when I first arrived in Thailand. Whenever a child is born in Thailand, either its parents will give the baby a nickname or they will take the child to a temple and a monk will select a name. Most commonly given nicknames are types of fruit or animals. The reason for the nickname is based on a superstition that using the name of a baby will draw the attention of evil spirits, especially when it is said that the baby is cute or beautiful. These nicknames are given to "fool" the bad spirits and protect the children. Real names are used on official documents and can be used by adults, but nicknames are the most common names used. I was given a Thai name, Anchalee, meaning respect. Anchalee was the name embroidered on my school uniforms; just about everyone however, referred to me by my nickname, Salee, which is a sweet Chinese fruit, similar to an apple or pear.

August 6, 2006

I got up early, while P'Nan slept in till about 10:00 a.m. We drove to P'Neui's house, another sister, and took her and P'Kip to lunch. This was only about one hour after I had eaten breakfast. After that, we were going to look at the market; it was Saturday, and there is no market on Saturdays, so we ate dessert instead. I think I ate a meal every hour or so. Thai people eat so much; I don't know how they can do it! One time, P'Nan asked me if I was hungry, and I said, "No," and that I was really full. She told me she was only going to give me a little bit because I was not hungry. The "little bit" that she gave me covered my whole plate! I was afraid to see what a lot would be.

We spent Sunday going to a Chinese temple and then to a beach. It was a lot of fun but very tiring. The Chinese temple was huge and had gold leaf on every part of the building. There were Chinese lanterns strung throughout the huge courtyard in front of the temple. Chinese women were standing around talking, and children were running all over laughing and playing games. We walked inside the building, and it looked even bigger inside than I expected. I followed P'Nan and P'Neui around, finally ending up in front of a statue of Buddha.

We went back to P'Neui's house, and I took a nap. P'Nan said that I was calling to someone in my sleep. I had never talked in my sleep before, at least not that I knew of.

I was supposed to go to Nakhon Phanom on Sunday, when they were going to have a big party for me, but P'Nan said that I could stay in Bangkok until Monday. I was glad she was going to let me stay a little bit longer. I was eager to see the rest of my host family, but I felt like I was getting attached to P'Nan, P'Kip, and P'Neui. I didn't want to leave. P'Nan took me shopping, and I really fell in love with the market. There were so many things for sale that I had never seen before, and everything was so inexpensive. I found a pair of shorts that I thought looked really cute and were a really good price. When I asked P'Nan's opinion, she nodded in agreement. A bit later, however, when she sensed that I was seriously considering buying them, she quietly said, "If you want to buy them to wear around the house, it's okay, but you can't wear them out in public." I was really surprised. They weren't really that short. I didn't realize that exposing the lower one third of my thigh was unacceptable. I declined to make the purchase. I was beginning to realize that I had a lot to learn about what was acceptable and what was not.

4

ARRIVING IN NAKHON PHANOM

August 8, 2006

P'NAN'S friend was going to Nakhon Phanom on the same flight as me, so she took care of me. I found out later that she was a Rotarian from my hosting club (as were P'Nan and another host sister, whom I have yet to meet), so I think it is a Rotary rule that someone had to escort me to my new home in Nakhon Phanom. It was a one-hour flight, and I slept. When I got into the airport, there were about 10 people waiting for me. They said that six of my schoolmates wanted to come, but it was too late for them to stay out. Late? I arrived at 8:30 p.m.!

When I got to my home in Nakhon Phanom, I was so excited to meet my family! I saw everyone except my mother, who was already asleep. I had been practicing how to introduce myself, along with the proper cultural gestures, ever since I found out my hosting country, although I felt as though I really hadn't learned that much. I really practiced the *wai*, which is used in place of our Western handshake because I wanted to make a polite first impression. The correct way to *wai* is to bow until the nose touches the thumbs. Many children become sloppy over time and only bow their head until their nose touches their fingertips. To be extra respectful, mainly when *wai*ing a monk or the image of Buddha, a person's thumbs should touch between their eyebrows, but that's really formal.

31

When we got out of the car, I *waied*, and said, "*Sa-wat-dee ka*," "Hello" in Thai. Everyone started talking in what was probably a normal speed, but it seemed really fast to me. I was listening as intently as I could to try to pick out a few words that I could understand, but everything in the conversation sounded incredibly foreign to me. My sister must have seen the puzzled look on my face because she turned to me to translate and explained that, "Our family is Vietnamese, not Thai." Surprise! She said that the family speaks Vietnamese mostly and really only speaks Thai whenever they are speaking to someone who isn't Vietnamese. During my preparations for my exchange year, Dad once mentioned that my host family might be bilingual. Well, he was right, but I bet he didn't mean like this!

My first host family was amazing! They own an electronics store, which is located in the front of their house. The access to their living quarters was through the store. The living quarters were fabulous! Even at first glance, it was obvious that this family was well off. They had large, oversized leather pieces of furniture, a beautiful wooden dining room table, a wooden staircase, and everything else was marble-topped. The sitting area upstairs had huge portraits of the family members on all the walls except one, which was completely covered in huge mirrors, running together. It reminded me of the studio where I took dance lessons when I was younger. There were three bedrooms and a hallway that led to a balcony, overlooking the store.

My first host family seemed huge to me. Paw, the Thai name for dad, was a very happy and welcoming person. He sat every day in the front of the store helping customers when they came in and watched TV or visited with different people when business was slow. He was always eager to speak English with me, although his vocabulary was not that developed. Mae, my Thai host mom, was very nice, though not as open-hearted as Paw. She never spoke in English to me and usually did not go out of her way to visit with me, focusing most of her attention on helping Paw with the store and keeping the household running smoothly.

Baa Thao was the family member I became closest to. In

Vietnamese, *Baa* means "father's older sister." When I tried to talk about Baa Thao to my second host mom, she couldn't figure out what the name meant because she spoke only Thai. Baa Thao was Paw's older sister and came to live with Paw and Mae when they came to Thailand from Vietnam. Baa Thao never married, although she did have an incredible love story that dissolved when she found out that she would not be able to have any children of her own. She did not want to burden her boyfriend by prohibiting him from having a family. I did not fully understand the extent of their connection until months into my exchange, when a man came to visit from a faraway province. Baa Thao told me that he visits at least once a year. As soon as he arrived, it was as if they had been happily married for years. Baa Thao spent all weekend with him and was obviously sad to see him leave. She explained to me later about her inability to bear children and how she did not want to burden anyone else with that. She said that he has a wife and many children in a province in northern Thailand, but they talk often, and he comes to see her as often as he is able. I was surprised that Baa Thao seemed to be the mistress in a happy marriage, but she convinced me that his wife knew and approved of their relationship and permitted him to see her every year.

Baa Thao got so close to me; she treated me like the daughter she never had. She gave up her room for me to stay in because most families in Thailand share rooms and even beds with other family members. Rotary International rules state that an exchange student must be given his or her own room. Baa Thao was exactly the type of family member I hoped to have. She was fluent in both Thai and Vietnamese; her English skills, however, were not that impressive. That didn't stop her, though. She would constantly talk to me every day—even if it was about nothing—allowing me to listen and get used to the Thai language and begin to learn new words, while I was listening to recognize the vocabulary that I had already learned.

Mae and Paw have five children: P'Nan the oldest, P'Neui two years younger, P'Nuan another year younger, P'Pond two years younger than her, and finally, NeungNoo, the youngest in the family.

P'Nan and P'Neui both lived in Bangkok; P'Neui was married and had two children of her own: Sinwia, three years old, and Nadia, just one. P'Nuan was 26 and spoke amazing English. It is a Rotary rule that the first host family for an exchange student must contain a Rotarian. P'Nuan was the required Rotarian in my family, and she really tried to follow the rules of speaking only Thai to me, although she helped me out in situations when I needed a translator. P'Pond was the only boy of the children. He was 24 and, like most boys in Thailand his age, spent all of his time either with his friends, his girlfriend, or on the computer. He would smile at me and say something occasionally, but rarely did we interact. NeungNoo was younger than me and spoke some English. Sadly, I only was able to visit with her for a little over a week before she went on exchange to the state of Oregon, in the USA. P'Neui's son, Sinwia, lived with us in Nakhon Phanom while she kept her daughter, Nadia, with her and her husband, P'Sia, in Bangkok. They believed that growing up in a quieter town would be better for Sinwia than living in Bangkok, but Nadia was too young to stay in Nakhon Phanom. P'Neui came home regularly to visit us; Sinwia would stay in Nakhon Phanom only until he was old enough to enroll in school. I hoped they were okay having a *farang* move in with them.

One of the Thai girls that I met in Grand Rapids explained to me what a *farang* (pronounced fa-LONG) is. The word basically means foreigner, someone who does not belong here, but it is really a term referring to Caucasians. It is a bit of a put-down, meaning that *farang*s are not of the status of Thais. A *farang* is someone who is out of place here, who does not know how to act in this culture, and who does not know how to show proper respect.

I had my first day of school. It was very long. I hung out with the teachers for most of the day. I had talked with my English teacher on the phone while I was at P'Nan's house in Bangkok. She said that they had put a picture of me in the hallway outside of the English department and that everyone was walking by, looking at it and talking about me. She was right: everyone in the entire school knew who I was.

Each morning, students sit outside in the courtyard. They line up in rows, depending on which class they are in. There were about 300 students and two dozen or so teachers. I was quickly introduced to a half French, half Thai, 18-year-old college student. He taught English while on his break. Then I met three Thai rebounds; Dear, Yee, and Peet, who had each finished their exchange in America a few months before I arrived in Thailand. Peet is a really nice guy but, like most Thai kids, prefers hanging out with friends of the same gender. He would talk to me occasionally, but we didn't socialize that much outside of school. Dear and Yee hung around with me for most of the day, when I wasn't sitting in the teachers' lounge. English camp was coming up in about a week. An English teacher talked to me for 20 minutes about what they do for English camp and what she wanted me to do. It was a little overwhelming, but everyone was so helpful. Dear, Yee, and I visited every English class in the school. First, they talked about the English camp in Thai and then they asked the kids if they wanted to hear me speak English, which, of course, they did. I basically gave the first part of my district speech in English, and everyone cheered at the end. I'm sure most of them had no idea what I had just said.

The name of my school was *Piyamahalachalai*. School in Thailand is very different from school in America. First of all, the high school was 7th through 12th grades, although they labeled them 1 through 6. Because I was repeating my senior year, I was in *matthayom* 6, abbreviated M6, or, in other words, grade 12. The students were grouped in classes based on their focus of study. There are four main tracks of study, but numbered 1 through 9, depending on how large the class size was. The class that I spent the most time with was focused on the Thai language and was known as 6/7. I think they put me in that class because the three rebounds were also in that class. I also had a lot of friends in 5/2, 6/2, and 6/3, which focused on English. Every morning, we would sit in class rows in alphabetical order in the courtyard area facing a statue of the founder of the school and the Thai flag. Each class had two rows separating genders. Every Monday morning we would stand and sing the National Anthem and then turn around toward the statue of Buddha and say a prayer. Then we would turn back toward the front and sit down to listen to announcements. To show respect, we were not permitted to stand during this time. Sitting on the concrete of the courtyard wasn't so bad. If, however, it had rained the previous night, we would have to squat so as not to get our clothes wet.

After the announcements, we were dismissed to go to our classes. I wasn't required to attend any specific classes, considering that I had already graduated from high school, but they gave me a bunch of options to keep me from getting bored. Mostly I preferred to stay with my home class, 6/7, but, by joining in other classes, I made a lot more friends. Upon entering any classroom, students were required to first slip off their shoes, place them along the outside wall, and then enter the room and sit down. When the teacher came in, the class leader commanded the class to stand, and then, unified, we would *wai* and say good morning to him or her. We then remained standing until the teacher said that we could sit.

Each class was different. The English classes were amusing because, in an effort to emphasize the different American greetings, the teacher would mix up what she said. Normally she would say, "Good morning class. How are you today?" but, every once in a while, she would walk in and say something similar to, "What's up?" The confused Thai students would then reply with their memorized lines, "I'm fine, thank you. And you?" I learned most of the Thai language in my English classes. Usually the instructor would just hand out worksheets and then leave, so students would then approach me, pointing to various Thai words, asking, "What is this word in English?" I would reply, "I don't know, I can't read yet. What is that word in Thai?" We played a lot of Pictionary, and all had a lot of fun and learned a lot, too.

After class was dismissed, we would all exit the classroom and have to find our shoes, which quite problematic for me, because everyone had the same style of shoes as part of our required uniforms. Everyone else didn't seem to have a problem finding their shoes, so I usually just waited and got mine last until I learned how to recognize the newness that only mine possessed.

Each classroom was different. Some had desks, which were

made of wood and were very old; others had short tables that three or four students sat around on the floor. There were a lot of windows and usually two doors in every classroom, which were kept open to allow for the maximum airflow because every day was hot in Thailand, and the school had no air conditioning.

August 9, 2006

Today, I had to play the piano in front of 30 students. I didn't have any sheet music, and I was really nervous, so I did not do well. Of course, everyone said I did great. I've never taken piano lessons, but, because of my high school choir instructor, I learned to read music quite well and loved to play around on our piano at home. I am definitely not good at it, but I spent a lot of time practicing and playing, so when Rotary required a picture of me engaged in a hobby, I chose one in which I am playing the piano.

Yesterday, I had to sing the American National Anthem in front of an English class of 30 people because the teacher was aware of my involvement in choir at Ottawa Township High School for four years. Tomorrow morning, I have to give a speech about myself, in English, to the entire student body. I advise anyone who wants to be a foreign exchange student: Be careful what information you state in the application process!

Everyone wants to practice their English on me, but it is still easy to learn Thai. They approach me and usually say the same thing. "Hello. My name is _____. Nice to meet you." Then they shake hands with me. Then everyone freaks out if it's a boy, acting almost as if we were in third grade again, and it is a huge deal to talk to a member of the opposite sex. If it's a girl, they ask Dear or Yee a question for me and eagerly wait for my reply. Once I say something, they pounce on the translator to find out what I said. Everyone is always so happy and excited.

I was renamed several times today. Everybody has been trying to think of hundreds of names for me—so I don't know what to answer to. It has been narrowed down to my real Thai name, Anchalee (meaning respect); my Thai nickname, Salee; Ashley; and Natalie. Most of the time, I went by Salee.

I wasn't sure who won the Miss Universe contest, but I am certain everyone here knows. Apparently, Miss Universe of 2005 married a Thai tennis player, so she has been followed like a celebrity in Thailand. "You look like Natalie. Do you know Natalie? You *wai* like Natalie. You're beautiful like Natalie." I didn't mind the compliments; I rather liked them. The first word I learned in school was *suai* (beautiful). I heard that about 100 times each day. Beautiful and pretty. They were fascinated with my eyes, too. In the picture that I used in my Rotary application, which was hung outside the English department, my eyes and hair looked darker. In person, they see that my eyes are a light blue color. They love my blue eyes, but it is kind of odd talking to someone and having five people staring at your face.

August 10, 2006

Because I had my uniform today, I had to go up in front of all 300 plus students and give a speech stating why I like being in Nakhon Phanom and attending *Piyamahalachalai* School. I wasn't quite as nervous as I imagined I would be, but my hands were shaking just *nit noy* (a little bit).

My favorite class was Thai. We learned about Thai poetry and read some poems aloud in class. It sounds like a song. I didn't know the Thai alphabet yet, but I learned the *cha*s and *hah*s at the end of the lines. Yee helped me a lot, and Dear was so supportive of my efforts. I was just worried that when the newness wore off, they would be less patient with me.

I went to dinner tonight with NeungNoo, P'Nuan, and a few other people. It was a buffet. It was really good, but, even better than that, I saw three elephants! I was so excited! P'Nuan was surprised that I had never seen an elephant before, and she paid 20 *baht* for my nephew and me to feed it. The monetary unit in Thailand is the *baht*. The exchange rate was roughly 30 *baht* to an American dollar. It was so cool, but I forgot to take my camera. I'm sure I will see them around later.

August 14, 2006

Today I helped out at my friend's mom's restaurant. I knew that the restaurants weren't as clean here as in America, but this was horrible. There were flies on everything, and some of the food was already prepared but didn't get served until 20 or 30 minutes later. The dishes we were preparing, however, really didn't need to be served hot. When we first got there, we started drying dishes. Then we washed our hands before working with the food. Later, we were touching raw fish and then went straight to preparing another dish without washing our hands. Another time, about five people sampled a particular entrée using the same spoon, and then the same dish was served to other customers. That's just how it is here, I guess. I mean, the food tastes great—don't get me wrong, it's just not what I am used to. Then again, that's why I'm here. Amazingly, no one seemed to get sick.

Ants were everywhere. The little red ones were in everything, probably on me and in my bed as I wrote this journal, but I tried not to think about them. In the kitchen, there were thousands of the red ants, as well as a bunch of the big black ones because they can easily find food. I opened my cereal box for just the second time since we bought it, and there were ants crawling through the cereal, as well as on the box's outside. Guess what I did? Wrong! I just poured my bowl of cereal and tried to sift through it as best I could and then poured milk on it and waited to see if any more floated to the top. None did, so I ate it. I just tried not to think about it. My host family bought a loaf of bread and a box of cereal just for me when I arrived. I think they were trying to help ease the transition to Thai food, which was really sweet of them. Therefore, I thought it would be rude to throw away the food that they specifically purchased for me, regardless of the recent inhabitants. It tasted fine; although, I made sure to store it in the refrigerator from then on.

Thais do not kill anything, not even the ants, because it is against their religion. Instead, they just shoo them away. Buddhists believe that killing anything is wrong because they think that even the insects could have been people in previous lives, maybe even their dead ancestors. Good thing I'm not Buddhist. I kill 'em every chance I get.

Mosquitoes were horrible, too. I wore capris and that awful school uniform all the time. I had mosquito bites all over my lower legs and feet but few on my hands and arms. No one else here seemed to have any mosquito bites. You'd think the mosquitoes knew I was a *farang*.

When I first arrived in Thailand, I could not distinguish easily between Thai, Lao, Cambodian, Vietnamese, Chinese, and Korean people. Now I can tell the difference—it seems so obvious—but I didn't have a clue before. Another surprise was to learn that just as Asians look the same to Westerners, *farang*s all look the same to Asians. We all have round eyes, larger noses than Asians, and square chins; most of us are a bit overweight. Because of this, I think I could convince them that I am a famous movie star.

August 23, 2006

Yesterday was the "welcoming of the freshmen." Every Wednesday, the boys who are enrolled in this program are required to wear green uniforms to school, and go through a military training exercise. The class is optional, but if a boy elects not to take it, he will be one of the first to enter military service in the event of a draft. So, nearly all boys enroll in this class. Once each school year on an unexpected day, the juniors and seniors get to command the freshmen to do whatever they want them to do. I felt so sorry for some of those boys. They had to crawl in waste canals from the rest-rooms. It was so gross! Then they had to roll around on the lawn that had just been mowed.

Occasionally, one of the commanders would pull someone out of his group and tell him to do push-ups or something. Kip, a boy in 6/7, was showing off and told five guys to stand in a line in front of me while yelling, "I love you, Ashley," louder and louder. I felt really bad for them at first, but Yee was having such a good time laughing at them, and she kept reminding me that the seniors had to go through this, too, when they were freshmen. I tried to imagine

Peet and Kip crawling in the canal. I was glad that the girls did not have to endure that.

Having to wear a uniform was incredibly uncomfortable. The skirt had to be worn up around my ribs and was tight, making breathing difficult when sitting. Of course, when I sat up straight, it was okay, but it was hard to sit up straight when sitting on the floor. The puffy shoulders made it impossible to raise my hand above my head. The shirt was a really light fabric, so I had to wear another heavy shirt underneath. The skirt was really heavy, so I looked forward to sitting down because the floor was cool. Whoever designed the uniform could have found a happy medium. Then the Mary Jane shoes and the bow for the hair—don't even get me started.

The uniforms for physical education are similarly uncomfortable; the pants were heavy and hot, and the shirt was somewhat see-through. At least we didn't have to tuck the shirts in, so I could wear the pants comfortably around my hips. Then I had the whole crotch issue to deal with. I could roll mine once, and it seemed to be okay.

Everyone wears uniforms here—I even saw a little five-year-old wearing one. God Bless America and the public school system!

I still haven't gotten used to seeing the Thai flag everywhere. I was watching my *Gaw-Gai* video the other day, and it got to *Taaw-toong* and had the Thai flag waving, and I completely didn't expect it. This video was made for 2 to 4 year olds to help them learn the Thai alphabet, as well as some other lessons. The A-B-C song in English just names the letters. In the Thai alphabet song, it names the letter (*Gaw*) and directly after, a word that starts with that letter (*gai*: chicken). *Taaw-toong* is the letter *Taaw* and the object representing it: *toong*, meaning flag. The Thai alphabet has 44 consonants and 32 vowels. While that may seem like a lot to learn, there are also no capital letters and no punctuation. Thai is a tonal language and that would eventually put me in an embarrassing situation.

Every once in a while, if I'm really tired or bored, I just think, "Wow, I'm in Thailand." It's crazy; I don't feel like I'm on the other side of the world! I think that e-mail helps a lot, though. Everyone here is so kind and loving. I don't know how anyone could be homesick. I mean, I miss my family, but I don't want to go home. Instead, I want them to come here.

I was watching a Korean movie the other day. I'm not sure if they were speaking Korean or Thai because they had Thai subtitles, but the voices didn't seem to match the lip movements. Anyway, it was the funniest thing I've ever seen. Every Korean movie is about two guys fighting over a girl and some old guy dying—that's my favorite part. They are such bad actors, and each scene has limited dialog. Maybe, once I understand what they are saying, it won't be as funny. I'm taking full advantage of it while I still can!

August 24, 2006

I just rode an elephant! It was so cool! I've never even ridden a horse before. It was at the same restaurant where I fed the elephant a few days ago. The lady originally said that the price was 100 *baht*, but Yee talked her down to 50 *baht* because I wasn't just a *farang*. I had only 100 *baht* with me, so I paid 60 *baht*, and she allowed me to feed it, too. Riding it was so scary. I stayed on for only a few minutes, but it was a big elephant. I left my camera at home, so Yee grabbed Peet's cell phone and took a few pictures. The guy sitting on the elephant's neck, Bor, told the elephant to sit, and then the lady helped me up. I felt bad stepping on her (the elephant) to get up. I know I couldn't hurt her even if I tried, but, like I said before, I've never even ridden on a horse. Once the elephant stood up and started walking around, I had nowhere to hold on, and her shoulders (which was basically where I was sitting) would move drastically up and down. Yee and Dear were yelling to me to just relax, and I yelled back, "I'm on a freaking elephant!" They were having a lot of fun laughing at me. Bor held out his hand to me right before the elephant was going to sit down, and I held on to it as though I was going to fall off a cliff, which I basically was. The getting off part was the scariest, but I'd do it again in a heartbeat. Just a buck-fifty to ride an elephant!

August 29, 2006

I've determined that there is a "Thai sick" and an "American sick." I had a long discussion with Yee about whether or not I'm sick, so we came to the agreement that I'm "Thai sick." I have a cough.

Today was so much fun. After school, it was raining so we decided to stay put until the rain stopped. We waited about 10 minutes and then decided to go because it was only drizzling. As soon as we left the school, it started pouring, and I was riding side-saddle on the back of Yee's motorcycle. I love the rain so I was having a blast, but Yee kept yelling back to me to stop having so much fun because I am probably going to "really" get sick and my host parents are going to kill her because she brought me home in the rain. At one point she glanced back and asked, "Are you that wet?" I almost fell off the motorcycle, I was laughing so hard. "I'm just as wet as you are!" As soon as I got home, I greeted Paw (as usual), and he started laughing at me and asked, sarcastically but in Thai, "Is it raining?" I just learned the word "rain" today so I understood! As I was making my way upstairs to change, I happened to pass every person in the house, who, of course, commented on how soaked I was. I love the rainy season!

August 30, 2006

I think I'm getting used to all the attention I'm getting. Just riding down the street on the back of a motorcycle, I've heard a dozen people yelling my name (or one out of three, anyway). When I first arrived, I would try to figure out if I had actually met them before. Now I just automatically smile, wave, and yell back, "Hello," to them. I am trying to be as nice as possible to everyone and not let the popularity go to my head. It's still really weird having a poster of me hanging on the door of the classroom where I spend 70 percent of my day. There's always a group of students who will walk past, then hesitate, walk back to the poster, and then start whispering amongst themselves. Then, one will look in the room, and I'll smile at them. Right away they will tell all their friends who are with them that I'm sitting right there and then turn back to me and smile back. Some groups will then wave and then walk away all excited because I waved back. Others will stand there and compare me to the picture, as if to ask, "Is that really her?" They stay there for a few minutes and then wave and walk to class. I guess they figured that because the picture was of a white chick and I'm the only white chick in Nakhon Phanom, it must be me.

I don't let it bother me too much. I just constantly smile. Thailand, "the land of smiles"— they're not joking. I've been here a month and have seen only two arguments. Some days it's a little too happy for me, but I remind myself that I'm only here for a year and try to be as happy as I can. It's not that I'm in a bad mood or anything; it's just tiring to constantly smile. Plus, half the time I have no idea what is going on.

Funny story. A while back, Yee asked me if I thought all Asians were really smart. I thought for a minute and said, "Well, all of the Asians that I have ever known are really smart, so yes, I think I would agree that all Asians are really smart."

She said, "That is so not true! I was so annoyed when I was in America and kids would approach me and say, 'Oh, you're Asian, you must be really smart!' Some Asians are smart, but some are not so smart. Asians are the same as any other race of people."

I pondered this but didn't think much more about it at the time. Later that day, we were walking in town with a group of friends, and we heard this music. It was a really up-beat tune. Yee grabbed my hand and said, "Come on, Ashley. Let's dance." I pulled back, saying, "I don't want to dance. I don't like to dance. I don't even really know how to dance." "Oh, come on, Ashley. You're American. All Americans know how to dance." I continued to pull back, and said, "Yeah, right. Just like all Asians are really smart." We laughed. I really like it here.

I am so thankful to have Yee and Dear. I would hate to have to translate everything. They are so sweet about doing it. I don't know what it would be like without them. I know that I wouldn't be having this much fun, though!

I think I've taken the "keep busy" mentality to the next level. I thought through what I wanted to get out of this year before I came. My number one goal is to be able to speak and write Thai fluently.

I think I'm doing a fairly good job at it. I've memorized the whole consonant alphabet and am beginning vowels, which should be faster and easier to remember. I love looking at a sign and sounding out the letters in the words. I think I'm learning a lot of words, too. I was told that it would take three months to be fluent, but I set a two-month goal for myself. I figure that if I can converse with a native in two months, then, in the third month, I can increase my vocabulary. I also said that I wanted to learn Japanese when I came. I don't know if that's going to work out because few, if any, people here speak Japanese. In addition to Thai, almost everyone here speaks either Laos or Vietnamese, and all are eager and willing to teach me. Laos is a lot like Thai, and Vietnamese is a little more like English. I think that it is possible that Laos started as a Thai dialect, considering that the two languages share many of the same words. The Vietnamese language is completely different, although the sentence structure is similar to Thai. I'm torn between which one I want to study after I learn Thai. I plan to focus 100 percent on Thai first and then branch off to Laos and Vietnamese. I learned that some of the local people are so eager to help spread their Vietnamese heritage that they give free tutoring lessons. That really interested me. Because they tutor kids, they should be fairly fluent in it; a lot of the people speak a little Laos or Vietnamese and aren't fluent in any language except Thai. It sounds like a lot, but I have 10 more months here and at most (hopefully), two more studying Thai, so it could be possible. Time will tell, I guess.

The most helpful situation for me learning the Thai language is playing with my three-year-old nephew, Sinwia. He loves having a playmate and talks nonstop, and I love kids anyway, so we've become good pals. He would tell me to do something and then, if I didn't do it correctly or didn't understand, he would take my hand and show me how to do it. One day I took one of his books and would point and ask him what color each thing was, and he would answer for a while with me repeating him; then he would start to ask me the colors, and I would reply in English.

September 5, 2006

Yesterday I went on a bike ride with my aunt. We were going home when we heard beautiful music coming from a church. She said the music plays every Sunday night. We approached the church, parked our bikes, and walked in. The church was so gorgeous at night, all lit up. Christian churches are few and far between in Thailand, and this was the first one I had seen. As we started walking into the sanctuary, I, for some unknown reason, started crying. The further down the aisle I went, the more I was crying. I don't know why. The inside of the church was so beautiful, and there was the beautiful music in the background. Part of me thinks it was because I miss going to church so much. Church is a huge part of my life at home, and, even though I read the Bible every night, it just isn't enough. A small part of me feels like it was guilt. I've been to so many temples since I've been here, and, just yesterday, I toured 11 or 12 temples. I felt almost guilty that I've been here a month and still have not even been inside a church. Maybe I really was feeling homesick, though.

Everyone keeps asking me if I am homesick, and then they proceed to tell me that I am. I honestly don't know if I am or not. I guess I miss my parents and friends, but I wouldn't give up this experience for anything. In my mind, I have kind of frozen life at home. I think I'm going to experience serious reverse culture shock when I get home and everything seems different.

It is difficult for me to express my feelings about this to anyone here because the same word is used to describe "missing someone" and "homesickness." They cannot understand how I can miss my parents and friends, yet not be homesick. At first, when they asked about it and I said that I was not homesick, they assumed that I was a child that behaved badly and that I must fight with my parents and was, therefore, glad to be away from them. Then, as they grew to know me and learned that my behavior was acceptable, they surmised that my parents must really be bad, and, for that reason, I was glad to be away from them. I want Mom and Dad to visit me in Thailand so that everyone can know that we have a very normal family and that I'm just not homesick.

Today was my first bad day at school. Well, I guess it wasn't bad, just frustrating. The beginning of the day was fine. We had a school tutoring lesson with a famous gay tutor. He was hilarious. At first I couldn't tell that he was a guy; then he started talking. Yee thought that I would be bored if I went back after lunch, so I went to the English department instead. I was fine with this because that gave me a chance to study Thai. When I walked into the English department, one of the teachers yelled at me because of my socks. I was asking for that, I guess, because the socks that I wore were not the "uniform" socks. I just blew that off. I seriously hated the school uniforms. I was studying the parts of the body when a teacher approached me and asked me in Thai what I was studying. I was trying to figure out how to say the word "clothing" because I didn't know how to say that in Thai. She kept repeating herself. I said, "I understand, but I don't know how to say this word in Thai," pointing to the headline on the page. She said something in Thai, but it didn't have the word "*thua*" (body) in it. I started to ask her if it should say "*thua*," and she cut me off by saying the same thing louder, obviously wanting me to repeat her. I repeated after her, and then I went on to ask her the same question, and she cut me off again, saying, "Why is it that you never speak Thai with me and you always say that you are trying?" I was so angry. Just thinking about the incident makes me frustrated. There were so many things I wanted to say to her, but no, I kept my temper; I didn't say anything. You'd better believe that I'm going to remember this incident the next time she wants me to teach her English classes for her.

When I first met Yee and Dear, they complained to me about how all the English teachers wanted them to teach various English classes after they returned from America, but Yee and Dear have their own scheduled classes to attend. Yee said that those teachers are so lazy that they are always asking them to teach English lessons. I've learned that it's true. Every day, I sit in one or two English classes with different grades, and, every day, each class has the same worksheet. The teacher walks in, usually late, hands out the papers, and then leaves to go back to the teacher's lounge. Some of my teachers in high school were not very good, but none of them could get away with just totally blowing off their responsibilities.

I was told to memorize five words each day, and I've done way more than that. I'm constantly making up new sentences in my head during discussions that I am sitting in on, but, by the time I have a sentence finalized, it's usually too late in the conversation to say it. I'm still trying to talk in Thai when I want to say something. Just because I don't talk that much to the teachers doesn't mean that I don't talk to anyone. My next host mom is a teacher, but she wasn't there today, so at least she wasn't the cause of my anger. I'm sure I'll get over it sooner or later, but, right now, I'm still ticked. It just makes me even more determined to learn Laos and Vietnamese.

September 7, 2006

Every time I sit down and place my arm on a table, at least one person will put their arm next to mine to compare skin color. Then it starts a whole game of, "who comes closest to Salee." It's funny because the same person will do it more than once, as if their skin will get two shades lighter in a week. Eventually, two people would put an arm on either side of mine and someone would yell out "zebra." It's fun though.

Every day around lunchtime or even earlier, I get so incredibly tired and sleepy. It's probably half because of studying and half because of the sun. It's frustrating because after school I am so tired, I just want to stay at home, and then I have to go to bed early. I get 9 or 10 hours of sleep, in which case I wake up completely rested before my alarm goes off, and the day starts all over again, and I am exhausted by lunchtime. I hope I get used to the sun soon because I hate being tired all the time. It doesn't matter all that much, though, because I don't have anything much to do after school anyway. Fye, a girl from 6/7, used to ask me every day if I wanted to play basketball with her. I've gone with her a few times, but recently I've started coming up with excuses. No offense to her, but isn't there more to do than just play basketball? The Thais seem to think that because I am "so good" at it that I must like to play a lot. Honestly, I don't really like playing basketball at all. It's okay playing basketball in gym class, but I'd rather do something else. I think we start dancing soon anyway.

It seems like kids in Thailand study constantly. Finding any activities to do after school is difficult because most kids come home around 4:30 or 5:00 p.m., eat dinner, and then leave again at 7:00 for a two-hour tutoring class. They usually choose classes that friends are also attending to make the tutoring more fun. I guess it wouldn't be so bad if I was used to going that often and had friends there, too, but I'm just so exhausted at night that I couldn't imagine having to go.

One thing that I have noticed is that, despite the obvious poverty of Thai citizens in general, they absolutely love their King. They are also happy with what they have, no matter how little. Americans, by Thai standards, are very wealthy. Yet, some Americans want, and expect, more, almost to the point of entitlement. In addition, many Americans are critical of the very system that enables one to pursue and attain a higher standard of living. I think it would be impossible to find a Thai who would criticize the King, unlike some Americans who can strongly criticize our government. I had to wonder, "Who is better off?"

September 13, 2006

A funny story happened a while ago, but I think I forgot to write about it. We were sitting at the table eating dinner, and everyone was trying to serve me more food. I kept saying, "No, I'm really full, thank you," but they kept trying to negotiate a smaller portion with me. Finally Paw said, "You know, there are people in Lao who are starving." I nearly fell off my chair, I was laughing so hard. Everyone else was laughing, too. Then, he went on to say, "Those people don't live in China anymore. They moved to Lao." It was really funny hearing Paw using a phrase that I thought was only used by Americans.

Before I came to Thailand, I don't remember ever talking about Laos. In Nakhon Phanom, everyone references it for one reason or another, but they all call it *"prathet* Lao" in Thai (*"prathet"* meaning country). When my parents came over to visit, they tried correcting me whenever I would address that country, saying that it was pronounced "Laos." By the time of their visit, I (along with an entire country of people) had been calling it "Lao" for so long that I couldn't change. To this day, I still find it awkward to pronounce the "s."

In addition to the school uniforms students are required to wear, teachers also have a dress code. In Buddhism, every day of the week is associated with a color. Because the King of Thailand was born on a Monday, his color and the color of respect for the King are yellow. The Queen was born on a Friday, so her color is blue. Every day, except Wednesday, teachers were required to wear black pants and a yellow shirt. On Wednesday, because the Queen's color is blue, all teachers wear blue to honor the Queen. I am not sure why Wednesday was picked to honor the Queen, maybe because it is in the middle of the week. Below are the colors for the days of the week:

Sunday	Red
Monday	Yellow
Tuesday	Pink
Wednesday	Green
Thursday	Orange
Friday	Blue
Saturday	Purple

Because I was born on a Thursday, my color is orange. When I first arrived in Thailand and was introduced to the Buddhist faith, I was often asked on which day of the week I was born. When I said that I didn't know, Thais would seem very surprised. Some would give me a shocked look, as if to say, "How could you not know that!" Each day also has a different pose of the image of Buddha. Tuesday's Buddha is reclining. Thursday's and Saturday's Buddhas are seated. The other four days the Buddha is standing but with his hands in different positions. Buddhists make merit by worshiping their day's Buddha.

Today, I played basketball at lunchtime. It was 6/7 versus 6/2. Did I mention that I don't like basketball? Anyway, the game was awful. It was a bunch of girls playing girls, and then me. I'm not saying that I was the only good player on the court. I wasn't because there were a lot of potentially good players, but everyone was so sloppy. Not catching the ball before dribbling, letting go of the ball so the referee doesn't call a jump ball, and many, many uncalled fouls, for example, shoving. I was trying to be a good girl out there, but, after being shoved around a few times and being down by however many points, I got angry, and took on a different attitude. "If you want to play basketball dirty, then let's play!" One of my friends, Alex, was told to guard me, and she was, really tight. Too tight, but the refs weren't calling it. She was trying to slap the ball from my hands, but she was slapping my arms in her missed attempts. So, like I said, I was annoyed. I grabbed the ball with both hands and threw my arms around a little to get my space. Of course, because I wasn't playing like that in the beginning, no one expected me to. I hit her only twice throughout the game and felt really bad about it. Both times it was her fault, but in America I'm not "friends" with the other team, so I don't care if they run into my elbows or not. Here, even though it was her fault, I felt like I shouldn't have been playing so hard, like I should have gone easy on them. Nonetheless, we still lost 22 to 26. In one instance, I was fouled while shooting, so I got two shots from the foul line. I made the first shot and then missed the second one, rebounded, and shot it again and made it for two points. Three total. I would estimate that most of the people in the stands were cheering for our team, but only because of me. A little embarrassing at first, but then it pumped me up. It was fun, but I wish we could have run some plays or something. I would say something, but the translation of it wouldn't fit the time frame of a time-out. Once I tried to show them how to set a "pick," but they didn't understand at all.

I went to a Rotary meeting again today. Rotary meetings aren't fun in Thailand. There is no food and half the time no people. Few people come, or they show up really late. Of course, we just extend the meeting for them. Today it was two hours, which is about the same as the last one I attended. It was so boring. Maybe when I can understand them, it might not be as boring. Doubtful.

September 14, 2006

I knew that there was going to be a "surprise" party for me at school, but I didn't know the extent of it. It started during lunch and lasted for three or four hours. There was so much food: fresh pineapple and watermelon, *pad Thai* (rice noodles stir-fried with eggs, peanuts, vegetables, sprouts, tofu, and meat), *kao pod* (fried rice), *som-thom* (a spicy Thai papaya-peanut salad), *moo* (pork), chips, ice cream, Thai drinks, and so much more. They decorated the room with pink and white balloons because they knew that pink is my favorite color. Many of my friends made me gifts. Bow and Yuy, two girls who were close friends with Dear and Yee and who I have become close to as well, made a beautiful heart of silk flowers. Everyone in 6/7 wrote something on a paper heart. Bow and Yuy used wire to attach them to the silk flower heart. There were dozens of pink paper hearts dangling from the centerpiece. It was so beautiful. The teachers gave me a huge bouquet of pink roses with one white flower in the middle. I was so overwhelmed with all the things I was receiving that I didn't know what to say. 6/7 gave me a card, which looks really nice, like they spent a lot of time on it, but, when I was coming home with Yee on the motor-cycle, it must have blown off because I don't have it anymore. I'm upset that I lost it. Part of me hopes that someone finds it and gives it to me, but the other part of me is embarrassed that I lost it and hopes that no one finds it.

September 15, 2006

I keep forgetting that this is not permanent and that I should write everything down, so that I'll have a record of it. The other day, I was learning some Thai in 6/7, and Peet told me how to say *kai jiow*, "omelet," or literally, whipped eggs. I can never remember the second part of it, though. At the basketball game on Wednesday, Than, a girl from 6/2, asked me what I had for breakfast because I don't know much Thai and that is one of the few questions that I can understand. So, I hesitantly said, *"Kai jiow"* forming the second word into a question tone. She laughed hysterically, then took me from group to group asking, "Salee, what did you have for breakfast?" To which I responded, "*Kai jiow*," using an even more pronounced question tone. Everyone was laughing, and I still didn't know what was so funny. What I didn't realize was that, because the Thai language is tonal, I was saying a different word by speaking the second word in an ascending tone. After the basketball game, I asked Than what exactly I was saying. She had difficulty explaining because she didn't know a lot of English. She used her hands to show a sphere, and would say, "Bowls, bowls." I still didn't understand. It didn't make any sense to me because 1) bowls are not spherically shaped, and 2) I'm sure "eating bowls" wouldn't be that funny. After she kept saying it for several more times, it dawned on me that she was trying to say, "balls." I asked, "Do you mean 'balls'?" Then she laughed and nodded and made the shape of a ball with her hands again, then pointed to one of the boys. Now I understood. By saying *jiow* in a questioning tone, the meaning of the word changed from "eggs" to "a guy's balls." So I was telling everyone at the basketball game that I had scrambled testicles for breakfast. Now I know why they found it so funny. I don't think I've said the word "omelet" since then and am still trying to avoid doing so. It was just my luck that the next day, in cooking class with *Adjant* (teacher) Sarapee, we made omelets. Go figure!

For dinner on Wednesday, Baa Thao bought *gai ka*, chicken legs. They should really be called chicken feet because they didn't have much leg on them. They were the feet, including the claws, of the chicken. They weren't bad to eat, but I wouldn't go out of my way to get them. Then I had the bright idea to feel the texture of it while it was in my mouth before I swallowed because it looked a little bumpy. Bad idea. I'm never eating chicken feet again, especially if it still looks like a foot.

Here is another funny story, which happened yesterday. Yee, Dear, Ging, Bow, and Yuy were getting ready to leave school, and someone, I forget who, offered to help me carry some of the presents that I got to Yee's motorcycle. While handing over some things, I guess I made a grunting-like noise, and Dear and Ging heard it and couldn't stop laughing the whole way to the parking lot. Apparently, that grunt was Thai (impolite at that), and they were just commenting on how quickly I'm turning into a Thai girl. It took about 10 minutes until Dear could tell me because she was laughing so hard. Not to mention that every time there would be a quiet moment in the conversation, Ging or Dear would grunt, and everyone would look at me and laugh. I'm having so much fun here!

September 19, 2006

I went to my friends' birthday party this past Friday. First of all, they told me to be ready at 6:00 p.m. and at the last minute changed it to 5:30, so I went outside a little after 5:30 (and I rushed to get out there when I did). I know Thais are notoriously late, so it would be okay if I had to wait a little. They didn't come until about 6:20! I was really upset. Once they came, I was more relieved, but I would rather have just gone inside or something. Baa Thao was waiting with me and kept telling me that they will come. She's so sweet. The party was a lot of fun, too. It was a bunch of people from my cooking class, whom I don't usually hang out with except for cooking, so it was fun getting to know them better.

Everyone here wants to learn English from me because of my native accent. So, every time they ask me what something is, they lean forward to get right in front of my face and then repeat it. I guess if they sat back in their chair, they think I wouldn't be able to hear as well. Anyway, at the birthday party we got on the subject of "boobs." Have you ever had seven Asian girls simultaneously lean three inches from your face and yell, "Boobs?" I was laughing so hard. I would have fallen off my chair, except we were sitting on the ground. Then we moved on to the difference between one boob and two boobs because there are no plurals in the Thai language. Later they were all walking around, patting their chests, saying, "Boob, boobs." Good times.

Eating the birthday cake was a lot of fun, too. They had a very small cake, and they cut two pieces (for the two moms) and then everyone grabbed a spoon and dug in. It was a lot of fun. I like it better than cutting individual pieces.

I went to a carnival today with P'Nuan, Baa Thao, and Sinwia. It was a very scary place. Occasionally, when I was younger, I would see a carnival scene on a scary, late night TV show. It was always a night scene, with creepy clown toys and rides that were rusted and had paint peeling off. The shows were always about someone dying or being murdered, complete with creepy music in the background. Well, I just walked onto the set. I forgot my camera, too, but the carnival will be here until October 2nd, so, hopefully, I can come back. First of all, I am afraid of heights. Secondly, I'm afraid of Ferris wheel rides that appear to be barely strong enough to hold a three-year-old, let alone two other adults. Yeah, that's right. I actually rode on it, and now I'm writing it down as a record of not dying! It wasn't even a big one either, maybe 15 carts, but I was still afraid. It did, however, provide a nice view of Laos. It was held in the temple, which is convenient because everyone who goes to the carnival has to walk past the donation box for the temple with six monks sitting behind it, looking at everyone.

September 20, 2006

Today I went with Baa Thao and P'Pin to the other house to help them clean. P'Nan has a travel agency business that she and P'Big run in Bangkok. P'Nuan helps out with the business, in this house. It's not a long walk from home, but I hardly ever go there during the day.

P'Pin is the housekeeper for our family. When I first got here, P'Nan told me about P'Pin but said that everyone tries to pick up after themselves and P'Pin just does the excess work and that I should do the same. Therefore, I took the initiative of doing my own laundry and ironing my own school uniforms. P'Pin is really nice, though. She is always smiling and makes sure to do her job the best that she can. It was obvious by the interaction between her and all the family members, especially my host siblings, that she had been with my family for quite a while.

When we got to the other house, Baa Thao wanted to clean the whole upstairs. It was really gross. Every time someone turned a box upside down, the bottom of it was almost completely rotted away, and there were maggots everywhere. I tried to hide the disgusted look from my face, but I don't think I did a very good job. They were both working hard, and I was just standing there. I offered to help, but I think Baa Thao knew that I was really grossed out and that I hated not doing anything. She told me to scrape away this moldy stuff that was on the stairs. It was tiring but not gross. I'm glad I could help. We also cleaned the bedrooms. She gave me a headband and a belt (that I think was P'Nan's) and tried to give me a huge stuffed Garfield—I "forgot" it upstairs. Out of sight, out of mind. It was really cute and so sweet of her to give me so much stuff, but there was no way it would fit into my suitcases to go home. We gave the dogs a bath, too. Well, actually, Baa Thao gave the dogs a bath, and I just sat there petting the one that wasn't getting a bath. Those dogs love me now because I tell them to jump on my leg, so I don't have to bend down to pet them. When Baa Thao and I go there to give them treats every night, they don't know which person to go to. I miss my dog!

I went to Fye's house for dinner tonight. It was a lot of fun. I was waiting for dinner to get finished, and Fye gave me a photo album to look at. I must have looked a little too excited because her aunt, who lives next door to Fye and whose house we were visiting, left to get two more stacks of photo albums. At first it was a little awkward, but then we ate dinner and talked, and, after the meal, I continued to look at them and talk at the same time. It was a lot of fun getting to know Fye's parents and her aunt, uncle, and brother. Most of the pictures were of Fye's cousin's graduation from college. Something really funny happened—but first, a little background. When asking a question in Thai, such as, "Do you want to play basketball?" The answer is either "play," or "no play." As an American, when someone asks me a question, I repeat the subject or verb in a question tone to make sure I understand the question and to give me time to think of my answer. I'm not really sure why. It's a habit, though, and it's gotten me into a few uncomfortable situations already.

Back to my story. We were talking about siblings while I was looking at what seemed like thousands of Fye's cousin's graduation pictures. Fye's aunt pointed to her son and asked, "*Law Mai*?" (Is he handsome?). I replied, "*Law, law*" (yes). Everyone in Thai says what they want to say at least two or three times. I personally think it is to take up more time in the conversation. What was I supposed to say? "No, your son's ugly?" Then her mom leaned over and said, "*Ao mai*?" I replied, "*ao?*" which they perceive as, "*ao!*" meaning to want. For the next half hour, they tried to hook me up with a guy I've never even met. They told me so much about him; being in this situation made me feel as though I was getting a "mail-order husband." They were all really nice and liked me a lot. They said that if my parents ever came over here that they should stay at their house, and I offered the same, if Fye's dad ever goes to America. I like them a lot and hope I'll be invited again for dinner.

The other day Fye took me to eat crepes at a shop. I've met the owners before with Yee and Baa Thao. The more questions they asked me, the more they started to like me. First was, "What Thai food do you like?" I said, "Everything," and the lady making the crepe said, "Everything except *som-thom*." I replied, "No, *chawp som-thom*" (I like *som-thom*). She got all excited and put the full amount of sauce on my crepe, which was apparently spicy but it didn't taste all that hot to me. Then we started talking a little in Thai, and they were impressed with what I've learned in such a short time. Then, she asked if I could speak Laos. Fye began to reply with, "Thai first, then Lao," but I cut her off, with my mouth full of crepe, and pointed to it and said in Laos, "*Sap*" meaning "delicious." Everyone freaked out. I figure that I'm not going to go out of my way to learn Laos before I can speak Thai fluently, but if I know the words, I might as well use them.

5

THE COUP

September 25, 2006

TODAY I finally found out exactly what has been going on for the past week in Thailand. So far, all that I knew was that Wednesday was a "holiday" for all students. We were told that it was because the Prime Minister went to Europe, and, while he was there, the soldiers said we don't have to go to school. Yes, that is what I get for not being able to speak Thai. Then, of course, if I ask what is going on, they say, "The Prime Minister is bad," and, *"Mai pben rai,"* meaning hakuna matata (no worries).

Yee filled me in on the situation, and I just read an e-mail from Dad to confirm it.

From: Ashley Krepps
Sent: Monday, September 25, 2006 8:13 AM
To: Krepps, Bob; Linda Krepps
Subject: Thai News

So I've been trying to watch the news as much as I can here, but I don't understand anything. Some people are trying to fill me in, but with the language barrier and everything, it's hard to understand. I don't have that much time to look it up on the internet, but if you could give me the low down on what's going on - thanks

Ashley

"Krepps, Bob" wrote:

Ashley,

I didn't know how much information was being circulated, so I didn't mention anything to you before. The Prime Minister, elected in 2001 is reputed to be corrupt. He was losing popularity for the past year and a half. He was expected to lose in the April, 2006 elections, but he won, amid allegations of election fraud. So if he is bad, and is manipulating the election results, the only way to remove him is by force.

So anyway, while the PM was in New York addressing the United Nations, the military took over the government. That happened last Tuesday (9/19) and spilled over to Wednesday (9/20). There were no reports of any violence, but there are tanks and soldiers on the streets of Bangkok, and groups of five or more are not allowed to congregate. The state department initially warned Americans not to go to Thailand, but the warning did not advise Americans in Thailand to leave. I think the travel warning was just a precaution, and may have been lifted by now.

The King is a "constitutional monarch," who really does not get too involved with the running of the government. The King has stated that he supports the military coup [I think he didn't like the PM very much] . . . . and the head of the military said power will be turned over to the "people" within two weeks. Everyone knows that the King is very popular among the Thai people. Presently the country remains under marshal (military) law. I am saving any articles that I find.

Not much news here. A lot of people from church and Rotary have expressed concern about the situation. A lot of people are looking at your blog. It would be great if you could post some new photos. Enjoy your day.

Love,
Dad

Hey Dad!

Most of this I already knew. I'm going to Bangkok on the 11th - do you think that there will be any soldiers still there? That would be really cool if there were!! Everyone here hates the PM. So technically has he been impeached or something? And I was told that he was in Europe, not America. Other than that - it's the same stuff. Except, I just found out all this today. I started break on Wednesday, but everyone else in my class had to go for finals for 3 days. They didn't go on Wednesday because of everything, but I couldn't talk to my English-speaking friends until tonight. (Went to a Korean barbeque - a ton of fun!) So technically I'm on break from school for a month - until Oct.23 - but my friend asked if I wanted to go to Nakhon Phanom University with her. So I start college tomorrow. I don't know if I will have to get a uniform for that or not, because it won't last that long. But maybe I will be able to talk my teachers into letting me take a college class or two when school starts up again. About 10 NPU students eat dinner outside right next to my house, so every night when I go with Baa Thao to feed the dogs, we stop and talk to them. So I already have a bunch of friends there, too. If you know any more info about the PM situation let me know. I got e-mails from both of my YEOs on Wednesday, just wanted to be sure that I was okay. Wow! District 6420 has really got a handle on how to run Rotary Youth Exchange.

Love you,
Ashley

I've been watching the news a lot but can only pick up a few words. *Taw-ta-han* is in the alphabet, so that came in handy. "*Ta-han*" means soldier. Just five weeks into my exchange year the government of Thailand was overthrown in a military coup. How cool is that? Although everyone here loves the King, the people do not like the Prime Minister. He is corrupt and does not work for the good of the citizens. He was in New York addressing the United Nations when the military took charge. He tried to address the Thai citizens in a broadcast from New York, but the soldiers stopped it by commandeering the TV and radio stations. This is really big news for Thailand; it's so cool living here during it! I am going to Bangkok next week. Wouldn't it be exciting if there are still soldiers and tanks in the streets?

Yesterday, Yee took me to a Korean barbeque. It was a ton of fun. The teacher paid for us, and there were about a dozen students, altogether. We ate for an hour or two, just hanging out with friends. I hadn't seen everybody for a week because of testing. Yee was putting the food on my plate, and she said to Dear, "Salee *gin yeu*." With my mouth full I said, "So, you think I eat a lot?" Dear was uncontrollably laughing, and Yee was trying to cover it up because she didn't think I would understand. It was so funny, and it really made me feel like I was improving on the language.

Just about every night, I go with Baa Thao to feed the dogs at the other house; sometimes we stop, and she tells me to read the signs on the shops that we pass. I can tell that she is really proud of me. I can read just about anything, although I still don't understand all of the words that I am reading. I feel like I'm getting really close to

Baa Thao. Every time we meet someone she knows, she always tells them how quickly I'm learning and that I can read already, and she acts so proud of me. I think I'm going to miss her the most when I leave. I'm sleeping in her bedroom right now; she is sleeping with P'Nuan and Sinwia in the other room, along with NeungNoo before she left to go on exchange to America. Rotary has a rule that all exchange students must have a room to themselves. She has told me several times that if I go to another host family and don't like it or if anything is wrong, then I can come back and have this room. She would go on to say that when she gets enough money, if she is strong enough, she is going to come visit me in America. I love her so much. I almost don't want to get too close to her because I know it will be so difficult to say goodbye to her when I have to leave in July, but I think it is already too late.

When I got home today, Baa Thao, P'Pond, and I went to my cousin's first birthday party. They were eating Korean barbeque, too. I met a Vietnamese girl who is studying on exchange at Nakhon Phanom University for three months. She can't speak Thai or English very well. She invited me to go to school with her for the month that I'm on break. I'm really excited to be going to the university. I taught there once, for an English day camp, so I've seen part of the school, and it's a really small school. I didn't ask what I'm supposed to wear, but I hope it's not my usual uniform. That would be awful!

6

ATTENDING NAKHON PHANOM UNIVERSITY

September 26, 2006

TODAY was a lot of fun. I had my first day of college. Apparently, I don't have to wear a uniform. The class is really informal, which is nice. I had two classes for two hours each and an hour lunch in the middle. There are about 30 students from Vietnam who are taking this course to enhance their Thai language skills. It was obvious that the other students knew each other well, but they always ensured that I felt included. The teachers tried to involve me in the discussion in both classes. The first teacher spoke some English, but the second one didn't speak it at all. In the second class, we discussed the body parts, which was awesome because I already knew the body parts, so I was on the same level as everyone else. We learned a few more that I didn't know as well, but I didn't take any notes today. After lunch, everyone went crazy with taking pictures of me. I was actually wondering when someone was going to ask me to pose, and once one person did—20 other people followed. Everyone is really nice. I love the class because they all speak Vietnamese as their first language, and none of them speak English, so they have to speak to me in Thai, and I have to speak to them in Thai. We actually talked a lot, which was great practice for everyone. I've decided that this is a good time for me to learn

Vietnamese. I've been here for two months and already know so much Thai by heart that I don't even have to translate some phrases anymore. These are now the phrases that I'm translating into Vietnamese. Well, I haven't done it yet, but I will start tomorrow. Baa Thao taught me my first Vietnamese phrase; *"un germ"* (eat rice) in Vietnamese means *"gin kao"* in Thai. I'm so excited to learn Vietnamese. I really want to get a dictionary but hate bothering P'Nuan to drive me to the store.

September 28, 2006

Today was my last day at NPU. Tomorrow they are taking an exam, and next week is break. Everyone is going home to Vietnam, and more than half of them invited me to go along with them. Unfortunately, my visa will not allow me to travel to other countries. Even if I was allowed to go, I wouldn't because I'm really looking forward to the light festival coming up in a few days.

About Thai boys being shy—they are so not! Going to NPU, all the girls sit in the front. Then there is one row of guys in the back and a group of guys right behind me. The only ones that weren't trying to sit next to me were either gay or had girlfriends in the class. One guy asked me out today. I can't even talk to him! I guess this doesn't count because these are all Vietnamese guys. The boys in *Piyamahalachalai* School are somewhat shy, but, if I even step out of our house, random 40-year-old men will sit around the house and just stare. Some of them are really creepy. Some people will stop by and talk with me a little, but usually they are the nice people that are not too creepy. I still live my life in that naïve nothing-bad-can-happen-to-me stage, so I usually talk with everyone. Hey, I'm just practicing my Thai.

One day I was sitting out front of my house waiting for Fye to come over to pick me up. A guy, who appeared to be in his thirties, walked past me twice, just staring. I tried not to pay attention, but, the third time he walked by, I looked up and smiled at him, and he made a big scene of choking on his juice in response to getting my attention. It was all just an act to make me laugh, but it was flattering nevertheless.

I keep forgetting to write these funny stories in my journal. Maybe because they don't seem important at the time, but, looking back on them, they are hilarious. I went to visit a temple housing the biggest Buddha in Thailand with P'Nan and a few other Rotarians. We were walking up this really steep hill, and I had to cross over this little stream that was running over the rocks. The water was muddy, though, and I slipped and fell. My jeans were covered in mud, and everyone started freaking out. I was laughing hysterically because there were five Asian girls using these little tissues to wipe the mud off my jeans. I really wish I had a picture from a third-person point of view. It was so funny. I got a new outfit out of it too, so it all worked out.

Remember me writing about that horrible Korean movie that I saw? Well, I was wrong; it wasn't a movie. It's a Korean soap opera that apparently is really popular here because we watch it every day. I'm actually getting used to the bad acting and am trying to follow the show, which is difficult because I usually listen to someone speak Thai and watch their mouth, but here it is dubbed over from Korean, so that doesn't work.

I'm starting to get really bored with studying Thai. That's all I ever do, or at least it seems like it. Now that I'm on break, I never get to hang out with my friends. Nothing happens during the day or at night because we are always home by 9:00 or 10:00 p.m. Leaving to go out at 6:00 or 8:00 p.m. means that we don't spend that much time doing anything.

It seems to me that the Vietnamese language is a whole lot easier to learn than Thai. I'm trying to learn the words that come naturally to me in Thai. It's crazy that I can say "delicious" in five different languages! I really don't want to change host families because I don't think *Adjant* Gannagar is Vietnamese, so she couldn't teach me things that I am able to learn here.

7

MORE LIFE AT HOME

October 1, 2006

I have been meaning to write this for a while. This house is definitely run by a three-year-old. Sinwia gets anything he wants, and everybody jumps through hoops to get it for him. He cries constantly, but it's like fake crying, with no tears and a sort of whine, and then it's, "Oh here, look, see, you can have it." Don't get me wrong; he's a good kid, but he's playing everyone in the house, and they let him. I don't get it. At meal times they chase him around with his dinner. He's three years old! He has no boundaries because if he wants something he knows he isn't supposed to have, he just cries until he gets it. The punishment system is crazy, too. If he does something really wrong, he gets hit with a stick as punishment, rather hard, too. It would definitely hurt. On the contrary, if someone is teasing or playing with Sinwia and he gets angry and cries because he didn't win or whatever, that person will be hit with the stick, just to make Sinwia happy. So what does the boy learn? With that and watching Power Rangers all day, he constantly wants to play fighting games. Then, I moved into the house.

I find it really humorous that I am the only person in this house who he doesn't hit no matter what I say he cannot do, and I can't even talk! Body language really is the most useful. I use, "Hey," a lot, too, in different tones. Today, he was trying to climb on the coffee table, which he knows he's not allowed to do. Every time he tried to put his leg up, I held it down. He'd look at me, and I'd give him that, "You know you're not supposed to do that," look. It was funny because he started to whimper, and he looked back at me, but my expression had not changed. He stopped, picked up my pen, clicked it open, and held it back like he was going to stab me with it and gave me a really angry look. I got face-level with him, put my finger up as if to say, "You don't do that," and gave him a look to match. Well, he grabbed the pad of paper from the table and stormed off to the other chair as if to tell me he wasn't going to play with me anymore. Then, of course, two minutes later, he had forgotten all about it. I don't understand why they give in to him all the time. He wouldn't cry as much if he had boundaries. He already knows the boundaries with me, and I can't communicate with him because I've been here only two months. I know that you are probably thinking that this kid is so spoiled, but every kid here is treated the same way. They chase their kids around with food at mealtimes until they're five to seven years old. Imagine starting Kindergarten and not knowing how to sit up at the lunch table to eat. I went to the park with Sinwia and Mae one day. Mae brought a bowl of food to feed him while he ran around. I thought that was a little much. I mean, in the house is one thing, but in a park? Then he met two other boys his age. Each boy had his mom chasing him around with a bowl of food, as well. Crazy!

I should mention that Thais can't imagine what the American version of daycare is. They ask me what my mom does, and I try to explain that she owns and operates a daycare center where she teaches really little kids. "Oh, she babysits." "No, she *teaches*!" "How many kids?" "There are 48 kids, in total." "Wow! How does she handle all of them?" I really wish I could demonstrate to them the way that American kids are expected to behave. They wouldn't know what to think.

October 7, 2006

I just got home from the illuminated boat festival. It is officially called the Illuminated Boat Procession. It is an annual event in Nakhon Phanom, marking the end of the Buddhist Lent. The festival is held on the Mekong River in front of the Nakhon Phanom Provincial Office. In all, more than 50 boats, elaborately adorned with lights and assorted offerings, were set afloat and lit up the entire Mekong River. Other activities during this festival include a colorful street procession and some cultural performances, as well as some traditional games. For once, we stayed out past 10:00 p.m.—it was actually 11:30 when we got home. The boat procession wasn't as good as I expected. I was a little disappointed because everyone had been telling me for a month how beautiful it would be; I kept expecting more. It was still fun, though. Around 7:00 p.m. we went to P'Lek's apartment, which overlooks the Mekong River. P'Lek is another Rotarian and good friends with P'Nuan. While there, P'Nuan and P'Lek were talking a lot, so I just watched the boats go by and watched all the people below. I was expecting there to be a ton of foreigners because of what people had told me, but there were only a handful. Most visitors were from other provinces within Thailand.

People here are so obsessed with looks. It's crazy! The first thing anyone comments to me about is my figure. During the Illuminated Boat Procession, I was walking the promenade bordering the Mekong River when a woman stopped me and began talking. She first asked me where I was from and then went on to comment about my petite figure and stated that most Americans were overweight. It is common for Thais to openly comment about another person's shape or weight, even if they don't know them. Honestly, the girls in my class won't eat a lot or are constantly on diets because they think they are fat. Maybe I'm being so critical because in America, I'm used to seeing people of all sizes, and even bigger people can be really pretty. It's common here to ask others how much they weigh. When I first arrived here, I didn't know how much I weighed in kilos because I was used to pounds, so I used that as an excuse. People would get really upset that I wouldn't tell them, like I should have checked my weight when I got off the airplane. I weigh more than any girl I have talked to, but 48kg is not heavy. I'm perfectly fine with it.

October 8, 2006

Happy 19th birthday to me! Today was so much fun. Mae and Paw went to Laos, so P'Nuan and I watched a movie that lasted all morning. I saw part of it last night, so I knew the characters and could understand some of the plot. It is a Korean movie with Thai subtitles, with an occasional scene in English so that I can catch up with what is going on. Compared with the TV programs here, this movie was awesome. It had 16 DVDs, each lasting about an hour. I think I might have seen eight of them yesterday and today. For lunch P'Pin bought *kao nio* (sticky rice) and *som-thom*, which was so good! I could eat that every day! Oh, wait, that's right; I do! Then an hour or so later, P'Nuan bought two Thai pizzas from the market near the house. They were small (four slices) and had hot dog slices, crab, peppers, and a tasty sauce that I can't quite describe. The dough was perfectly seasoned. I had really been craving pizza for a while. Later in the day, P'Nuan took me to dinner, and we met a few other people there, mostly Rotarians. Then we went to karaoke, ordered drinks, and then a whole bunch of Rotarians and their friends came. P'Nuan brought in a birthday cake with two candles, a "1" and a "9." They all sang to me and showed me how Thai birthdays are celebrated. The first piece of cake is given to the oldest person in the room. It was a lot of fun. In the morning, Baa Thao called me from Bangkok to wish me a happy birthday. I had a feeling she would, but I didn't want to get my hopes up. I miss her. I don't know what I'm going to do when I switch families.

October 23, 2006

I got home from Bangkok this morning around 2:00 a.m., so I relaxed all day and slept till noon. This was my last day of vacation. I love Bangkok—everything about it! There is always something going on, and it's never quiet. The whole reason P'Nuan and I went was to sell knick-knack things at a mall for a week. P'Neui and P'Sia own a company that made and sold the knick-knacks. Among the items were small plastic Buddha statues, cat statues with a waving arm, and necklaces, which consisted of a cheap plastic pendant and a thin string. The items that they sold were marketed to the superstitious aspect of Thai society and as souvenirs for foreigners. These pendants and statues are rumored to bring good luck and prosperity to the owner. They mainly sell these items wholesale to other stores, which retail them individually. Because they mostly sell to other stores, P'Neui's house is not separated from their shop like Paw's electronics store is. When I first walked into P'Neui's house, I immediately noticed that the first floor contained 10-foot-high stacks of boxes. There is only enough room for a walkway to the kitchen, located in the back of the house. There is also one other room on the first floor, which is where the workers assembled the knick-knacks. I spent a morning during my stay sitting in a circle on the floor with about 10 other workers, stringing thread through pendants for necklaces and listening to their conversations. On the necklaces that were ready for shipment, I noticed a sticker on the cellophane that read, "MADE IN THAILAND." After my return to America, I began to notice where different items that I owned were made. It was neat to be able to be a part of the assembly of something that one day might be sold in America. Near the kitchen in the back of the house was a staircase leading to the second floor. The staircase opened into a small open room, which was also stacked high with boxes. There was a sliding glass door that separated the office area, just two desks with computers, and a bedroom from the rest of the upstairs. These were the only two rooms in the house that were air conditioned.

Selling the knick-knacks in Bangkok was a lot of fun. There wasn't much to do, but I like watching people and listening to their conversations, trying to understand. I said, "*Cheun chome dai, na, ka*," more times than I can count. Translation: "Feel free to come have a look." I got to walk around the streets of Bangkok by myself whenever two people were already working our booth. It was so nice being given a little freedom. I even bargained a little! I ran out of shirts a few days before we were coming home, so I had to go find some. The cheapest one was only 80 *baht*! It's really cute.

The night market is my favorite in Bangkok. Most of the merchandise is secondhand and incredibly inexpensive. I went only once and just got batteries. There are so many people—I love it, but going with P'Nan, it's run here and run there. She takes me to really cool places, but I wish I could just get dropped off for a few hours and be able to take my time looking at things.

After the week of selling things was over, we went to a very nice restaurant. After we ate, we got on a boat and cruised the Chao Praya River, which is the main river running through Bangkok. It was really pretty. Going up the river, I didn't really get to see much of anything. P'Nan was taking a million pictures with me in them, so I just stood where she told me to and smiled. Then on the way back I got to look around. They had platefuls of fruit and drinks for everyone. It was really nice. They got a huge discount for it, too, because P'Big always takes her tour groups there, so she pulled some strings. P'Big and P'Nan work at their travel agency in Bangkok, and P'Nuan works with them from our other house in Nakhon Phanom.

After the cruise, they told me that they were taking me to see "entertainment." Naturally, I expected a show of some sort. We stopped at a nightclub. I was excited because I really wanted to visit a nightclub in Thailand. The one I went to in France was a ton of fun. To make things even cooler, patrons must be at least 20 years old to get in because they serve alcohol. My big sister, who happens to be a Rotarian, lied to get me into the nightclub. How cool is that? We got drinks and food, enough for three times as many people as were with us. After a while, more people joined us, all girls. I'm thinking that it's really weird that no one is hanging out with any guys. An hour later the whole place was packed—with girls. I had never been in a gay club before, but it was fun hanging out with everyone. Then, as the hours flew by and the vodka bottles emptied, it became a little too much for me. Not to mention that I was the prettiest one there, which was really awkward. P'Nuan and I basically had our own little party with peanuts and Pepsi. It was a good night.

The next day everyone else was hung over from partying the night before, so I just watched TV with Sinwia and read a little. That night, we went to the movies. It's really cool because at the beginning of every movie, everyone in the audience stands up to respect the King. A short picture slide show of the King and royal family is shown while the National Anthem is played. I saw two movies while I was in Bangkok: "The Ant Bully" and a Thai ghost story. The Thai movie was confusing, perhaps in part because of the translation subtitles. It wasn't all that scary, just characters popping out, which I hate, but I'm glad I saw it. It was actually more of a comedy than a ghost story. It was interesting to me to observe the small cultural differences evident in the movie. In one scene, university students were evacuating the "haunted" dorms. The characters were obviously terrified in this scene, but even the scary background music didn't stop me from laughing at the fact that every person was carrying a rice cooker, amongst boxes of other things.

The next day we went to the crocodile farm and zoo. It was so cool! I got to hold a real monkey. It was the cutest thing I've ever seen. I also saw a camel and hippos for the first time. The big attraction was the crocodile show. I thought it was mean because the guys would drag the crocs on stage by their tails and poke them in the face with sticks to show the audience how loud the sound is when they bite. All in all, it was a lot of fun. Again, I would like to have stayed longer.

October 27, 2006

There are two things that bug me about Thai people. First of all, apparently it's hot for guys to have long fingernails. I mean my fingernails are cute, but they wouldn't look good on a guy. Long nails are apparently against my school's rules, but the school hasn't made me cut them, at least not yet. I'm going to try to keep up the, "Oh, I'm just an exchange student" act, so maybe they won't make me. My nails are a nice length, filed down slightly to make them less noticeable, but the guys' fingernails are gross! It is either their pointer finger or their pinky, and the rest are filed completely down. In college, students are allowed to have long nails, so the guys' pinky fingernails are at least twice as long as one filed completely down. It is so unattractive! They always point with that finger as if to show off or something.

The second thing I can't get over is how Thai people pick their noses. I mean, seriously, do they realize how gross that looks? I'll be sitting in class, and the teacher will be talking about derivatives or something, the one subject that isn't completely foreign to me, and then he decides to dig for some treasure. When I first got here and saw people picking their noses, I just pretended I didn't see. It's a little difficult when the person is in the middle of a sentence or telling a story and then there goes a finger. I, however, seem to be the only person noticing these moments. In America, I recall many parents scolding their children to stop picking their nose. I guess no one here was ever taught to be embarrassed by that mannerism.

October 31, 2006

Happy Halloween! I love Halloween. Halloween is my all-time favorite holiday. Well, besides Christmas, but seriously, Christmas is so much more than a holiday that it shouldn't even be in the same classification. Anyway, today I got to school at 5:30 a.m. Well, I waited for Yee at 5:30; we didn't get to school until later because everyone in Thailand is late and because we stopped to give food to the monks and to get ourselves some breakfast. We spent all morning painting our faces and getting into our costumes. I was a Japanese ghost. I got to wear a Yukata, and a few girls played with my hair while a few others put make-up all over my face. This was the first year that *Piyamahalachalai* School celebrated Halloween, so it made me feel really special. I was surprised that none of the kids in the school had ever heard of Halloween. Right after announcements in the morning, Dear, Yee, and I addressed the entire school. I read a speech that I had written in Thai script about the Halloween holiday. I was so nervous about it that I started shaking worse and worse as I went on. Eventually, Dear had to hold my paper for me. I did fairly well, thanks to her for some help with the hard words, but speaking in public is not my thing. I think I'm getting better at it, though. After announcements, the rest of 6/7 walked around and handed out candy to everyone. I think I have a million pictures of today. Once classes started, we went to some of the rooms of the younger kids and handed out more candy, but only if they said, "Trick-or-treat." It was nice because I got to go home at noon, although then I had to go renew my visa. It's a shame I didn't get out of school for that.

Yesterday, I went to my first Thai wedding. It was so beautiful. Everyone was dressed in formal attire, and it was held in the best hotel in Nakhon Phanom. Once we got there, we had our pictures taken with the bride and groom. I kind of felt bad for them because they stood for pictures for at least an hour, with all the people that were coming and the small conversations they had with each group. Actually, in retrospect, I could see it serving as a nice account of the people who attended or have the picture sent with the thank-you cards as a keepsake for those who attended. Apparently, the couple got married in the morning, a ceremony that I wasn't invited to, but Mae and Paw attended. Last night's event was just a party, much bigger than the actual ceremony. P'Nuan was trying to explain to me that the party that we were attending is about the equivalent of an American wedding and the ceremony that Mae and Paw attended was usually attended by just family and close friends. There were a few hundred people at this ceremony, and this was considered to be a small wedding. I'm told that usually there are around 600 or 700 people in attendance. Once everyone arrived, the bride and groom went on stage with their parents, and then some guy gave a speech. A lei of flowers was placed around each of their necks, and then they cut the cake, together. It was totally just for show because the cake had 10 tiers, but only the bottom tier was real cake, and no one got to eat it! There was karaoke for the rest of the evening. Paw sang, "Judy, I Love You," solo, and I took him the rose that was the centerpiece of our table. I get to go to another wedding this week, so I'll be able to compare a little. The next one is going to be a lot bigger, too. I love weddings!

November 10, 2006

I have been incredibly busy since the last time I wrote. The day after Halloween, the teachers conducted a uniform inspection at school. Basically, the teachers went amongst the students to see if anyone's hair was too long (longer than right below the ears). If it was, a teacher would cut a chunk of it off! That made it look really bad, which is what they wanted, so the students would have to go to a barber and get the rest of their hair cut to that length. It is okay to have really long hair because it can be put into a ponytail. If the hairstyle is short, and the student has allowed it to get too long for that style, then that is unacceptable. I have long hair, anyway, so nothing would have happened to me, but, just because I'm an exchange student, it probably wouldn't matter about my hair length. There is so much special treatment for me.

For the past few weeks, everyone at school has been preparing for Sport Festival. The whole school was divided into four colors, depending on the student's concentration of study: Mathematics (Yellow), Science (Blue), Thai (Pink), Foreign Language (Purple). All of my friends were in Pink, and all of the English teachers wanted me to be in Purple, so they let me decide which color I wanted. I think it took me all of five seconds to pick Pink.

To prepare the reader (and myself) for the following information, I would just like to reinforce the principle that, as an exchange student, I will not say no to any opportunity. Contrary to many beliefs, the world did not come to an end, and no anvils have fallen from the sky. All right, I will actually say it: I became a cheerleader. Wow, it looks even worse when written down on paper! Just to keep my sanity, I have chosen to call it "hand dancing." I learned only six or seven songs (out of about 20) because I joined the squad later than everyone else and because I wanted to be able to do other things in the festival, too. I also played basketball, but we didn't practice at all for that.

The best part of the festival was the last day. I had to get up at 3:00 a.m. to go to the school and get my hair and makeup done for the parade. I was so excited to be wearing a Thai dress with a ton of accessories. The best part—my friends in America would be completely jealous—was that I got to be carried on this platform by eight guys all wearing Thai classic dance attire. It was so unbelievably cool. Everyone was taking my picture and made the boys pose about 50 times during the parade. The boys were so sweet, too. They definitely treated me like a princess. For instance, I could see them sweating and could sense that they were getting really tired, so I said, *"Nak mai?"* (Is it heavy?) One replied, *"Mai nak, krub"* (No, it's not heavy.) and another said, *"Mai, hen mai"* (No, look at this), and he carried his bar with one finger. Then, all the other guys started yelling at him because that put more weight on them. My face was starting to hurt from smiling so much, but then I would look at the boys and have to laugh. More than once, we would get to a stopping point in the parade, and they would set the platform down and let out huge sighs at the relief of the weight and would stretch their arms. Yee came over during one of the breaks and started yelling at them, playfully, that they were all weak and to pick me up so she could get a good picture. Another funny time was when half the guys wanted to put me down, but the front guys could see the line beginning to move, so I was holding on as best I could, with the position I was in, at the mercy of all the guys.

Once we arrived back at the school, we had to stay in the line of our color, but everyone got to relax while we waited to be judged. The boys all stood behind me with a sheet to block the sun, and one was next to me with a hat fanning me. We were all having a really good time. Every time someone moved so that the sun hit me a little, one of the guys would punch him teasingly, and then the rest of the boys would all start yelling at him. It was so much fun to be a princess for a day!

One evening my mom, P'Nuan, and I were standing in the shop waiting to be picked up to go out for the evening, and Mae tells me, in Vietnamese, to have a seat. I walked over next to her and sat down, and she commented to P'Nuan how impressed she was that I could understand Vietnamese. I tried to explain to her in Thai just how I understood what she had said in Vietnamese, but she and P'Nuan couldn't understand the point that I was trying to make. Giving up my attempt at their language, I sighed and pointed to the dog and said, "Joey understands Vietnamese. I always hear you telling him to sit." P'Nuan started laughing so hard that she had trouble translating what I said for Mae. Of course, Mae was laughing and told her friends about it when they came. Now whenever her friends come to the house, they stop and have short conversations with me in Vietnamese, asking me if I've eaten supper yet, and, if I am standing, to sit down. I can't believe I'm learning a third language—from a dog.

November 14, 2006

Today in gym class with 6/7, we began dancing. We are learning ballroom dancing, which I am really excited about. No one here is a good dancer, though. I really want to learn how to ballroom dance, and I found out that there are classes on Monday and Wednesday nights taught by my parents' friend, but I can't speak that well and don't have a partner. Speaking of partners, today in class we got to pick our own. I had not yet seen a fight at school here, but today I was definitely the cause of one. It was quite embarrassing, actually. The guys were only pretending to beat each other up, but if I had picked a guy myself, I would have never heard the end of it. At last, I was matched with Thong, a really tall, really dark guy (appointed by the teacher). At every break, other guys would come over and dance with me, too. It was a lot of fun.

On my way home today, riding between Yee and her sister on the motorcycle, out of the blue I got pooped on by a bird. I've never been pooped on by a bird before, let alone while zig-zagging on a motorcycle. It was so gross. Yee almost wrecked the bike because she was laughing so hard. Tomorrow morning, after everyone at school finds out about this, I'm going to be a whole lot more popular than usual. A few years ago, on a trip to France, my friend, Chad, got pooped on by a bird. It was not nearly as funny when it happened to me. I've got to laugh about things like that, though. What else can I do?

Yesterday, I ate my first meal of KFC. Nakhon Phanom doesn't have any fast food restaurants, so when Yee left for college testing in Sakhon Nakhon, a neighboring province, she promised to bring me something. She brought me a chicken burger and fries with cheese and crispy things. She brought it over so late, though, that I had to put it in the fridge and eat it the next afternoon. By then, the lettuce was wilted, the fries were soggy, and the cheese was cold... it was heaven on a plate! I savored every bite as long as I could. Oh, how I miss fast food!

November 15, 2006

I broke my door. Don't ask me how. I locked it so I could change without anyone coming in, and, when I left, I checked the outside knob; it was still locked. After trying everything that I could think of, I still couldn't get it unlocked. Of course, due to my luck, no one was around. Usually P'Pond is on the computer all day and all night, but the one time I need him, he's gone. Fortunately, I have keys so I could lock my door when I go to school, which I never do. I stuck one in the door and kept the other one in case someone decided to come and take that one.

Not only that, but my air conditioner is broken. I think Baa Thao had something to do with that because she came in this morning. I had already woken up, but my alarm didn't go off yet. To block the sunlight, I pulled the covers over my head. I think she thought that I was really cold, so she left the room, and, when she came back, she said it was broken. Whether she just unplugged it or it really is broken, I don't know, but I'm really hot and hope it gets fixed soon.

November 16, 2006

The other morning my mom drove me to school, but she was running late. As she dropped me off beside the gate at the entrance to the school, I noticed a teacher was standing there with a group of other students, who had all come in late as well, collecting them for punishment. She motioned for me to join their group, and we stood and waited for announcements to be over. When the principal was finished speaking, the teacher holding us hostage began yelling at us in Thai. She then walked over to me, stood on the sidewalk curb so she would be closer to my height, even though she was still shorter, and continued yelling in Thai. I just held my head down, nodding occasionally, partially to acknowledge her anger toward us and partially to hide my laughter. Having an Asian person get so worked up, angrily yelling at me in a language that I can't fully understand, is just funny. She got to the end of her monologue and finally yelled at me in Thai, "Do you understand?" I lifted my head and with an innocent smile replied in Thai, "I'm sorry, but I don't understand." Everyone who was there, including the teacher herself, burst into laughter. She asked if any of the other students could translate for me, and one girl looked over and said in broken English, "Not come late."

Tonight, I was listening to Paw sing karaoke, and the phone rang. Of course, no one else is home, so Paw told me to run and answer it. I think I repeated what he said three times, and it was obvious that I was supposed to hurry. I "hurried," secretly praying that the party would hang up before I got there. No such luck. I even answered the wrong phone at first and got a dial tone and was completely relieved until the other phone rang again. Our conversation started out okay:

"Hello, Sa-wat-dee ka."	"Hello, (Hello in Thai)."
"Sa-wat-dee ka. Koun Mae pai nai?"	"Hello. Is your mom there?"
"Mae pai leeo."	"Mom left already."

Then she said something in Thai that I didn't understand. I looked up, and Paw was walking out on the balcony so I asked him where Mae was, but, because of the distance, I couldn't hear to pronounce it correctly. It was so horrible. Paw was yelling, "*Krai?*" and I asked her, but she talked too fast and slurred her words. Of course, she had to make a complete compound sentence so I couldn't decipher which word was her name. Then I repeated it for her, and she said it was right, so I screamed it to Paw, but he didn't understand. Finally, I pronounced where Mae was correctly, and the other lady was relieved, too, that she understood and we could finally end the conversation. I have a feeling it was one of the ladies that comes to our house every month for karaoke, so I know I'll hear more about it when I see her again.

November 17, 2006

Shortly after I learned that Thailand would be my host country, I was given a brochure about three optional tours that Thai Rotary offers to all exchange students. One is to Phu Kradung, which is an area featuring the highest mountain in Thailand. It is a nice area but requires a lot of walking and climbing. The second is to Chiang Mai and Chiang Rai, including different hill tribes living in Thailand and featuring the Golden Triangle, which is where the borders of Thailand, Laos, and Myanmar (formerly Burma) meet. The third is to southern Thailand, which is where a lot of vacation resorts are located. It is also the area hit by a major tsunami in 2004, as well as being the setting for the James Bond movie, *Man with the Golden Gun*. These tours are well received by the inbound exchange students because they can spend some time with friends, share stories of their exchange experience, and speak English with someone. The timing of the tours is during the Western holiday seasons, which serves to ease the homesickness at times of traditional family get-togethers. The first tour is during Thanksgiving, the second during Christmas, and the third at Easter.

8

PHU KRADUNG TOUR

December 2, 2006

I just got back from Phu Kradung! It was so much fun. I'm going to try to write down everything that happened, but I don't know if I'll have enough time. First of all, I thought I was going straight to the mountain on Sunday, so I made plans with a bunch of people for Friday night and Saturday. Well, as always, plans changed, and I was the last to know. When I got home after volleyball practice on Thursday night, they told me I was leaving tomorrow in the after-noon. I was already planning on taking Friday off to do laundry, so luckily my teachers already knew. I was able to do one load of laundry on Thursday night. In Thailand, most homes have just a washing machine and a squisher. The squisher wrings out the water, and then the clothes are hung on a line to dry completely. Friday I packed and went to the market next door to buy other necessities. I got on the bus at about 1:00 p.m. and didn't get to Udon Thani until 7:00 p.m. We live only about a three-hour drive from Udon Thani, but, because the bus stopped so often to let people on or off, it took more than twice as long to get there. I spent that night and the next night with Mary, who is an inbound from New York. I didn't really get a chance to hang out with her on the mountain, so it was nice to talk with her before and after.

November 18, 2006

Basically, I spent the whole day touring Udon Thani. I hung out mainly with Mary and the other exchange students living in this province: Zoe, inbound from Canada; Theresa, inbound from America; and Heidi, another inbound from Canada. It was fun to be able to go wherever we wanted and buy our own lunch whenever we were hungry. I visited the mall, which was fun, but we didn't really shop that much. At night, Heidi went to another house, so the four of us went back to Mary's and made spaghetti and cream of mushroom and ham soup for dinner. It was so good! I really do miss American food, but I did notice how much my appetite has changed. I barely ate anything because my stomach has gotten used to eating about 20 small meals a day. After dinner, we watched TV for a while, then went to bed. Zoe was sharing my queen-sized bed, and we got to sleep kind of late because we stayed up late talking.

November 19, 2006

We got up about an hour before we had to because Mary and Zoe wanted me to experience their favorite breakfast place, and we had to walk to it. It was at the other end of town, and we practically ran there, ate as fast as we could, and ran back, but it was really good! We rode in a van with Katie, inbound from Ontario, Canada; J.D., inbound from Quebec, Canada; and Sazoke, inbound from Japan, along with Max (who was an exchange student last year to America), a Rotarian, and a driver. Everyone was so excited to get to know everyone else, and, although we were a little overwhelmed and tired, no one slept. We were the first ones to get to the hotel. I talked a little with Sazoke, but it was boring until more people came. There were two more groups of people, and when everyone got there, it was so crowded! There was never a moment when I was alone. Everyone was eager to meet everyone else, so it was a lot of fun. Of course, by meeting 45 other people in one night, remembering names and countries was impossible. Jennifer gave me a *kwai* (water buffalo) key chain for "saving her at the airport." She is the sweetest person! She's in a province with Erika (from New Jersey) who, as soon as I met her, said, "Oh, you're Ashley!

You're all I hear about from Jennifer." I'm glad that she appreciated me staying with her when our flight landed. Really, I just think that everyone was so excited about their arrival in Thailand that no one else realized just how horribly sick Jennifer was feeling. Anyway, we all exchanged cards and pins, except I completely forgot to bring mine. Oh well, the exchange student tour to Chiang Mai in northern Thailand is only two weeks away. I'll hand out my cards and pins then.

I hung out with Erika and Jennifer in their room for a long time, my motivation being that I wanted to take a shower there. Only two of the rooms had warm water, and I knew that the temperature at the top of the mountain would be freezing. I went back to my room with Kelly and Theresa at about 11:00 p.m. and didn't get to sleep until about 3:00 a.m. because Theresa and I stayed up, talking. I forgot to say that earlier Marie (from Canada) and I ate a quart of chocolate ice cream together; it was so good!

In addition to the Rotary blazers, district 6420 provided business cards for the outbound students. The cards have a picture of the student, information about our hosting and sponsoring Rotary clubs, and contact information. They make it really convenient when we are meeting other exchange students because we don't have to worry about quickly jotting down all of their information and then worry about losing it. The pictures are intended to help us remember who each person is.

The blazers are great. Rotary intends for them to be a keepsake of our experience abroad. Many students will either buy or make pins featuring something about their home country and exchange them with other students. Exchange students make it an unspoken personal goal to put as many things as possible on their blazers. Along with numerous pins, mine has key chains, patches, stuffed animals, and my biggest attachment, a water gun (story about that later). Each item carries a story of how it was received and a memory of that event.

November 20, 2006

Morning came quickly, and stuffing my suitcase with everything was nearly impossible, but I did it. 11 kg! We had two breakfasts, one at the hotel and another when we arrived at the mountain. I didn't really eat that much. I ate enough, but I didn't want to be too full for the long climb up the mountain. I started up Phu Kradung Mountain with Jennifer, Erika, and a bunch of friends, but they were walking too slowly. Maybe it was excitement, but I didn't want to wait. I double-checked with Jennifer and Erika to be sure that they were okay with me leaving them to go ahead. Then Erika caught up to me at the rest stop. There were four rest stops, complete with refreshments, about .5k apart and completely paid for by Rotary. I walked with Erika for almost 3k, but she was going too slowly for me. I wanted to see what my time would be if I just kept going. Talking was difficult for the last .5k because the steep and rugged terrain caused shortness of breath. Then I met a Thai kid who just happened to be there with a group of his classmates for a senior trip. He told me that he went to Germany last year with American Field Service. He spoke English very well. It was really cool to talk with him but, at the same time, really hard to walk. It was kind of a relief when we had to let the porters through. Oh, guess what? I got a picture of the porter with my bag! I'm so excited, but, at the same time, I felt extremely bad for him because of how much weight he had to carry. Every time I passed one going down with a load, he would smile at me because I am a *farang*, and I would thank him for carrying everything and ask him if he was tired or if it was heavy. They were really sweet people and weren't upset about doing it. Probably it was because they were making so much money; 15 *baht* per kilogram, and each porter had between six and eight bags. The whole trip could have been kind of expensive. The entrance fee for climbing the mountain is 40 *baht* for Thais and 400 *baht* for *farang*s. That's not an exaggeration: 400 *baht*. If we had two different prices in America, we'd have so many discrimination lawsuits that every lawyer in the country would be busy, but this is Thailand. Anyway, I arrived at the top in about three hours. I'm not sure about the exact time because I checked the time when I got to the *Champ*, which was the snack shop where we were told to meet. Rotary had already worked it out that all food and beverage charges for us at the *Champ* were already paid for. I hung out at the top of the mountain for a while before waiting for more friends to walk with for the remaining 3,000 to 4,000 meters to the *Champ*. This whole trip was really just about talking to everyone, and all of the exchange students agreed that we really needed this.

November 21, 2006

Of all the people in my dorm room, only Erika and I got up at 4:00 a.m. to watch the sunrise. As Prapart put it, we got up early to "say hello to the sun." Exchange students from last year said that it wasn't worth it, so I didn't expect much and definitely got what I expected. Basically, I wanted to spend as little time as possible sleeping on this tour, so that was just a reason for me to get up early. The sunrise was pretty, just not worth the hike to see it. There was hot chocolate waiting for me at the *Champ* when we returned. After I ate breakfast and got changed for the day, we went on a 20k hike. That was a lot of fun, but it was really hot. We walked in open fields a lot. McKinsey, an inbound from the St. Louis area, and I got sunburned on our necks but just the left side. My face and arms got sunburned too, but it's my own fault for not using sun block. We stopped out there for lunch and then continued on. Everyone was tired and sore. We saw a few waterfalls and a bunch of cliffs. Some people saw a wild elephant off one of the cliffs. I wouldn't have believed them, but they got pictures. I was so jealous. We ended our walk by watching the sunset on one of the cliffs. When we got back, we ate dinner and then sat around our camp fire and talked. I talked with McKinsey and J.D. for a long time. That was a lot of fun. I enjoyed the times that we would spend in smaller groups because it helped us to get to know each other better. Last night, one of the girls got a leach on her foot, and, throughout today, a lot more people got them, so now everyone is terrified and walking around with their pants legs tucked into their socks. It makes me laugh when I think about it—just another funny memory of Rotary Youth Exchange.

November 22, 2006

I slept in till about 7:00 a.m., today. There were a few of us who wanted to go to see the sun rise again, but none of the Rotarians wanted to go. I had a sore throat from talking so much during the past few days, plus my whole head was just stuffy. I walked to the *Champ* and made myself some Ovaltine. The lady there was really nice and kept offering me things. I told her that my throat hurt, and she made me some Thai tea. She was really sweet, and, throughout the rest of the trip, she would always approach me if she needed to say something to anyone, such as telling people they couldn't sit at certain tables because they weren't Rotary tables.

This was the day of the trip when there was nothing planned. There is only so much to talk about. McKinsey, Alicia, and I decided to go for a walk on a different path than we walked yesterday. Alicia is from Japan. She is really quiet and shy but fun to hang out with. She doesn't speak English all that well, though. On the way back, I had to go to the bathroom, and we were still about 3,500 meters from camp. We were walking kind of fast when all of a sudden a white pickup truck came toward us down our path. That was the first and only vehicle I've seen on the top of the mountain. I had to wonder how the truck ever got to the top of this steep mountain. The driver asked if we wanted a ride, and I said, "Yes," and McKinsey said, "No," simultaneously. We discussed it for a few seconds and then hopped on the back. Pretty quickly, we were barreling through the field toward camp at a roller coaster speed. The path wasn't flat either, so it was a lot of fun. We were all taking a ton of pictures. When we got back, McKinsey realized that she had lost her cell phone somewhere on the path. She went back to look for it, and Alicia and I went to the *Champ* to hang out. McKinsey got back fairly quickly. She met the same guy, this time on a motorcycle, who helped her look for it. Surprisingly, they found it at the last cliff we went to. Then a bunch of people decided to go to a waterfall. I wasn't really expecting a good waterfall because all of the ones that I had previously seen were so small, but this waterfall was really big. Jason and Greg decided to go swimming in the freezing water;

that was fun to watch. Greg is from California and is doing his exchange in Korat. I wanted to explore past the waterfall and pond, so McKinsey and I started to cross over. She was almost over a big rock when I saw a spider on the other side. This spider was huge. I told her about it calmly but quickly, so she wouldn't hang around it. Well, she is apparently terrified of spiders and totally freaked out, almost falling off the rock that she was balancing on. Everyone looked over when she screamed from almost falling. I caught her, and then Greg swam over and poked it with a stick and discovered that it was dead. Oops! In my defense, I didn't know that it was dead when I first saw it!

November 23, 2006

I was so tired that I slept really well. Rotary rented two large dorm rooms for us; one for the guys and one for the girls. The girls' dorm room had a dividing wall in the center. Our side was overly full because we had four beds and six people, but the other side had five beds and just Nano sleeping. I think everyone was expecting the other girls to come back, so they didn't want to take their designated beds; no one came back, and Nano had five beds to herself. Nano is one of the oldies, having arrived in Thailand this past January. Because the South African school year is different from the American school year, she will complete her exchange in the middle of winter. The rest of the girls were hanging out in the guys' dorm and must have fallen asleep over there. I know that two guys slept in the girls' dorm because in the boys' dorm there was an all-night party. We weren't allowed to sleep in the opposite sex's dorm, so at breakfast, the Rotarian who was in charge totally freaked out. It seemed at first that we were in trouble because no one was being careful in the morning when coming out of the wrong dorm. That, however, wasn't the issue with Rotary. They were upset because the guys' room was a complete mess, including a bunch of food that they didn't eat. I kind of felt bad for the kids that got called out on it because a lot of other people slept there, too. Nothing, however, happened because of it. The Rotary rules seemed really relaxed on this trip, at least until now, but I'm expecting the rules to be better enforced on the Chiang Mai tour because we won't be secluded.

I started down the mountain with McKinsey, but she was going too fast, so she went ahead with J.D., and I hung back. There was a big group, but I didn't feel like walking with them, so I went by myself, enjoying the quiet. I like walking alone because then people talk to me when they're walking the other way. I stopped to talk with another *farang* from England. He has been here for six years, just *pai tiow*ing (sightseeing), but doesn't speak any Thai at all. He was really interested in the birds and other wildlife here. It was nice to talk to someone that I didn't know. After I left him, I kept going, eventually catching up to Steffen and Henrietta, who had passed me while I was talking to the *farang*. We talked a little but basically watched out for each other. They are both from Germany but are fluent in English. We were getting close to the bottom of the mountain, so it was kind of steep again, making it difficult to talk. Once we got to the cafeteria at the bottom of the mountain, we met up with others from our group. I bought two shirts at the gift shop, partly because I knew I was staying in Udon Thani for two days and I had no more clean outfits. We drew names for Secret Santa because we would be spending Christmas together in Chiang Mai. I was really hesitant about this idea when we were at the top of the mountain, but I drew Kelly's name, so I felt more relieved. At least I know her a little bit; that's all I was worried about.

All in all, Phu Kradung was a ton of fun. I can't wait for the Chiang Mai tour, and I really don't have to wait long. In just two more weeks, we will be together again. I was glad that this was our first tour because it was the shortest one and was a good way to become acquainted with the other exchange students. I know I switch families in a few days, so I spent today cleaning and reorganizing. Once Christmas is over, I will have a lot of room in my second suitcase. I was actually thinking of giving my Christmas gifts to my family and friends in Nakhon Phanom before I go to Chiang Mai. Then I can begin to refill my suitcase with gifts bound for home. I don't want to switch families, but I'm kind of eager for a change. It's just a new phase of my adventure.

9

BACK TO SCHOOL

❦

December 4, 2006

STARTING off the day at school, things were fairly normal. I avoided the English department all morning because I knew that *Adjant* Gannagar, my next host mom, was going to ask me when I was moving, but I didn't know. I'm always the last to know, anyway. Exchange students are required to have more than one host family during their year abroad. Rotary has established this rule to allow the student to experience different perspectives of their hosting country. Just as American families differ, those in other countries vary by size and living style.

When I was getting ready to go home, Yee's sister, Gate, told me that *Adjant* Gannagar wanted me to see her before I left. I couldn't get around that. At a quarter after three, I walked into the English department and told everyone, a million different times, how fun Phu Kradung was. Then *Adjant* said that she talked to P'Nuan earlier and that she was coming over at five this evening to pick me up. She asked if I had packed yet, which I hadn't, and then said that it's okay if I wasn't ready. She'd just come to get me and that I could get my stuff later. Well, I obviously didn't want to do that, so, despite having volleyball practice after school, I went straight home and began packing as quickly as possible, only breaking for 10 minutes for a snack of *som-thom*, my "last meal." I expected *Adjant* to come a little early because I knew she was excited. When she came, I still wasn't ready, so P'Nuan and P'Pin helped me get the last of my things into bags, while P'Joey carried my ready suitcases downstairs. P'Joey is the only employee in our shop in the front of our house. He would often talk to P'Pin on his break, but rarely did I talk with him. When we got to *Adjant*'s house, P'Nuan had called a bunch of Rotarians to come over to get some pictures. I had been collecting a lot of things for my blazer and just finished sewing and pinning all of them on last night, so I was happy to be able to get those pictures.

I really think I will like living here. I have two siblings. Oak, my brother, is 17, and Euy, my sister, is 15. Euy likes to practice her English and is very eager to talk, so that's good. The only thing is that this is Asia, and it seems as though every kid in Asia likes to play on the Internet. How boring! I'm sure I'll find something else to do with my time. My new dad likes to talk with me too, and, when he does, he speaks in a normal speed, so I can get used to hearing normal conversation. Hopefully, I will be able to pick up words more quickly. I hope to decorate my new house for Christmas as soon as possible. We don't have school tomorrow because it's the King's birthday, so maybe I will get a chance to do that. Yee was going to take me to buy a cell phone on Wednesday, but my dad said he was going to give me his extra one. I'm excited about that, but I hope he will let me pay for it with a calling card or something because otherwise I will feel bad using it to call my friends. I hope I can keep it until I leave, but I think that is what my dad intended anyway.

December 11, 2006

Well, I've been here for a week now. I guess it's okay. I was really worried about my move because I was afraid that my new mom would speak only English to me. Well, that is partially true and partially a problem. Whenever I have a conversation with her, I always try to say my part in Thai first and then mix in the English that I don't know the Thai word for yet. She will sometimes play along and speak "Tinglish" back, so that's good, but she constantly makes Euy speak to me in English. It's so annoying because I don't want to speak English! I've even told her about this, but she says that I have all day at school to speak Thai, so I should be okay with speaking English at home. How ridiculous is that? I'm an exchange student. I'm here to study the culture and language! Then they wonder why I can't remember the words for different things because they tell me once and then seem to never say it again in Thai but say it all the time in English and even use English sentences to describe it. Other than that, this family is okay. My siblings don't really like to talk much, probably because it's too difficult for them to say anything in English. They mainly keep to themselves, or they're on the Internet. I've been able to find things to do. Paw is awesome. He really likes to talk to me, and he speaks to me in Thai at a normal speed, so I am getting used to listening to that. He also wants to learn English, but he doesn't know even one-fourth as much English as I know of Thai, so we talk in Thai a lot. I really enjoy talking with him.

Last Friday, I went to a military base with a friend from 6/7. All of the male students at school have to study to be a soldier for three years. The program is voluntary, but, as I stated earlier, the boys who do not volunteer for this course of study would be selected first in the event of a military draft, so, basically, everyone volunteers. Once each year, all the school's student soldiers get together at the military base and watch the real soldiers practice and then the boys practice marching, field drills, and other military activities. I was able to see it this year, and it was so cool! They had smoke bombs and huge guns and were completely decked out in uniforms for battle. I talked with many of the soldiers and their teachers. Of course, everyone loved me. This was probably because I'm white and because my friend, A, her older sister, and I were the only girls there among a few hundred guys.

I went to a bunch of weddings last weekend with P'Nuan and some friends. Saturday morning I wore Baa Thao's Vietnamese dress, which was dark green with white silk pants. About five minutes before we went back to my first host family's house, my Aunt Flo came to visit, completely unexpectedly. I hadn't realized that it was that "time of the month." On the way home, I was obviously embarrassed but wasn't really nervous about how anyone would take the news. I've definitely gotten used to the Thai style of living; no one ever gets worked up over anything. Everything is always so *sa-bai* (relaxed). I got home, and, just as I expected, they didn't really care and gave me some pads. This was about 10:00 a.m., and I didn't have another wedding until 3:00 p.m., so I stayed and visited with Baa Thao along with Mae and a few of her friends, who had come over, as well. Baa Thao was really glad that I was home, even if it was only for a visit. I think Mae was glad, too. I had a conversation with her, and she always speaks fast (but she's spoken fast ever since I got here), so practicing the language with my new Paw helped a lot, and I think she was impressed with my improved Thai. About 2:30 p.m. I fell asleep on the couch and didn't wake up until 4:00 p.m. P'Nuan decided not to go to the next wedding, probably because I looked tired, so we went to the one at 6:00 p.m. Baa Thao thought I was spending the night there, but I had already told Yee that I would spend the night at her house because I had to get up early the next day. She was disappointed, but I'll go back and visit again this week. I want to show her my pictures of Phu Kradung.

I went to Yee's house that night and only got about four hours of sleep because I had to get up at 3:30 a.m. for the parade. This time, it was just a lot of waiting; there were so many people. The parade didn't even start until 1:00 p.m. I was dressed as an angel for the parade. I was, of course, given the primary seat, only because I'm white. I tried to sit upright the whole time. I caught myself slouching a few times, but, of course, I smiled during the entire parade. The other girls didn't understand why I was smiling; they were all tired of smiling. The way I look at it is that I am being shown off during the parade, and everyone wants to see a good parade. Regardless of the outfit I'm wearing or my hairstyle, I won't look good if I'm not smiling. If I look hot and tired and bored, then the whole float won't look good. I'm guessing that, because most Thai kids are involved with parades when they are very young and are in so many, that it's just not fun for them anymore. It's a normal thing to do, so the expressions on their faces match their emotions. Maybe it's because I was in a dance program for so long, too, but I feel like I have to put on a good show in situations like these. Who wants a picture of a bunch of people looking bored?

Today, Paw came home from Bangkok and brought me Christmas lights! I was so excited! I put them on the tree right away and continued decorating it with garland that I made by cutting magazine pages into strips and looping them together. The "tree" that I was decorating was a potted shrub that Mae placed decoratively in the family room. It was the only tree in the house, so it would have to do. I did all this while listening to the Looney Tunes Christmas CD on my iPod. That's the only Christmas CD that I have on my iPod, and I am starting to get sick of it, but it's not Christmas without listening to the Looney Tunes Christmas CD at least once. The Rotary exchange trip to Chiang Mai is only six days away. I still haven't gotten anything for Kelly yet. I'm thinking about something Christmas-related and maybe a necklace or a pin. She doesn't seem to be a girly-girl type so maybe a bracelet of some sort. I'm having trouble with the price range of 200-500 *baht*. Everything in Thailand is so cheap. Maybe I'll get her a Christmas stocking filled with little things. Soon I will be able to wish everyone a Merry Christmas!

December 14, 2006

Today, I was cold.

December 16, 2006

Today was the best day ever! I still hadn't purchased Kelly's Christmas gift, so when I woke up I was determined to do that first. I met Mae in the hallway, and she said that she wanted to go along. I told her I wanted to walk, so we compromised by riding our bikes. I couldn't find a stocking, but I got her a cute watch, bracelet, and some candy and put them in a light-up Santa hat. I thought it looked cute. When we came home, I made macaroni and cheese with Mae. She said that it was okay, but I don't think she really liked it. It was so good; I ate about three-fourths of the box. I think I finished eating in five minutes because I missed American food so much. After that, I wanted to make Rice Krispie treats. I bought all the ingredients the other day and had everything ready to make them.

They turned out okay. Mae liked them. I don't like the cocoa Rice Krispies, but they didn't have the regular ones in the cereal section of the grocery store in Nakhon Phanom. Mae really liked the marshmallows alone. She was so excited that they contained only 80 calories, but then I showed her the serving size (1/4 cup). I think I burst her bubble. She kept eating them, anyway. Thai women are so weight conscious.

I spent the rest of the day wrapping gifts. I really enjoy wrapping gifts, as well as deciding who gets what gift. In the evening, I went to aerobics when Mae went for a run. The aerobics class today was really boring and easy. I like going on weekdays better, when Mae's friend is the teacher. When we got home, I continued wrapping gifts until dinner. I only ate a little bit of dinner because I was still really full from lunch. After dinner, I finished wrapping as many gifts as I could before running out of paper. I brought them downstairs, wearing the Santa hat that I bought for Kelly and fixed my tree. I posed for pictures with everyone, and then NeungOak turned off the room lights and NeungEuy turned on Christmas karaoke music. I sang *Jingle Bells* with NeungEuy and then other songs with Mae. Then we got to the Christian hymns. No one else knew them, so I sang with the microphone by myself. I even surprised myself with that, but I think that shows just how comfortable I feel with this family. NeungEuy left at the beginning to practice her speech for school, so it was just me, Mae, and NeungOak because Paw was still out. We continued singing Christmas hymns and it was fun until we got to *O Holy Night*. I was actually doing well until I reached the "Fall on your Knees" line. My voice cracked, and I started tearing up. I told Mae how this was just normal because I always get emotional when I sing that song. I also told her about how we always sing at church on Christmas Eve and that, during the last song, we turn off the lights and everyone holds a candle. She told NeungOak to play the song again as she left the room. When she came back, she was holding a lighted candle. It was really sweet how she tried to make it like home for me. We played every Christmas song and sang along with them. Then Paw came home, and he and Mae sang some Thai songs until about 11:00 p.m. I, of course, still hadn't started packing, so I took a shower and then packed for the Chiang Mai trip. I packed really quickly and light; I have way more room in my suitcase than I did for Phu Kradung, and this trip is going to be twice as long. I just want to make sure I have room for souvenirs. Today was a great day!

10

CHIANG MAI TOUR

December 27, 2006

I just got back from the Chiang Mai trip. I thought that Phu Kradung was fun; this trip was about 20 times more fun! I think it helped because all of the exchange students basically knew each other already, so we just got to know each other better, and all the long bus rides gave us a chance to talk about anything and everything possible. We did so much in the 10 days that we were there, but one thing we all did very little of was sleep. I'll catch up on that later.

December 17, 2006

P'Nuan was supposed to pick me up around 7:00 a.m., and I was going to get on the bus. Being Thai, she came late, but I had already expected that. I got on the bus around 7:30 a.m. and still had to wait another half an hour to leave. My new host mom was seriously afraid I would starve, so she packed me four Rice Krispy treats, three cartons of milk, and four sandwiches. (Keep in mind that, although the bus ride is somewhat long, we were stopping for a pre-paid lunch). For breakfast, I ate one of the sandwiches and then snuck one of the cartons of milk back into the fridge. When we stopped for lunch, I didn't know how to get the food, so I followed some old ladies around, to the bathroom first, and just did what they did; it worked. When I got to Korat, a security officer told me to wait on a bench and then motioned for a Rotarian, who was obviously pacing at the other end of the bus terminal, waiting for me. We drove to the hotel, and he took me to the luggage room to drop off all my stuff. There were, obviously, a lot of other exchange students already here. Then he told me to hang out with the other inbounds in a different room. When we got to the other room, no one was there, and the receptionist said that they all went that-a-way, pointing to the door. The Rotarian had to leave to go do something, but he didn't want to leave me there alone. Luckily, right before he left, McKinsey came, so I hung out with her. About 5 or 10 minutes later, everyone else came back, all holding ice cream cones. We all started talking as though we had seen each other just yesterday. I joined "The Game", and I know I'm going to kick myself every time I reread my journal for writing about it.

The Game is a game in which, because you know about The Game, you are automatically playing the game. There are a few different versions that I've heard of since I've started playing, but this was the one I was told about. The object of The Game is to forget about The Game. When you think about The Game, you have to say aloud, "I thought about The Game." You then have 30 minutes to forget about The Game. If you fail to do so, you have to say, "I lost The Game." However, because even after losing The Game, you still know about The Game, you are continuously playing The Game. So, now, forget about The Game (or at least try to), and let's get back to the Chiang Mai trip.

My pins were in my suitcase, but I gave out my cards to all of the other exchange students because I had forgotten to bring them on the Phu Kradung trip. I love my cards, and every other exchange student loves them, too. Most Rotary clubs provide outbound students standard business cards, but the ones we got from district 6420 were blue printing on a white background. They looked fine but were just not the way I wanted to present myself, especially compared with a full-color business card I received from an inbound student from Australia at one of the Rotary conferences that I had attended during preparations for coming to Thailand. I understood, though, that because of the large number of students that District 6420 was sending on exchange, they would have to be frugal; I was just jealous of other business cards I'd seen. Therefore, I talked to my dad about seeing if I could get nicer business cards, and he found a person in the neighboring town of LaSalle. Mom and I met with him, and I described what I wanted. Basically my card is my high school senior picture (in color), only the size and shape of a normal business card, with the usual business card information on it. While meeting with him, we learned that he is a Rotarian, and, because of that, he offered to print them for free. There are so many benefits to being associated with Rotary. He did an amazing job on my cards; I've gotten so many compliments on them. After exchanging cards, pins, and just catching up, we ate dinner at the hotel. As usual, there was a lot of food, but it wasn't very good. After dinner, there was an awards ceremony for all the oldies, and we were introduced to one newbie from South Africa. She is staying only a few months, so I don't know if she is going to Phuket (the trip to southern Thailand) or not. After all of that, about 7:00 p.m., we got on the bus with a long night ahead of us. I think I fell asleep around 2:00 a.m., but, on the bus, it wasn't very *sa-bai*.

December 18, 2006

I woke up around 6:00 a.m., and we arrived at our hotel about an hour later. The hotel was really nice, but all of the planned activities were outdoors. It was just the beginning of being cold on this trip. I was assigned to room with Heidi, who is doing her exchange in Sakhon Nakhon. It would have been fine rooming with her, but everyone switched to room with closer friends, so I roomed the entire trip with McKinsey. McKinsey and I became really close during the first tour.

Breakfast at our hotel was amazing! I usually hate breakfast, but *farang* food is heavenly. I had some kind of cereal, French toast, toast with jam, and hot tea. After breakfast, we went to our room to freshen up and change. Jason came over, and we hung out for a while, talking. Then McKinsey and I left to watch some movies in another room, and Jason went back to his room. A few hours later, we all got back on the bus and proceeded to the Chiang Dao Cave. No one really wanted to go. It seemed that everyone on this tour has become so lazy. I really wanted to see the cave but was a little disappointed when we got there. The cave was cool, but we were only allowed to go a short distance and then had to walk on the path. Everything here is Buddha-related, which is really neat to see. There were alters all through the part of the cave that we were allowed to tour. When we got back to the hotel, there was really nothing planned for us to do. We walked around the hotel and found a tree house. That was pretty cool, but I didn't get any pictures. Then we basically hung out in the banquet hall, waiting for dinner. Dinner wasn't that good. I've learned to appreciate the breakfasts on Rotary tours so much that I eat only enough lunch and dinner to get by until breakfast. I mean, it is nearly impossible to mess up cereal and toast that I make for myself. No one knew what to do after dinner, so we decided to watch "Pirates of the Caribbean II". Because McKinsey brought her computer, our room became the party room throughout the whole tour. I liked that a lot because then we could do our own thing and the party would come to us.

December 19, 2006

We got an unnecessary wake-up call at 6:00 a.m., so we had a lot of time in the morning to ourselves because we weren't scheduled to leave until 8:00 a.m. The first stop of the day was at the Maesa Elephant Camp. The elephant show was really cool! We had really good seats, but I stood the whole time anyway. The elephant ride was awesome! I rode with McKinsey, and some Rotarians gave us sugar sticks and bananas to give to the elephants that we were riding. The elephant behind us really wanted a treat, though. Part way through the ride, I was talking with McKinsey and then "discreetly" an elephant trunk came slowly in between us. It was really funny because we didn't want to get elephant boogers on us. Of course, after we fed it once, it wanted more. McKinsey got a long streak of elephant slime on the arm of her sweatshirt. Other than that, the ride was amazing. The trail was really difficult and really steep at times. We were both sliding under the bar of the seat and had to really hold on. It was a half-hour ride.

After that, we went to eat lunch in town. Kelly, McKinsey, and

I got into a discussion about why it is that when someone sees us, they immediately start to speak in English. We surmised that it would be really cool if we knew a language that no one else knew. We began inventing a new language, which we called Zuombong*om. The things we come up with when we're bored. We probably look and sound really stupid speaking it because it's just a combination of different grunts and weird noises, but that's half the fun.

After lunch, we dropped our stuff off at the hotel and headed straight for the zoo. The only reason I was excited about the zoo was that I wanted to see the panda bears from China. They were so cute. They had to be kept in separate areas to control breeding. The exhibit looked like a stage with a wall dividing it into two sections. The part facing the audience was open, and there was a pit surrounding the exhibit that was about six feet deep, which distanced the audience from the animals. There was also plexiglass in front of the viewing area. The male didn't like being separated from the female and tried to climb around the wall. He almost made it, but the female swatted at him, and he fell into the pit. Everyone in the audience screamed. That became a big topic of discussion for the rest of the day for the exchange students: cruelty to animals. The panda didn't get hurt, and the people managing the zoo know how to take care of animals, so I just listened to the discussions. A small group of us went to see the rest of the zoo. People drifted away, and after a while it was just McKinsey and me.

We had seen most of it, and we were walking back toward the bus when I remembered that I wanted to take a picture of the camels. As we walked over, the camels started moving toward each other and then started rubbing their necks. It was so cute. We were about to leave when the camels looked like they were fighting, and they started biting each other's necks, so we decided to stay. Then, they started biting other parts of their bodies, and McKinsey and I were thinking, "What are they doing?" Then, we saw the female lie down on the ground. We both just turned around with looks of shock and cracked up laughing. We both instantly knew we had to get a picture of it to show the rest of the exchange students and laugh about it. Well, I start focusing my camera and was just about ready to take the picture when a monk walked in front of me. How embarrassing is that? McKinsey was practically rolling on the ground laughing at me. So, we got a picture of the "activity" and then a picture of the sign that read, "One-Humped Camel." Other than that, we saw giraffes on our way back and got to feed them. After the zoo, we went back to the hotel, dropped our stuff off, and then went shopping at the night bazaar.

This hotel was huge, and there was no third floor button on the elevator, so McKinsey and I decided to go exploring at midnight because everything is more fun at midnight. Jason tagged along. We found the third floor: a parking garage that is not yet completed. Then we decided to go to the top floor and look out over the city. We got up there and realized that there were more stairs leading up. We went up and under another staircase, and there was a door to a balcony. It was really pretty, but then we found a ladder that led even higher. We climbed up to the highest point on the roof of our hotel, above the elevator shaft. The view was so gorgeous. Because of all of the lights from the night bazaar, we could see for miles. We were so cold up there, but no one wanted to get down. Because we were turning into human popsicles, we finally got down and promised ourselves that we'd go back tomorrow.

December 20, 2006

In the morning on the bus, we got yelled at because of the people who went to the clubs and got drunk. Gui, our tour guide for all three Rotary trips, also went to the club to watch out for them, but I heard that he lost control of the group and got frustrated. Everyone was having a good time but apparently got a little obnoxious as the night went on. I don't know the extent of the misbehavior because I wasn't there.

Gui was a lot of fun. He spoke excellent English and got really close to all of the exchange students. The whole morning was spent at a bunch of random shops. We stopped at a leather shop and a silver indenting shop where they made portraits from thin sheets of silver, using only a hammer and a nail. We also stopped at an umbrella painting shop and then, finally, arrived at a huge flower garden. We were supposed to stay with a group of 10 students while viewing the flower displays, but we divided the lunch money up as best we could and then split up. I hate being stuck in huge groups and then not being able to see everything because of having to do what everyone else wants to do. After looking around a little bit, we got an urgent call from one of the exchange students who had been in our group, saying that Rotary wanted us to go to the lake to see the water show. So, we ran there but then had to wait once we got there. We sat all the way to one side of the viewing area for the show, next to the pipes that went to the lake. The ground was completely soaked around there, but we didn't think that we'd have enough time to find the others before the show started. The show was really boring anyway, so we decided to leave halfway through it. Steffen had the bright idea of walking through the muddy part of the hill instead of rudely making our way through all the people still trying to watch it. Long story short, I fell, face first. My whole outfit was covered in mud and so was my bag. I was having such a hard time getting out; I almost fell again while holding on to a wire fence and then a third time while holding on to Steffen. As soon as we got out, Alicia handed me a wet wipe. Keep in mind, half of my body was literally covered in mud, and she handed me a Kleenex-sized moist towlette. It was so cute and unbelievably Asian. Luckily we got on the bus and headed straight back to the hotel, so that I could shower and change clothes before dinner.

Yesterday we ate a Khantoke dinner. A Khantoke dinner is a customary northern Thai style of eating in which food is served on low tables, while the diners sit on mats on the floor. They also had a show, featuring Thai dancers. We couldn't see the show from where we were seated, so we sat at another table, where we started talking to a family from Israel. Everyone in their tour group was a dentist. They were really interesting people to talk with. McKinsey asked them how to say, "Hello," in Hebrew and then could have kicked herself when they said, "Shalom" because we already knew that. Hebrew is a cool language.

Anyway, when we got back to the hotel, I changed, and then we went out shopping with Kelly. I got a really cute piece of jewelry, which was originally 900 *baht*, but I got it for just 420 *baht*. Just a little more than five dollars; that's awesome! When we were walking back, I heard these people talking in what sounded like Hebrew, so I turned back and looked at McKinsey to see if she recognized it, too. She had the same look on her face, so, we stopped and yelled back, "Shalom," and the guy looked up and smiled and waved. We got really excited that we recognized that language and could use our newly acquired knowledge in a real situation. The guy seemed amused. That was so much fun.

We had just arrived at our room when Katie came out of her room in tears. Something about Jason, so I tried to calm her down and planned to go with McKinsey to find Jason because we knew that he would tell us what was going on. Katie seemed to be calming down, but someone must have asked her about whether there was anything between her and Greg. She answered in a very loud and unquestionable tone, "I don't like Greg!" As soon as those words left her mouth, Greg walked around the corner toward his room, stopped, looked back, and awkwardly said, "Okay?" Katie ran into her room from embarrassment, and I, along with everyone else, burst into laughter. Then McKinsey and I left and called Jason to see if he wanted to talk. He was already on the roof, so we ran to McDonald's before meeting up with him. When we finally got on the roof, we only got to talk for a little while until some other exchange students came up. We then decided to leave the roof, and we went to this nook on the 22nd floor and talked until about three in the morning.

As it turned out, Katie and Jason had started seeing each other since Phu Kradung. I guess Katie liked Jason a little more than he cared about her. Anyway, Jason didn't want to lead her on and could sense that she really liked him, so he started hanging out with McKinsey and me. To make the situation even more complicated, Jason, apparently, has had a crush on me for a while, but, thankfully, he hasn't really pressured me about it. I really like hanging out with Jason and McKinsey; I can tell that they are going to be people that I will keep in contact with after my exchange year is over. I just hope that he doesn't ask me out or say anything that might make our friendship awkward.

December 21, 2006

Reading the schedule, we were to get up at 6:00 a.m. and go down to breakfast shortly thereafter. Our schedule was changed yesterday because everyone was complaining about getting up so early.

We went to the bottom of the mountain and into our *song-taew*. A *song-taew* is a type of public transportation. It's kind of like a full size pickup truck with the usual cab, but the back of the truck has a roof and sides. It is like a bus but completely open so that people can hop on and off easily. It has benches along the three sides and poles on the two sides of the opening for people to grab onto when boarding or exiting the *song-taew* or to hold on to if it is too crowded to sit down. *Song-taew*s usually travel on a specific route. If a person desires to go to a place that is on the route of the *song-taew*, it is a very inexpensive mode of transportation.

I was in the "large" *song-taew* with five other inbounds. It was so much fun going up the mountain because we started off by making fun of our *song-taew* and how we could walk faster. Then the curves started getting to people, so it became the "sick" *song-taew*, and I was joking about always having to be surrounded by the sick people. We all still managed to laugh the whole way to the top of the mountain. We got a group picture and saw the highest point of Thailand and stood there for a while. Then we came back down. The trip literally went that quickly, too. On the way down, one girl was trying to dry her tongue, and then everyone else started trying it, too. By "drying our tongues," we were all hanging our heads out the side of the *song-taew* with our tongues out. Then Erika looked back and realized that the people in the car following us were videotaping us. That was so funny. She pretended to be taping the scenery, but then, the next time I looked, she was taping us again. The things we do while on tour; I'm sure we looked ridiculous.

On our way down the mountain, we stopped at a waterfall. The waterfall was really big and really beautiful. We walked all the way down to it, and we were close enough to feel the mist. Actually, we got really wet because of the mist. Then everyone made their way down some big rocks. My shoes were already really muddy and really wet, so I wasn't taking any chances of falling. I was following Jeff, who I had first met at the Central States conference in Grand Rapids and had to grab on to his hand a few times, but I'm glad I got there. The water was freezing. Then we got back in the *song-taew*s and went to lunch: *som-thom* and *kao nio*, always my favorite. We had a long bus ride to dinner, and then we got yelled at for leaving our blankets on the *song-taew*. We were on our way to the restaurant where we were going to have dinner, but I think we were early because we stopped at a random street and were told to go shopping for a half an hour. I went with Kelly and got a cute purse. We eventually went to dinner, but no one seemed to eat much. With so many fast food places within sight of our hotel, it's no wonder no one ate. We had a celebration for Prapart's anniversary and another Rotarian's birthday. We all knew what that meant: free cake. Everyone did eat cake.

We got back to the hotel and did a little shopping nearby. Everyone was rather bored with shopping by now, so that didn't last too long. We then had the great idea to get pizza from The Pizza Company for dinner, but we had to call. According to Gui, they spoke great English and were open all night. I tried calling twice with J.D.'s phone, but no one picked up either time. Then J.D. tried and got through, but I wouldn't take the phone back. We finally ordered a large pepperoni and sausage pizza, deep dish. We wanted two, but then we decided to tell the delivery guy we wanted another one when he got there. We hung out in our room waiting for the guy, and every time someone would want to come in to hang out we'd all get really excited and then really disappointed because of how hungry we were for pizza—what a welcoming crowd.

The guy came with our "large" pizza, which was the size of a small Papa John's pizza, and the place had just closed, so we couldn't order any more. The pizza was really good, but we each only got one piece. I paid for it, but McKinsey and J.D. chipped in a little. While we ate, we watched the movie "SWAT". Our room was very small, and, considering that we had eight people crammed into it, some people left part way through the movie. It ended up being J.D. and me on my bed leaning against the wall with Marie at the foot of the bed and then McKinsey, Kelly, and Jason on the other bed. Our beds were on wheels, so all of a sudden J.D. and I start laughing at the movie, the bed starts to roll, and he said, "I think we are getting down." I love his English vocabulary with his French accent. Once the movie was over, Marie and J.D. were the only ones left in our room, so I took J.D. to go see the roof because I had promised him previously. On the way to the roof, we met a few other exchange students who had not seen it either, so they tagged along. It was really cool being able to show off my find. They really liked it, too. We took a picture but didn't really stay up there very long. It was cold, and by this time everyone was tired.

December 22, 2006

We got up and ate breakfast, but I hardly ate anything at the hotel. Instead, I went to Subway because we were leaving the hotel, and I still had not eaten at a Subway in Thailand. I got a foot long and gave half to McKinsey because there was no way I could have eaten it all. Because there were free chips and soda on the bus, I just bought the sandwich. Rotary had provided a huge variety of snacks and drinks for the bus rides on each tour. We went to another temple by *song-taew*, and, even after the *song-taew* dropped us at the top of the hill, we still had to walk up another 300 steps. The temple was pretty but not any more beautiful than every other temple I've seen. After we went back down, we got into our *song-taew*, and Hayley, an inbound from Canada, showed us her puppet that she had bought for 4,000 *baht* (originally priced at 10,000 *baht*). She is definitely in love with that thing. Standing upright, it came up to about my chest and was very intricately designed. Then we got back on the bus to head to Chiang Rai.

We arrived in Chiang Rai about 4:00 p.m. Because we had some extra time before dinner, McKinsey and I decided to walk around and explore the area. I bought a really cool sweatshirt with an enormous zipper but hideous pockets. It was cool because, when we walked to the shop, the lady yelled for someone else who spoke English, and I said, "*Poot Thai dai, ka,*" (I can speak Thai). She was really taken aback. I bargained a little for the sweatshirt, but I know I paid too much. By American standards, it was quite a good price, and it was an awesome sweatshirt! The guy came over anyway and wanted to practice his English. We talked for a little while and then headed back for dinner.

After dinner we went shopping again with a big group. They were still looking at shirts. I was basically waiting, and I felt something on my ankle. I looked down, and this huge black cockroach jumped on me. I yelled and began flailing my legs, trying to shake the enormous creature off. I'm sure everyone was staring at me, but I was too busy brushing nonexistent bugs off of the rest of my body, as well as running in circles. Hayley caught me while I was freaking out and took me in a big comforting hug. She is so sweet. By this time, I was completely ready to go back to the hotel. Everyone else was cold, too, so we headed back. A small group of people came to our room to watch "The Illusionist." It was obviously pirated and kept messing up. We never did get to see the end of it. During the movie, we wondered why the room was so incredibly cold. We wondered if the hotel did not have a heating system or if it was just turned off. Kelly and I were snuggled in my bed, and Jeff and Jennifer were in McKinsey's bed. In between was Jason, wearing someone else's sweatshirt, and McKinsey was altering my new sweatshirt. She was really excited about doing it, so she was content with being on the floor. Part of the way through, I realized that we hadn't taken a before picture, so I tried it on and held the pocket up so it looked like it was completely attached. Then I looked at it, and the part that was supposed to still be attached had cuts all through it. I just gave her a look, but I trusted her. Once she had finished, the sweatshirt looked so much better. I've gotten so many compliments regarding my huge zipper. I then took the longest hot shower of my five months in Thailand, and I'm still surprised that the smoke detector didn't go off. Finally, I jumped into bed and fell asleep as quickly as possible. I was sure I could see my breath.

I forgot to mention a funny incident that happened earlier tonight, right before the cockroach incident. Hayley was browsing at the street mall, and a man was sitting behind, well, kind of next to, a display of a bunch of cute socks. He kept saying, "Yes?" and gesturing toward her, and she kept replying in Thai, "No, I don't want any."

As he kept gesturing, her voice more adamantly began reiterating how much she did not want those socks. Finally, the man gave her a somewhat surprised, yet mostly confused look, wondering why she was stating so firmly to this lone beggar on a street curb, hoping for a little bit of change, that she did not want any socks. Hayley finally realized the situation and, incredibly embarrassed, ran back to catch up with the rest of us and explain the whole story. We couldn't control our laughter.

December 23, 2006

I was freezing when I woke up. I must not have slept well because McKinsey said that I was yelling at her in my sleep while she was trying to get ready in the morning. Apparently, while she was trying to be quiet, I yelled, "Why are you making so much noise?" "God!" and then, "Are you finished yet?" in an irritated voice. Then I remember opening my eyes and seeing her head toward the door with a backpack, so I, consciously, asked, "Are you leaving?" and "Where are you going?" She annoyingly replied, "I'm not leaving. Just go back to sleep." I didn't know why she sounded so grumpy until breakfast, when she told everyone, "I love sharing a room with you. You are so funny in the morning." Then she proceeded to do impressions of me. So that was the joke of the morning. I always knew I was grumpy in the morning, but I'm glad I could provide some entertainment.

We got on the bus and went to the King's mother's garden house. It was really pretty. It was in a hilly and mountainous area. The King's mother went to Switzerland every year until she became too old to travel. The King then brought Switzerland to her, with this garden house. It was one of those things that I'm glad I saw, but I don't necessarily want to go back. We ate there and then proceeded to visit the hill tribes. Everyone was incredibly excited about that. We got there by *song-taew* again, and basically it was just a bunch of shops. Everyone was dressed in traditional clothing and begging us to come in and look around in their shop. I have a feeling that they all shared the profits that they earned because no one would haggle prices and they weren't fighting each other for our attention. Once we got all the way down the mountain, we visited an actual tribal village. The women all had metal coils on their necks and legs. They didn't speak much Thai because they spoke their own mountain dialect, but we had little conversations with a few. I talked to a mom and asked if the coils on her neck hurt, and she said that it hurt occasionally. She lifted up the bottom coil and showed me the bruises all around her neck. I think that was because she had recently gotten another ring of coil added. Another woman said that it hurt to sleep. People had said that if they take the coils off, then they would die because their neck muscles are too weak to support their heads. Nevertheless they were selling pictures, and some of the pictures were of them taking the coils off, and others showed women wearing no coils at all. I guess if they are really careful when taking it off, then it's okay.

We were there for only a half hour or so, and that really annoyed me. We spend so much time shopping and sleeping at the hotels, why can't we just get up a little earlier or go home a little later. This, visiting with people from different cultures like the hill tribes, is why I came on youth exchange.

On the walk down the hill through the shops, there was a guy along the road who was smoking marijuana from a huge bong. If stood on end, I think it would have reached my neck. So, of course, everyone got pictures, and then the guy asked if we wanted to try it. One of the exchange students got really excited. It was obvious from the smell of the smoke that it was weed and not tobacco. Gui was standing right there, so the guy looked at him for approval, and Gui actually allowed him to do it; I have a picture to prove it! That is a bit surprising about Rotary in Thailand. I think it would have been different if Gui was a Rotarian. Maybe the exchange student wouldn't have been permitted to smoke if an actual Rotarian was there. That would never have been acceptable in America. I wonder if smoking marijuana is actually legal here or if it was only allowed because we were in the tribal village.

After that we went back to our hotel. It was actually a nice day outside, almost warm. I asked Kelly and McKinsey if they wanted to go swimming because some other people said that they were thinking about going, and the sun probably heated the water in the pool a little bit. They told me that I was crazy, but then I convinced McKinsey to go with me and Kelly said she would go down and take pictures. We went down and met three other exchange students. Erika also went, but, as she put it, she just went to laugh at us. The pool was really gross on the surface, so McKinsey was cleaning it, and a few people were watching us from their balcony. We tested the water with our feet and found that the sun had done nothing for the temperature of the water. It was so cold. We all decided to jump in together. As soon as we hit the water and resurfaced, everyone scurried to the edge to get out. Nano was standing at the edge, laughing at us because she didn't jump in. She did her own count and then chickened out again, so McKinsey came from behind her and pushed her in. McKinsey wanted another picture, so I jumped in again with her. We got a bunch of pictures, and then someone had the bright idea of playing tag to get warm. That lasted a whole five minutes. My skin hurt so badly from being cold; I felt as though I had sunburn all over my body. We went back to the room, and I took another very hot shower. Kelly was hanging out in our room so we started watching "Lord of War" and, again, went to dinner late. After dinner, everyone came to our room, and we decided to play a card game called Egyptian Rat Screw. This game is fast paced and involves players slapping a pile of cards in the middle of the table when certain sequences appear. The object of the game is to slap the pile first in order to gain more cards. If a player is quick enough to slap the pile of cards first, that player will usually get the back of his hand slapped by the other players in their failed attempt to win the pile. Jason, McKinsey, and I were quite good. Kelly was too slow and then decided that she didn't want to play, so she kept track of the Christmas music. It's really hard to concentrate on the game and sing at the same time. Then Greg came into our room to play, and, let's just say by the end of the night, my hand felt as though it would have been relieved if it had fallen off. It hurt so badly! Jason and Greg would hit their hands on the table really hard, so they were both in a lot of pain, too. It was so much fun! Then, because everyone was in so much pain, we switched to poker. I didn't want to play because I'm awful at it, and I didn't really understand how to play, so I was the constant dealer. McKinsey always showed me her cards, though, so I guess I learned a little bit. This night was even colder than last night. We both slept horribly, actually looking forward to the morning.

December 24, 2006 (Christmas Eve)

Repacking was difficult because of all the souvenirs I had purchased, but really I didn't get that many. I turned into a cheapskate. "Four dollars for a shirt? Are you kidding me?" We ate quickly and got on the bus for a really long ride, during which everyone slept. Our next stop was at the Golden Triangle, where visitors can see Laos and Myanmar from Thailand. It was really cool. I got a shirt there, too. By this point of the trip, I had no clean shirts left and desperately needed to buy more everywhere we went. We went to a nearby temple to buy some incense and candles for tonight because we wanted to have our own Christmas Eve service at our hotel. We got back on the bus, and McKinsey and I played a card game for a while, and then we fell asleep. We ate lunch at Phayao Lake and then got back on the bus for another long bus ride, during which we all slept.

As soon as we got to the hotel, we threw our stuff into our rooms and left to go exploring, trying to find the roof. We had to sneak into a banquet hall to get there. It was a lot of fun but, this roof wasn't nearly as cool. We weren't the only ones with the idea, either. A few other exchange students came up only seconds after we got there. We got a picture, and then everyone left, but we were last because McKinsey was in a skirt and had to go extra slow. I stayed back with her. Because everyone else had already left, we decided to stay and explore a little bit more. We climbed another half flight of stairs and came to three closed doors and one open door. The room with the open door was kind of boring, so we debated about looking in the other doors. We had time before dinner and everyone else had already left and was probably in their rooms by now, so we decided to go for it. I reached out my hand for the closest door and BOOM. We both jumped to what seemed like at least 10 feet, and McKinsey flew down the stairs and flung the door open. I was trying to catch up with her, but I was laughing so hard. We followed the same path we used to get there, so we ran into everyone that had been on the roof. They were all having a cigarette with Gui. They all stopped their conversation and were staring at us with concern because our faces were so pale and we were out of breath. We both started telling the story simultaneously while trying to catch our breath. Everyone was confused; I'm sure we didn't make much sense, but we still had a good laugh over it. It was probably just the elevator shifting. Nevertheless, it was scary at the time.

After we calmed down a bit, we went to the store so I could get some blank CDs for other people's pictures. We came back for dinner but didn't eat much. Because today was Christmas Eve, we wanted to eat something unbelievably good, even though we hadn't decided what exactly that would be. After dinner, we were heading to Big C, which is a large grocery store, with Jason, Greg, Katie, and Marie. We ran into some other exchange students on the elevator, and they said that they were leaving to look for a church and wanted to know if they should call us if they found one. We told them that we would do that, too, so we agreed that, if any of us found one, we would call the other group. That was a great idea; we hadn't even thought about the possibility of going to church. We headed to Big C and had to get directions a few times after heading a few blocks in the wrong direction. We were almost there when we saw a Protestant church. We knocked on the door and looked around a little, but no one was there. Just as we were about to leave, a guard came to lock the gates, and we asked him if they were going to have a midnight service or anything. He said no, but he told us that the Catholic church was. He then gave us directions to get there. We thanked him and wished him a Merry Christmas and then went to Big C.

We split away from the group when we got there because McKinsey and I had the great idea of finding Christmas cookies. We could only find Thai cookies, which taste horrible compared with American cookies. Then we changed our plan and went on a search for cookie dough. The best part in making cookies is eating the dough; everyone knows that. We asked some clerks at Big C about it, but they just had the powder mix. It took an egg and butter. We decided to try it anyway, without the egg. We bought milk, too; after all, what's cookie dough without milk? We caught up with everyone at the checkout, and then Marie wanted Swensen's ice cream, so we told her to go and get three spoons. We sat down at a table there and began trying to melt the butter with our hands and the heat from our breath. Needless to say, that didn't work. Then we added milk and ate it. It tasted incredibly delicious!

Marie wanted to go to church with us, but no one else did, so we split up again. We were power walking because we didn't know exactly where we were going and we wanted to go back to the hotel and change before the service. It was only three intersections away, but the intersections were really far apart. At one point, we could see that we had just thirty seconds to cross the street. We were trying to talk to three exchange students, who we just ran into, while at the same time eating our cookie dough and running to the other side of the street. We probably looked really stupid. Let me rephase that; we did look really stupid. Now we can say that we ran to church on Christmas Eve in Thailand eating cookie dough.

We stopped a bunch of times to ask directions and to make sure that we were going in the right direction. We were. Finally, when we saw the church, we all broke into a run only to discover that the church was open with lights on, but no one was there. We could hear voices in the distance but not at the church. We started walking toward the voices and then decided to ask the gatekeeper instead of barging in. He said that there was a service in the recreation center, so we decided to go. We got there, and they were playing Bingo. We talked to a few people, and they said that the little kids' play was over, but in a minute the older kids would have their performance. We went in and sat down. Marie called the other group, but they decided not to come. The play was really cute, but it was a really short performance. The angels did a dance that was obviously based on the Thai dance techniques to common English Christmas songs and then a short reenactment of the nativity scene. We were all singing along with the CD. After it was over, we had our pictures taken with some of the kids. Then everyone got into a line, and someone held the Christ candle in the front and walked to the sanctuary while everyone else sang about 10 verses of *Joy to the World* in Thai. The church service was okay. It was a lot of fun trying to follow what was going on and sing whenever they were singing Christmas songs. After the service, they gave out plaques with the Pope's picture on them and calendars depicting different photos of the King for each month. After the service ended, we were about to leave but were approached by some people who wanted to talk. We took a bunch of pictures in front of the nativity scene with various people.

We started walking back but realized that we were rather far from the hotel and it was really late. We turned around and went back to the chapel to asked some nuns if there were any *tuk tuk*s nearby. I told her that we preferred riding because we were scared, which was true, but more so because we didn't know how to get back to the hotel. A *tuk tuk* is a three-wheeled vehicle, a bit like a motor-cycle, but with a passenger seating area in the back. It is less costly than a taxi but is also not as comfortable because it is not enclosed. There apparently were none in the area, but some boys generously offered to take us back on the school *song-taew* if we would just wait a minute. We talked to them on the way back, took lots of pictures, and thanked them for the ride.

We had only a half an hour until midnight, so we ran back to our room and invited everyone to participate in our Christmas Eve service. We got candles when we went to 7-Eleven, so we just needed a lighter. Everyone was smoking and hanging out in a nearby room, so finding a lighter shouldn't have been that difficult. It was. I think that they were afraid that they weren't going to get it back. I finally got Steffen's lighter and ran to our room with it, lit one candle, and then ran to give it back to him. We went out to our balcony and lit the other candles and incense. Kelly and Jennifer came over, too. We had a complimentary Bible in our hotel room, but we couldn't find the Christmas story. I know it is the Gospel of Luke, chapter two, but this Bible was a weird version, printed in both Thai and English on every page. We sang Christmas hymns until we found it, then we took turns reading parts of it, while holding a candle. After we finished, it was past midnight, so it was Christmas. We wished each other a Merry Christmas and sang some fun Christmas songs. We went back inside because it was cold and because everyone started coming in.

Our room was definitely the party room. A lot of them were drunk, but, nonetheless, it was fun. We stayed up and talked until about 3:00 a.m., and then I took a shower and was about to kick everyone out, when they all voluntarily left; most likely because I had changed into my pajamas and was getting into bed.

December 25, 2006 (Christmas Day)

Merry Christmas! We were supposed to get up at 6:00 a.m. for the gift exchange, but, apparently, I was wakened and asked if I wanted to get up, and I supposedly said, "No". So because McKinsey agreed, we slept in until 7:30 a.m. when someone came to ask if our bags were ready to be taken to the bus. I retrieved my gift from under the tree and opened it at breakfast. I got a puppy purse, a chocolate bar from Starbucks, a bracelet, and a silver King's bracelet. I really like my silver bracelet. I asked Kelly what she got, and she was wearing her hat and said enthusiastically, "I got a battery charger!" At first I panicked, thinking someone switched gifts with her, but I thought, "Oh well; at least she's happy with it."

We got on the bus, and I gave out all my pins and then slept until lunch. We stopped around noon at a hotel to eat. They had a huge buffet, but I basically ate only *som-thom* and rolls. We got back on the bus and headed for the historical park. I asked Kelly if I could see what her battery charger looked like, and then she opened it and found the watch. It was really funny, and I still give her a hard time about her looking at her "battery charger" to see what time it is.

We got to the park and had to get into two small train-like vehicles. McKinsey and I sat right up front. Then Gui said that if we didn't want to learn anything about the park to get into the other train. A bunch of people got off ours, and then a few got on. I would have been surprised, but then reminded myself with whom I was traveling. Both vehicles traveled the same tour route, but we had an actual tour guide from the park, and the other train had Gui as a guide. Why would anyone pay to go on a tour and not want to see the sights and learn something? I think that some of the exchange students are just too immature to realize the opportunity that youth exchange provides. I swear that they act like they are just on a year-long vacation and have no interest in learning the culture or the language. Some are actually making no effort to try to fit into Thai society. One incident that happened early in the exchange year involved the theft from an exchange student of money that was to pay for his three Rotary tours. Another exchange student from the same host club was very outspoken about the issue. She was adamant that it was the maid, and she probably was correct. She insisted that the maid repay the money to the student and be given appropriate punishment. Unfortunately, that is not the Thai way. In this case, the hosting Rotary club paid for the three tours for the theft victim, but the ill feelings caused by the incident did not go away. It was mostly the exchange student's attitude that caused friction. She did not work to learn the Thai language and culture and, therefore, either did not understand or did not care about showing the proper respect. She didn't fit in with what was expected and didn't even try to, holding the attitude of, "Hey, I'm an American. Just deal with it." She was asked to move five times during her exchange. I was able to visit her and stay with her host family for a few days during my exchange. Her host mom was a really sweet person. It is unfortunate that some of the kids' immaturity limits their exchange experiences.

After the tour, we did a little souvenir shopping, during which I bought nothing. Then we got back on the bus for another long bus ride. Today was mostly riding on the bus because we were heading back toward Korat. When we got to the hotel, McKinsey and I were going to go exploring because this was the nicest hotel of the whole trip, but we started watching "Coach Carter" and couldn't stop. It's a good movie. We didn't have that much time, but we decided to go to Big C before dinner. We wanted to get a Thai board game to play that night. They didn't have any good games—all were lower quality—so we decided to find something else to buy because we didn't want to have wasted the trip. We looked for a Christmas movie but couldn't find any. Then we settled on cookie mix and milk. We had five minutes to be downstairs for dinner, and we still needed to change into nice clothes. We again ran back to our hotel room to quickly change. Thankfully, it didn't take either of us very long to get ready.

Dinner was amazingly delicious; I had four plates of food! There was pasta, salad, and a whole table covered with fruits and desserts. It was a huge all-you-can-eat buffet, and I took full advantage. After we had finished eating, some people sang karaoke, and everyone else went to the dance floor. McKinsey had studied dance for 14 years, so she taught me a lot of different steps. Then Steffen cut in. Germans are required to study dance through all 12 years of school, so they made a really talented pair. I was taking pictures and talking until Jeff grabbed my hand. He's the worst dancer ever, but he tries, so I've got to give him credit. The best part was when most of the other people had left, and Jeff was determined to swing dance. It was a lot of fun. Then McKinsey and J.D. were dancing, and we did the tango through them. Afterward Jeff tried to dip me, and we both fell over, but that just made it more fun. Everyone was planning on going to a club that night, so McKinsey and I went upstairs to freshen up, and then we all met downstairs. About 20 of us piled on the back of a pickup truck to go to the club. We arrived at the club, Discovery, and it was empty. I think the hotel was more fun, but then the enter-tainers stopped singing and just play acted. Jennifer, McKinsey, and I already agreed to leave at 1:00 a.m., but really it was more like 2:00 a.m. Everyone was getting drunk as the night went on, so it was becoming less and less fun. We did enjoy watching them getting on and off the stage; although a few times I thought someone was going to really hurt themselves. At 2:00 a.m., a group of us decided to leave.

We went to 7-Eleven, and I bought a phone card. Then we started walking toward where we thought the hotel was, looking for a *tuk tuk*. A food stand attendant that we passed told us that the *tuk tuk*s were in the opposite direction from the way we were walking. Everyone else was hungry, so they stayed and ate, and McKinsey and I left to find a *tuk tuk*. We had only 50 *baht* and a phone card, so we decided to look for a free ride back to the hotel. We started walking, and some boys yelled something to us from a shop. We kept walking at first and then decided to go back. We went to the shop and saw their mom sitting behind the desk with a baby. So we, being sweet, innocent girls, asked politely where the *tuk tuk*s were located. She asked where we wanted to go, and we told her. She seemed really surprised because we were pretty far away and it was late. We explained that we had only 50 *baht*. The two boys (presumably her sons) were jumping with excitement in the background. Finally, their mom said that it was okay for them to drive us back to the hotel on their motorcycles.

McKinsey and I each got on the back of different motorcycles and headed toward the hotel. We stayed together for a while, but were separated when McKinsey's driver turned, and we kept going straight ahead. I was worried because we weren't going in what I thought was the direction of the hotel. I was already wondering about where we were headed, and then we were suddenly in the marketplace. Everyone we passed was teasing the boy that was driving me and gesturing toward me. One of the people teasing the boy was a butcher and was using his knife to point. It was something that would normally be in a scary movie or book, but this is Thailand, and people are a lot different. I would have never done this in America. Once we got through the market, we met up with McKinsey's bike and then lost them again and had to wait for them at the hotel. We tried to pay the boys for giving us a ride, but they wouldn't take anything. It was probably payment enough to be able to show off "beautiful *farang* girls" to all their friends while taking us home.

We got back to our room, and I took a shower while McKinsey called home. When I finished showering, she had just finished her call to her parents. We made cookie dough, and then she helped me call home using her cell phone and my calling card. I called Mom's cell phone, but she didn't recognize the number of the incoming call, so she gave the phone to Dad to answer. It surprised me a little when he answered, but I just said, "Hi, Daddy. Merry Christmas!" They had just arrived at my grandparents' home in Pennsylvania, so I not only got to talk with Mom and Dad, but also Grandma, Granddad, and Uncle Den. It was nice to be able to talk to everyone at home, but I could have done without it. I knew everything we talked about already, but nonetheless, it was nice. When I left for youth exchange, my parents had said that they were there for me if I needed them. They said, "Call, if you need to call; e-mail, if you need to e-mail," and explained that if I wanted them to visit, they would come. This was my first call home from Thailand, other than my mandatory call when I arrived. We talked for only a half an hour. I didn't want to run up McKinsey's phone bill, but, even if I had, she wouldn't have told me to cut the call short.

J.D. called a little later to see if we wanted to hang out, but McKinsey said that we were already in bed. Which was true, but we could have visited. Neither of us really wanted to have a drunken party in our room at 3:30 a.m., considering that we had to get up at 8:00 a.m. the next day. I fell asleep thinking that this was the best Christmas ever!

December 26, 2006

Today, we got up late, as usual. Breakfast was just as good as dinner was the night before. We were being rushed onto the bus, and I had a lot to carry, so I had two croissants in my mouth because I couldn't hold them. Gui was making fun of me, but those croissants were awesome. I think I ate five already! We tried to talk all the way to lunch because we knew that this was our last day together, but, because we were all so exhausted, we fell asleep. At lunch, there was a lot of food, but I was still full from breakfast, so I just filled up on *som-thom*. Between McKinsey and me, we ate three plates of it and then ordered another plate for the other eight people at our table to share. It wasn't as good because it wasn't spicy. I could have eaten it with *kao nio* (sticky rice), which would have helped me get full sooner, but the *kao nio* wasn't that good either.

We arrived in Korat about 4:00 p.m. and had only a few minutes to say goodbye to everyone. I had gotten really close to only about half of the oldies, so I gave them each a big hug. Nano started the tears, which got a lot of other people going. That is what happens in the life of an exchange student, becoming close friends with people we know we'll never see again. I was getting a ride home with Heidi by van because we live in neighboring provinces, so we had about an hour to just hang out. People began leaving one by one. They had taken all of the snacks off the bus, so, while we had the chance, we all stuffed our purses with our favorites. I was stocking up because I couldn't get that kind of stuff in Nakhon Phanom!

We left at about 5:15 p.m., and I got home about 1:00 a.m. I thought that Rotary had already contacted my host parents, but I was wrong because they weren't expecting me. Everything here is so *sa-bai*.

Chiang Mai was so much fun. I can't believe that it's over already, but, during the trip, the days went by relatively slowly. We had the opportunity to do so much, see so much, and talk about everything possible. There are so many memories. It is sad to think that we will never all be together, again. I am really looking forward to the District Conference in March in Rayong, but, at the same time, I'm also dreading it because the oldies won't be there. Although, I'm sure it will be a lot of fun, it won't be as much fun as it could have been with Nano, Jono, and Jade. I know that the next half of my exchange year is going to fly by. I already have plans with Kelly to visit McKinsey in either Korat or Bangkok. We both want to go to Bangkok, but, if McKinsey switches homes, we might not be able to go. This year is going by way too fast!

11

HAPPY NEW YEAR

January 2, 2007

bought myself a cell phone yesterday. I'm so excited! It was only 1,370 *baht,* so that's not too bad. I left it at home when I went to eat dinner, and, when we got back, I already had two text messages from Jennifer and Marie. It's awesome having contact with all of the exchange students outside of Nakhon Phanom. I really like being the only exchange student in my town and having a lot of Thai friends, but sometimes I am annoyed by the immaturity of my peer group.

Speaking of immaturity, everything here is cute. I hate cute! For the Christmas party that they threw for me at school, a bunch of teachers gave me gifts. Some of the gifts were really nice, but then I got a white furry purse "that you can use when you go back to America." I would resemble a grade school kid if I wore that in America. I really appreciate the thought behind it because Thai kids my age would love a gift like this. In 10 months, I'm going to be 20 years old. I'm not going to walk down the street wearing a Hello Kitty shirt and have a bow in my hair to match my purse. My new fashion phase is "Goodbye Kitty." I hope we have it in the U.S., but, if not, maybe the exchange students can bring the fad home. It's basically just different ways of killing Hello Kitty. One of the other exchange students has a black sweatshirt with Hello Kitty on the back and a bullet hole through the middle of her head and a tag on her toe reading, "D.O.A." Apparently, there is a bunch of Goodbye Kitty merchandise available in Korat, so I may have to plan a trip there. I should try to visit someone there, anyway.

The Christmas party at school was really nice. They decorated the classroom and had Christmas music in the background. Everyone brought a present to exchange. They prepared a special "American-style" lunch for me. We had fried eggs and hot dogs served on fried rice; the Thai version of American food, I guess. I gave my presents to them, as well. I really don't think anyone liked the presents. I just needed to get rid of them so I would have more room in my suitcase. Most of my presents were Christmas related, so they just took them. My dad really liked his gifts, though. I gave him a USA shirt and a USA hat. He put them both on right away. Even if he hadn't liked them, I think he would have acted like he did, anyway. I love my dad.

We have a festival hosted by the Red Cross for the New Year's celebration. There was a battle of the bands type thing, too, and my little brother was in it. We don't know what place they got yet, but we watched all four of the bands. We all agreed that Oak's band most likely placed third. My dad doesn't approve of Oak spending his time practicing music rather than wanting to study, so we didn't tell him about the competition. I guess what he doesn't know won't hurt him.

January 7, 2007

One day last week, I spent the night at my first host family's house. I went over to give them their Christmas presents, and P'Nan was there. It was also her birthday. I love going back to visit because everyone wants to talk to me and always tries to feed me, regardless of the last time I had eaten. P'Pin always runs out for *som-thom* for me. I wonder what it will be like years from now when I come back to visit this host family.

My favorite thing to do at my second family's house is conversing with my host dad. He is always really eager to talk with me, and it pushes both of us to think in the opposite language. He will either read the paper or watch the news and then explain to me in easier words what is going on and what everyone is saying. Then we'll go off on tangents about our personal views or the difference between countries. I really miss being able to express my opinion on different matters intelligently, but talking with him is better than just talking with my friends about Korean movie stars that are "so handsome."

I've had my cell phone only a week, but so far I've already gotten and written many text messages and talked on the phone a lot. Yee calls me a lot, and I've also talked with Jason and Kelly. I love my phone.

I've been sending a lot of e-mails to Mom recently about her and Dad planning a trip to visit in May and about what is going on at home. I love Thailand a lot, but, even before I got here, I was really excited about getting home and having a bunch of stories to tell and being able to speak another language. During the first few months, I would always remember that my parents were coming to visit, so that would keep me studying. It still does. I am having such a fun time here, but I've always been looking forward to going back home. Thailand just isn't a place where I could live for years. Everyone, including most adults, are so incredibly immature. Everything is so superficial here, as well. The adults wear so much makeup that it covers everything on their faces, except their eyes. It is caked on to the point of being ugly. Kids in Thailand seem to be constantly afraid of getting fat. Even little kids are told not to eat ice cream because they will get fat. I'm called fat at least 10 times a day. By American standards, I am considered to be quite thin. I am five feet, four inches tall and weigh a little more than 100 pounds, but they still say how fat I am. Then, if I eat just enough to be full (so that I can eat at the next meal that will usually be only two hours later), they say how scared I am of being fat. That makes absolutely no sense. Most of my friends are so skinny. In their school uniforms they look cute, but, when they wear regular clothes, they look sickly thin.

I just got myself into a "great" situation. We went to eat at P'BaiThong's restaurant (it is a buffet-style restaurant called Ran LookThan), and we started talking about how they wanted me to work there. I said that I'm too lazy to work, but that I would work if I didn't have to go to school anymore because school is so boring. Walking to the car, Mae filled me in on the whole conversation. Apparently, I will be working there as a "trial week" from this Tuesday to Friday from 4:00 p.m. to whenever. In addition to working, I still have to go to school. P'BaiThong said something about helping out at another province, but I guess that doesn't apply to this situation. Before I left, she said to "pack my bags" so I don't know if I'm sleeping there, too, or what is going on. At least, it's only a week, and, as pay, I get to eat dinner! Great. I'd rather just take the 89 *baht* and starve. Cheap labor.

January 8, 2007

The other day I went to *Adjant* Sin's house and enjoyed a Korean barbeque. He has a really nice house and two really cute puppies. The older dog was about one year old, and she was really well trained. It was so funny because, obviously, the dog was trained in Thai. He said to sit in Thai, and everyone was impressed because the dog responded quickly. Then he commanded the dog to shake saying, "*Sa-wat-dee*" (translation: "hello"). I started laughing. I wonder what the command is for "speak."

We have only about two more months until the school year is finished, so all the kids in M6 purchased a blank book for all of their friends to write in. It's called a "Friendship Book" in English. One page is for personal information, such as likes, dislikes, favorite color, etc. Then on the other, friends write something that they would normally write in a school yearbook. They have never had yearbooks at *Piyamahalachalai* School, so I guess this is what they do instead. I just learned that this year is the first time for getting yearbooks at school. I'm really excited about getting one, but I already bought a "Friendship Book." Although I'm excited to have one for when I go home, I think the information page is a little unnecessary. I plan to get another book like this one for all of the Exchange Students to sign. I really hate the fact that all of my friends from *Piyamahalachalai* are leaving to go to college, but I also think that saying goodbye to them now will make going home in July a lot easier.

The school year in Thailand is completely different from that of American schools. School starts in the beginning of May and ends mid-February. They do not observe Thanksgiving, Christmas, or Easter, but they do have other breaks for significant Thai or Buddhist holidays.

I got home from Yee's house, and my house was locked. I went to go through my grandma's house, which has an adjoining wall to our house and shares a courtyard. She seemed to want to talk, but I was having a hard time understanding her pronunciation. Finally, she told me to sit down and told the servant girl to get me some milk. When she gave it to me I thanked her and started to drink it. Apparently, I was supposed to thank my grandma, not the servant. Grandma reminded me, and I corrected myself, but I still felt bad. Then she gave me a cookie and a napkin, but this time she had the servant girl give it to her, and then she gave it to me. I *waied* and thanked her for everything. I felt really awkward, and then Oak came home the same way, so I followed him into our house. I always enjoy talking with people, but, whenever I'm in a situation like the one with the grandmother with a definite language barrier, I always want to leave because I feel so awkward. Looking back on the situation, I'm glad I tried as hard as I did to communicate.

January 9, 2007

As always, I get myself into situations that I'm not looking forward to, but, they turn out to be a ton of fun. So I'm just going to go through the days as if this experience were a trip.

I slept more than 11 hours last night and was completely exhausted all day. Therefore, I didn't really do much at school. After school, I packed, not knowing how many days I was packing for, and waited for Mae to take me to the restaurant where I would be working for the next week. We were just getting ready to leave when P'BaiThong and Shannon came to pick me up. Shannon is a little girl whose mother is Thai and father is Australian. They live in Australia, but they are here for vacation and to visit family. They come here every other year for a few months. Shannon was really hyper and excited that I was staying with her and talked all the way to their restaurant. Baa LaWang, P'BaiThong's mother, greeted me with a *malee,* which is a very fragrant small bunch of flowers strung together, and was just as excited as P'BaiThong that I was staying there and working. I put my apron on and basically followed P'BaiThong around to kind of get to know how things worked. We didn't have any customers except for the entire Rotary club. I helped clean up and wash dishes, and we got home around 11:00 p.m. Little did I know that that would be an early night.

January 10, 2007

I asked Shannon if she wanted to go along with me to school, so that was my excuse to basically not do anything at school the next day. It was actually a lot of fun hanging out with her for the day. Even though she is only 10, it was nice to be able to speak English for once. We ditched most of my classes, went out with Yee for some errands, and went back to the restaurant around 3:30 p.m. We changed clothes, and at 4:30 p.m. I went with Shannon to her Tae Kwon Do class. I don't think anyone there was over the age of 12, excluding *Adjant* Beer, but it was still a ton of fun. Everyone wanted to be next to me. The teacher was really patient with me and really tried to help me learn the steps. Actually, he seemed eager to practice his English with me. We discussed prices a little, and then I decided I'd go back on Friday with Shannon again and talk more about that. After class, I went back to the restaurant and worked. At 12:30 a.m., we went to the market to get fresh veggies. I was pretty tired by the time I went to bed around 2:00 a.m.

January 11, 2007

I woke up around 10:00 a.m., and we left to go work at noon. We prepared everything at the restaurant, and at 4:00 p.m. we packed the truck and went to the badminton court and set up. We were catering the food for a badminton event/tournament. P'BaiThong went back to the restaurant, so I basically looked after Shannon at the courts and watched the games a little. P'BaiThong came back around 5:00 p.m. and allowed me to cook the steaks. They tasted really good! I saw a few people there that I already knew.

P'Pond came in with his *faen* (significant other; girlfriend in this case). He talked to me when we were cleaning up, which was really surprising, and he spoke in English; I don't know where that came from. Then, after we finished talking, I went to finish cleaning up, and he left to smoke a cigarette. I thought that was really amusing. I was going to tease him about his *faen*, but I thought that would be mean (and I didn't know how to formulate the sentence in Thai). It would have been extremely funny to see how he would react. It is more than obvious that he has a crush on me, but he already has a *faen*!

We got back to the shop and unloaded everything and then had to make another trip back to the court to get the oven and bottled gas. By now, a lot of the local people were drunk and were eager to talk to me. It was a lot of fun and humorous, too. Now that I can speak better, it is a lot more fun to talk to guys, especially the ones that are in the 25 to 35 age group, who think that they have a chance with me. They get so frustrated! After we finished cleaning up, we left for P'BaiThong's house and got to bed at around 2:00 a.m.

January 12, 2007

School wasn't bad today. I made *som-thom* for my Thai cooking lesson. It was good, but I'd rather buy it from the market. I was getting bored, so I called P'BaiThong at 2:00 p.m. and left to go to the restaurant. I didn't really do much of anything there, either. We went home to get Shannon and then went to Tae Kwan Do. I got my outfit and white belt, so I was really excited. This was Shannon's last class, so her parents came to take pictures, and I took pictures, too. Then I went back to the restaurant and worked hard because we were pretty busy. After things settled down, we went to the Rotary meeting and realized that my booklet wasn't completely finished. The booklet contains all of the pertinent information about where I am living and who I am staying with, in the event that Rotary would need to get in touch with me immediately. P'Nuan quickly drove to my current host family's house and had Mae fill it out. While there, I opened a package Mom and Dad sent from Illinois and looked at all the pictures with Mae, Paw, and P'Nuan. We stayed for about

40 minutes and then went back to the Rotary meeting. We went to Nano-oke after the meeting but didn't really stay that long. We just socialized with friends and ordered way too much food.

Then, P'BaiThong said that I could drive the truck home. It was so cool! It had a standard transmission, so I had to change gears using the stick shift. When I took driver's education back in Illinois, my parents required me to learn to drive a standard transmission before I took my licensing test. I know how to drive a vehicle like this but haven't done it for a while. I thought it would be difficult to shift using my left hand because the steering wheel is on the right side of the car. I have to admit that shifting with my left hand was a little different, and the turn signals are on the opposite side of the steering wheel from my car at home. I was pretty nervous at first because I hadn't driven a car in five months, let alone driving on the left side of the road! I don't know when the last time was that I drove a car that was a stick-shift, but there were hardly any other cars on the road, and I did fine. I know, I just broke one of the "D" rules.

January 13, 2007

Today I had to get to Nano-oke at 8:30 a.m. to work for Children's Day. It was really boring. Nano-oke is a karaoke business in Nakhon Phanom. The owners named it Nano-oke after their first son, Nano. I'm not sure how commonplace it is to name businesses after children, but I know that Ran LookThan is named after Baa LaWang's first daughter, P'BaiThong's older sister.

At this event, I was told to work a booth with a member of my host Rotary club. Our job was to write a Thai word and then students would have to translate and spell the word in English. It was hard coming up with words because the Rotarian that I was working with couldn't understand my Thai and he knew only a little English. Part of the way through, he left to go to the bathroom, leaving me to work the booth alone. I was alright being by myself until someone came; then I didn't know what to do. I began drawing pictures because I pronounce words in Thai, but I didn't know how to spell them. Then, when the Rotarian returned from the bathroom, he wouldn't come into the booth. Instead, he stayed back with the other Rotarians and talked about what I was doing. They thought it was pretty clever; so did I. Finally, we were done working around noon or 1:00 p.m.

I then went with Yee to get my face scrubbed. I was so tired. The attendant massaged lotion onto my face and then put a heater on it. It felt really good, and I think I fell asleep for a few minutes. I was in there for about two hours, and it cost only 200 *baht*. I have to go back on Saturday to do it again. It didn't really hurt until she got around my nose and cheeks, and then it was rather painful. After that, we went back to Yee's house to practice Thai dance for Monday. I was so tired and not in the mood to practice, but I humored them. I really am awful at dancing. I got to the restaurant with enough time to run to P'BaiThong's house and change my clothes, but they had already brought my clothes to the restaurant.

We got to Tae Kwon Do, and, again, it was a lot of fun. Shannon and a younger girl, Melanie, who was six, were constantly trying to get my full attention so that the other one getting less would become jealous. Melanie's father is from England and taught her to speak English really well. She lives in Thailand, and her father hasn't been back to England for about a dozen years. Melanie was behaving just fine this evening, but Shannon was trying to cause trouble by telling me stuff about Melanie and that I shouldn't talk to her. Melanie is only six, and she was being perfectly fine, just wanting to talk to me like all the other kids. With her command of English, she actually could. Shannon just didn't like the fact that she wasn't the center of attention around me. After Tae Kwon Do, we went back to the restaurant. Business was really slow this night, so we cleaned up at 9:45 p.m. and got home around midnight. I started watching "The Lord of the Rings," but it was in Thai, so I could only understand parts of the movie. It does look like a good movie; I'd like to see it in English sometime. I went to bed around 1:00 a.m.

January 14, 2007

I didn't really do much today, sleeping in and getting to the restaurant at about noon. I went to 7-Eleven and got a grilled ham & cheese sandwich. I really hate ham, but I've missed eating cheese so much here that I just put up with the ham. Once the restaurant opened, we were really busy. Soon we had four kids (two from Tae Kwan Do class, Shannon, and Melanie), and all of them were acting like Thai kids. P'BaiThong was getting a little upset with them, as was Baa LaWang. Melanie's dad was talking with Shannon's dad, and then two *farang*s came and joined them. I was having a really good time because we were busy and there was always something to do.

One incident happened tonight. I was in the kitchen waiting to be told what to do, and Shannon was half hugging Baa LaWang and looking toward the buffet, so I asked, "What's going on?" Baa LaWang said that Melanie doesn't like it when Shannon gives her kisses and hugs, so Shannon is waiting until Melanie starts to come back to give her hugs and make Melanie jealous. How immature is that? I mean for Baa LaWang to play along with Shannon like that. I would have said, "No, there is enough of me to go around, and it's not very nice to make someone else feel bad." I lost a little bit of respect for Baa LaWang for acting that way, and I don't know why she doesn't like Melanie. I mean Melanie is a normal six-year-old who is a little obnoxious and a little loud at times, but she's only six years old, and she's Thai. What else can anyone expect? So she was being extra loud that night. No wonder; she wanted attention.

Later that night, we got on the topic of kidnapping, and Shannon was acting really scared. I really thought that she was just looking for some attention. I said, "It's okay for me to talk to the man (the one that she was afraid of) because I'm older and he can't do anything to me." She responded with something like, "Yeah, and I'm little and everyone would want me because I'm so beautiful." I was shocked. Yes, she was being completely serious. She is a pretty girl, but her attitude about appearance is all wrong. She is going to have a hard life ahead of her if she thinks that she is more beautiful than everyone else. I'm sure she gets told that all the time. Another time she said to me that everyone wants to take pictures of her and not Melanie because Melanie's not pretty like her. Shannon has the face of a Thai, but her skin is white like a *farang*. Melanie is the opposite. As soon as she started talking about being beautiful, I was ready to put her on the bus back to Bangkok because it annoyed me so much. The fact that Baa LaWang plays along with Melanie escalates my frustration and doesn't help the situation.

After the shop closed at 10:00 p.m., I went to Yee's house and slept alone in her room. I think they might have been testing the situation because I might be living with them as my third host family. I doubt it, but I'm really not sure.

January 15, 2007

Today, we had an exhibition at school. It was somewhat like the science fairs I had participated in during middle school. I got ready for the day at 6:30 a.m. and went to get my hair and make-up done. Yee and I stayed at our booth for quite a while, and then one of the teachers allowed us to wander around because I had never seen the exhibition before and I really wanted to see it. Bank, a friend from school, came over to our booth at one point, with two goldfish in a bag, and gave them to me. They were so cute. He came back a few minutes later with two more. I think he kept those. When it was time to dance, they said that they didn't have the instrument that I've been practicing on, so I was supposed to dance free-style in front of the drums. Those were the longest six minutes of my life. Thai songs are so long anyway, but free-style? I ran out of things to do within the first minute, but I'm glad I did it. Now I have pictures, and it looks like I knew what I was doing. After that, Dear, Yee, P'BaiThong, and I went for ice cream. Dear and Yee were pretending to try to kill my fish because I was gawking over them so much. They kept trying to throw napkins into the cup that I had them in, but it was all in good fun.

I went to a Rotary meeting with everyone later that night. The food wasn't all that good, but it was nice having friends to talk with for a change. P'Nuan gave me a package from Bill (my YEO in the Marseilles Rotary club). That was so nice of him; it felt like Christmas!

After dinner, we went to karaoke and then dropped Yee and

Dear off before going to Barnana. Barnana is a bar that I had heard about but had never had the chance to go. I was so excited! The bar opened at 10:00 p.m., and we got there a little bit after that, so no one was there yet. We decided to leave for a half an hour and just walk around to waste some time. When we returned, we got a table in the back, and P'BaiThong ordered two beers because she still didn't believe that I didn't drink. She ended up drinking both of them and then ordered more. It was a lot of fun hanging out with her. A little while later, in walked a Rotarian. He was with a bunch of guys that were sitting near our table. He, also, happened to be friends with another group of guys in front of us that were talking about me. He saw me and started walking over to our table. I hid my face, acting all embarrassed and everything. By then he reached the table, so I *wai*ed him. He had this huge grin on his face. I'm sure he had a few drinks by this point. P'BaiThong was talking to him, and I said that, "Yeah, I was scared." Not really being honest because what would Rotary do anyway? I wouldn't be sent home for just being in a bar and not drinking, so why be afraid? I felt like it was expected of me to act like I was scared, anyway. He was just laughing and said that he wouldn't tell Rotary and then said that he was offended that I didn't ask him to come along to the bar, too. All in all, it was pretty funny.

Then, P'BaiThong had to go to the bathroom, and I was sitting there alone waiting for her, and the group of guys that were friends with the Rotarian called me over. I was alone and bored, so I figured I'd go over and talk to them. I thought that it would be fun to see if I could get them to buy me a drink. Not that I was planning on drinking it but just to see if I could get them to buy it for me. I think beer is disgusting, anyway. I'm a *farang*, so I knew it wouldn't be too difficult. I was talking with them with the little bit of Thai that I know, and, although they didn't buy me a drink, one guy poured me a glass of beer from his bottle. I guess that counts as half. Then the Rotarian turned around and looked at me, and this actually *was* embarrassing. I mean, not five minutes ago P'BaiThong was saying to him that I was such a good girl and I didn't even drink alcohol. Now I was sitting with a group of five guys with a glass of Heineken in my hand. He just gave me a smirk as if to say, "Good girl, yeah right." Then he said something to the guys about how he knows me; a big brother sort of thing, I suppose, from what I actually understood of the conversation and then went back to his table. We didn't stay much longer. It was kind of boring. They had some dancers for entertainment, but they were fat for Thai girls. They didn't look very good in the bikinis they were wearing, and they couldn't dance very well. Even I could dance better than them, and I don't dance well at all.

Once we left, P'BaiThong started to get really antsy about going home to face Baa LaWang and was seriously starting to freak out. She called her friend to see what to do for a hangover and then sent me into the 7-Eleven to buy her a "hang" drink. The name of the beverage that she wanted was "Hang." Well, everyone in the store was staring at me for buying it. I awkwardly commented, "Uh yeah, it's for a friend." "The exchange student bought a hangover drink" is not a rumor that I want to get started around town. Then she asked me to buy a bunch of other things, so I went to 7-Eleven three or four times. Then we got noodles because she was supposed to eat or drink something with it, but she talked on the phone the whole time and barely ate a spoonful. Then I told her that I would not give her the bottle of Hang until she gave me the car keys. Normally she would let me drive without hesitation, but now her excuse was that if we got pulled over, it would be a bad situation for her to be in. What? There were no cops around! My point was that, if I drove, we might not die. She lost the argument in the end, and I drove home just fine. Baa LaWang was already asleep, and P'BaiThong wouldn't let me get a shower because it might make too much noise, so I got to bed around 1:30 a.m.

January 16, 2007

P'BaiThong woke me up at 8:00 a.m., still really nervous about having to face Baa LaWang. She was still asleep, but I think P'BaiThong wanted me to be with her when she woke up. Nothing happened that I know of. I left them alone for 5 or 10 minutes, but everything seemed okay when I went downstairs. P'BaiThong took me home, but I couldn't get in the house because everyone was still asleep. Mind you, this was about ten o'clock already. Finally, NeungEuy let me in.

January 19, 2007

It took me a few days to write the above entry, so I already had another story to write about that happened yesterday. I'll start out with a funny story. Mae, Paw, and I were sitting at a red light, and someone on a motorcycle ran the light because no one was coming the other way. Paw said something about that, and they were discussing it. I wanted to be a part of the conversation and said, "*Ni sai mai dee*" which translates to something like, "That's a bad habit," and they both freaked out at me, saying, "No, don't say that!" I was laughing because I've said that a ton of times and didn't know what the big deal was. The phrase is basically judging the person, saying that they are doing something wrong. Apparently, it is very inappropriate for young people to state any such judgment about or toward adults. Young people must have respect for everyone who is older. I didn't even see who was on the motorcycle, but, apparently, it was an adult, so I just won't say that anymore around my parents. My friends say it all the time around me, so that's why I started saying it, too.

Later on, we got home, and my fish tank was really dirty, so I asked Mae how to sterilize the water because I would normally use bottled water, but I knew they have to pay for that, and I didn't want to waste a bunch of money by using it every week. I suggested that I boil the water and then let it cool overnight, and then it is sterilized. She went through how to clean the bowl (like I'm two years old) and told me to change only half the water and leave the other half there because if all of the water is changed, then the fish will go into shock and die. The way that I saw it was that by doing that, I would have to change the water twice as many times. We had goldfish at my mom's day care center in Illinois for a long time. None of those fish ever went into shock when we changed all the water. I told Mae that, and she said that this type of fish is very sensitive and that she used to raise them. They are called *pla thawng,* which is literally translated as "fish golden." I said, "Yeah, they're the same type I used to have at home in America." My father (who could follow only part of the conversation) said that their heads are really, really small. I agreed but went on to say that their bodies are really small too, so everything is in proportion. I wasn't sure if that was correct, but neither were they. My mom then stated that we'd only had them for two days, and I replied, "Correct, but they have been alive for more than two days; they weren't recently born."

I thought we were having a normal discussion, but apparently not because my mom got really upset. I think it was because she couldn't think of any more reasons to support her theory. My mom pointedly stated in an angry tone, "Fine, do it however you want," and my dad brought the trashcan inside and motioned as if to just throw them all away. I apologized and said, "I just didn't understand why, but I'm sure you know how to do it because you used to raise them, and they are still small." Then I added some more bullshit along those lines, just hoping to smooth it all over.

I was really angry that night. Just because she has been alive longer than I have doesn't mean that she knows more than I do about everything. I hate how the respect thing works here. Young people can't have a discussion with a person of an older generation because they would be disrespectful if they disagree. Therefore, the issue at hand can't even be discussed. I was also annoyed by the fact that my dad sided with her while not even knowing what was going on. I do know a little about life and have my own opinions and knowledge about different things. I just didn't understand how anything could get accomplished, if nothing can be discussed.

At school, in the line this morning, I was still a little mad about the whole situation. Yee walked up to me and said, "Okay, when you say, '*ni sai mai dee,*'" and I cut her off, asking if my mom had talked to her. I told Yee that she had already talked to me about that. Yee said, "No, but *Adjant* Seanporn asked Dear if we said that to you a lot." I just looked at her, and she went on to say that *Adjant* told Dear that I said "*ni sai mai dee*" to my mom when she wouldn't buy me a gold fish.

That just sent me over the top. First of all, that never happened.

Secondly, if it had, who does my mom think she is to go running her mouth about me to the whole English department? If she wants to say something about my vocabulary, say it to me. I'm just learning how to speak Thai; I don't even know the full meaning of anything I'm saying so far because I can't literally translate expressions like this one! If I ever said that directly to my mom, I was never corrected, and I can't remember doing it. The reason that I'm positive that that never happened is because she didn't even buy me the fish; I bought them myself along with the rocks, scenery, oxygen, and food. All she paid for was the tank, and I tried to pay for that, but she wouldn't let me. She even wanted more fish than we got, but I told her that three in total was plenty about five times, and finally she let it go. That just made me so mad because if I say something wrong, I want to be corrected right then, especially if it is something really bad that I shouldn't say. I'm still annoyed about that, but I guess that is just another cultural difference. Correcting someone at the time of a misstep could cause them embarrassment, and that is not the Thai way.

A while ago, Yee told me a story about something that happened during her exchange to America the year before that was similar to this situation. A group of her "friends" taught her the phrase, "fuck you." They told her that using that phrase would cause people to laugh. She soon found that to be true. Every time she said it, people would stop what they were doing, look at her, and laugh. She was having fun with it and began using it more and more, eventually even to her teachers and her host mom. One evening after dinner, her host dad said that they needed to talk. He asked her about the phrase and where she learned it. He then asked her if she knew exactly what it meant. She admitted, "No, not really." He told her that it was something that was very inappropriate to say in nearly all situations and that it should never be said outside of a group of really close friends. He went on to say that many Americans find the phrase very offensive and would never say it in any situation, ever. Some Americans will not even associate with people who frequently use that type of language. She never said it again but later learned what it meant and was embarrassed and angry that her so-called "friends" had played her like that. So I guess I should be thankful to know that "*ni sai mai dee*" is a phrase I should refrain from saying in the future.

January 20, 2007

I had English Day Camp today at another school. More than a week ago, the *adjant* asked my mom if I would attend, but my mom waited until just two days ago to ask me. If I had any other plans I wouldn't have gone, but I was free. My mom actually woke up early in the morning (usually she sleeps in really late) and asked me if I wanted her to go with me. I said that it didn't matter to me and asked if she wanted to go. She replied, "No, I don't really want to go. Do you know any of the *adjant*s that will be there?" I said that I didn't, and she said, "Well, I guess I can go with you then, since you don't know anyone." I don't remember if those were her exact words, but she made it sound like she was bending over backward for me. Again, I'm not a Thai kid. I came to Thailand, alone, with two suitcases, planning on staying in a completely foreign country for 11 months and not knowing a single soul; I think I can handle going to a school 20 minutes away for 6 hours. Just to make sure, she gave me a pep talk, saying that if I want to come home to just let her know right away, and she will find a way for me to get home. I guess I'm still upset with her from when she told the whole English department about our argument revolving around my goldfish. I think that because Mae studied English and Western culture, her mannerisms elicit my American stubbornness and temper. I suppose it is good that I feel comfortable enough with her to show my frustrations.

When we got in the English Day Camp van with the others, she got her 10 minutes of fame by talking about me; but the entire day, she was just pushed around. It was obvious that she felt out of place, and the *adjant* who was in charge there didn't know what to do with her. By the end of the day, I saw her napping in one of the chairs. I had a lot of fun in my room, though. The whole day was a lot of fun. I was called beautiful so many times today. I really am going to miss it because in Nakhon Phanom everyone calls me fat rather than beautiful!

January 21, 2007

I had to go back today to get my face cleaned. Today, she didn't really do it for all that long, but she still said for me to come back in a week. She kept asking if it hurt, and I wouldn't lie; it hurt pretty badly. So I think that's why she didn't continue any longer. I wish she had, though, because I don't want to go back every week, but the things they do before and after the face cleaning are really nice and relaxing. I fell asleep again today for a few minutes.

After we were done with that, Yee took me to a Thai sauna. I've never even been to a real American one (only the ones by the pools in some hotels). It was all outdoors (as everything is here) and very naturalistic. They had a ton of plants and trees and little huts where patrons can buy things to eat. We changed into a sarong and then smeared this organic goo all over our arms and legs and then yogurt on our faces and some other kind of cream for our hair. Then we went into this really small room that would fit eight or nine people, if they all sit properly. Heat was rising from the floor, so everyone had their legs on the benches because otherwise it was way too hot. There was no door; instead, a thick tarp was attached at the top so that people could easily get in and out, but, when no one came in or left, it kept all the steam inside. The room was pitch black; we couldn't see anything at all. Those who were already in there guided us to a part of the bench that was open. Every time someone came in or left, it allowed enough light in to see an available space for a few seconds. Our eyes adjusted somewhat to the darkness. We stayed for an hour or two, going in and out of the sauna and just talking. It was really fun.

Today was the first time that I outright lied to my mom. I told Yee that I would eat dinner at my house because I thought my mom would be expecting me, but she wasn't home, and I wasn't that hungry either. We didn't really have that much to choose from, anyway. So I ate bananas with milk and sugar and then a few pieces of bread because the banana soup made me a little bit hungrier.

Oh, and then I had blueberry yogurt milk. My mom came home and asked me what I had eaten for dinner, and I just told her I ate at Yee's. At home, in America, Mom would ask, "Are you sure you don't want anything else?" I would say, "No," and that would be the end of it. Here, if I had told her what I had eaten, she would consider it to be not enough food for me and try to pressure me into eating all the other kinds of food that we have in the house. She worries so much that I'm going to starve, and I hate it. If I'm not hungry, I won't eat. Whenever I get hungry, I'll find something, and, if nothing appeals to me, then it's obvious that I'm not that hungry. I do admit that I had started eating a lot healthier foods and no junk food since I moved into her house to lose weight, but that's because I could barely fit into my jeans, and everyone at school was calling me fat.

I did gain a lot of weight initially, about 12 kilos in all. Now I've lost all of that, and I'm sure I've lost more, but I don't know how much. I'm not dieting in an unhealthy way, though. My mom makes it sound like I'm anorexic or something. If I eat somewhere that she doesn't see me eating, then she just assumes that I must not have eaten and tries to get me to eat more. It's really getting to the point that I simply don't care. All the teachers at school say, "Oh, what are your parents going to say if they see you and you look so skinny?" Well, what would they say if I looked really fat? I don't think they would say anything, either way, and I don't think it really matters what they say. If I'm happy and healthy then does it really matter? Another thing about my weight is that every month I have a week when I barely eat anything at all. Then, afterward, I eat so much, you'd think I was eating for three people. It's always been like that; I can't help it. I'm sure being in a different environment does affect my body, but it's not going to change my eating habits that drastically.

I don't know if I'm just in a bad mood, but I am really counting down the days until District Conference. It's been almost a week since I started the countdown. I am so bored with the monotony of each day. It is fun to hang out with my friends at school, but they have classes to attend and I am always stuck studying Thai in the

English department. Every night I go to bed looking at the calendar and thinking, how many more days until February.

Next month is high school graduation. Soon after that, all of my friends will be leaving for college. After that, I hope to just travel until I go home. March: We have District Conference. April: Songkran and the exchange student tour to Phuket. May: Mom and Dad come for two weeks. June: Get packed and say goodbye. The only reason I don't want my year to be over yet is because I still don't know the language that well. It's really frustrating, but it's so hard to learn and tiring to try to study the same things.

March is going to be boring because school is over and some of my friends will have already left for college. I think P'BaiThong is going to take me for a week to another province to hang out with her and her friends. That is going to be so much fun because she is about 23, and we are at about the same maturity level. For a Thai person, that is really unusual. Basically, I have two weeks of fun events every month until I go home, not including my plans for independent travel to visit my exchange student friends in their towns. School starts again in May, but I really don't want to go back. Because I was almost 19 when I arrived in Thailand and the oldest students at *Piyamahalachalai* School were only 17 or 18, I naturally made friends with the older students. Now, they're all going off to college. I have heard that some of the other exchange students don't have to go to school anymore. I don't know if I can swing that. I am now 19 and a half years old, and I don't want to be in classes with 16 and 17 year olds, whose maturity levels are about the same as 13-year-old Americans.

I want to work at P'BaiThong's restaurant instead. It would keep me busy, and I could even stay there for my third host family. If I can't skip school, I'll just be "sick" for my 20 percent of the school year and then do some traveling to miss more school. I have used only one "sick day" since I started school, so I figure I have a few saved up. I would be fine with going to school half days just to continue studying Thai, but I don't know how I would be able to get out of the school for the other half. I'll think more about that later.

My Thai Family and My American Family

Standing in Class Lines for School Announcements

Hanging Out with Friends Between Classes

My Rotary Blazer Midway Through My Exchange Year

Feeding an Elephant on the Street

Loy Krathong Festival

Touring the Long Neck Hill Tribes

The White Temple

Touring Temples With Monks

Thailand Inbounds

Swimming at a Thai Beach

The Meat Section of the Market in Nakhon Phanom

The Floating Market

The Food Line at My Temple

Visiting Chiang Dao Cave with Other Exchange Students

My Temple

January 23, 2007

Tonight was a lot of fun. I got out of school at 3:30 p.m. (an hour and a half earlier than usual), which is always a good start. Then, I started walking to Tae Kwon Do at 4:30 p.m., so that I would arrive there by 5:00 p.m. I love Tae Kwon Do so much. It's a lot of fun to learn, and it really does give me a good workout. It's more stretching than cardio, but I come home sore after every lesson. During class, everyone respects me because I'm the oldest (and probably because I'm a *farang*), and they all help me to understand what's going on and just talk to me about anything, which helps me with my Thai, too. *Adjant* Beer is really awesome. Today he seemed especially more attentive to me. He always makes sure I understand and is very encouraging toward me and constantly corrects my stance so that I get it perfect and have a good base. Today was great because it was the first time he made me do push-ups. Usually I'm treated like a *farang* and I didn't have to do anything I didn't want to do, but today he made me pull my weight. Apparently, I wasn't yelling loudly enough during the punches, so I had to do five push-ups. He actually got a bit angry with people today, which was a side of him I had not seen before. I actually liked it because I felt like we all learned more because he was so serious. I think he's just being harsh because we have a test on Friday for a new color belt. I don't know if everyone else feels as I do, but I am so excited! I've been attending class for only two weeks, and I might get my yellow belt! He told Baa LaWang that I was a really quick learner and that he was impressed with me. I'm starting to get bored with the white belt, so I'm excited for the next lesson on Thursday because it's my last practice before the test, and then, hopefully, on Saturday, I'll be able to study something new. Classes are from 5:00 p.m. to 7:00 p.m., plus an extra half hour afterward to practice for competition. I didn't know about it until tonight, so I couldn't stay late, but on Thursday I'm planning on staying later.

Another funny story happened before class started. I arrived early because when I walk to class I always allowed extra time so that I will not be late. *Adjant* Beer was finishing up some paperwork in his office, so he told me to hang out in the playroom upstairs. There were two boys from my class in the playroom, and, despite the numerous toys there, they were just watching TV: a "Tom and Jerry" episode. I joined them on the couch. Something happened on the cartoon episode that caused all three of us to laugh simultaneously. It suddenly occurred to me how, regardless of what language we speak or what country we live in, kids are the same everywhere. I noted while watching the rest of the episode that there were few lines of actual dialog, but the various actions of the cartoon characters elicited the same reactions from the two boys and me. Although that moment probably didn't mean anything to the two boys, it really gave me a whole new perspective on my exchange experience. I felt oddly tied to the Thai people. During my exchange thus far, I had been focusing almost entirely on the differences that I'd encountered and the new experiences that I've had. I had yet to step back and observe just how incredibly similar we all were.

P'BaiThong picked me up after Tae Kwon Do and took me to a rather desolate area so that she could give me my first lesson on driving a motorcycle. It was so cool, but I found it to be a little bit difficult to learn. Just starting the motor took a lot of practice, but, once I did that, driving wasn't so hard. I'm just not used to working the clutch with my hand and shifting gears with my foot. My next lesson is sometime next week, so I think I'll pick up on it fairly quickly. P'BaiThong seems to think that I learned really fast.

25 January 2007

Wow! I just totally wrote the date in Asian style without thinking. Anyway, after Tae Kwon Do today, I went to help work at P'BaiThong's restaurant. Today just wasn't a good day there. First, Baa LaWang was hurrying to make salads to go and slipped on something or other and fell down. She insisted that she was okay, but I know she has had surgery on her knee previously, and she admitted later (in Thai) that her wrist was hurting, but she wouldn't make a big deal about it. Later, she dropped a glass dish, and it shattered. I don't know if the fall just shook her up or if her wrist really is injured. She is going to the hospital tomorrow to have blood taken, so I have my fingers crossed that everything goes well. A little while after that, Loong Thao (Baa LaWang's husband) was cooking steak, and the whole stove caught fire. I think that all the oil around the stove contributed to this. It was a pretty big fire, too; the flames reached a few feet above the stove. We doused it with water right away, so everything is okay now. A lot of excitement for one day, though.

When I got home today, I knocked on my mom's bedroom door because tomorrow I wanted to go help P'BaiThong while Baa LaWang went to the hospital (we didn't have school tomorrow). I just wanted to be sure that she was okay with it. I didn't want to have to wake her up in the morning because everyone always sleeps in so late here. She said that she wants me to go to school tomorrow, after all. So, apparently, we do have school tomorrow. My grade, M6, doesn't, and yet she expected me to go. What am I supposed to do there? Nothing, but sit in the English department all day? So then she proceeds to give me a guilt trip for missing so much school. (This would be the second day that I would miss excluding absences for Rotary events.)

Then she changed the subject to the fact that I should do my own laundry every week because the maid (not even her) does everyone's laundry on Saturdays. Her reasoning was that, because I practice Tae Kwon Do on Tuesdays, Thursdays, and Saturdays, I should do all of my laundry on Sundays. I had been doing all my whites on Sundays already. She said that the maid has to do so much laundry or something to that effect. (This conversation was all in Thai, so I'm sure I missed a few words.) If that were the case, then why doesn't she do her laundry separately? Or Oak? In three months, he's going to be in M6 too, so why do I have to do my own laundry? The fact of doing my own laundry doesn't really upset me. In fact, while staying with my first family, I did my own laundry every week. What upsets me is that it suddenly became a problem for the maid to do my laundry. I've already been here for two months. Eight weeks of laundry, and now it's a problem? Maybe I am missing something in the translation because I don't know why this suddenly became a problem. When I said that I wanted to help out P'BaiThong for the next three days while her mom is recovering from the wrist injury, she suggested that I just sleep there, too. She suggested it in a "pushing me out the door" type of way.

I don't know why she gets this way. Maybe she's mad that I enjoy having an after school activity rather than sitting at home and reading a book. Ever since I started Tae Kwon Do, I stopped going to exercise with her at night. She seemed supportive of my new after school activity when I started attending lessons. Maybe going with Mae to exercise at night meant more to her than I thought. I should try to spend more time with her, but I've made a lot of friends and gotten involved in many activities. I don't want to sit around the house all evening.

Maybe I'll move out of this house in late February. That'll be three months here and then four more to go. It'd be cool to live with P'BaiThong for the first two months and then my "third" host family for the last two months. I still haven't talked to P'BaiThong about that. It would just be easy because I could work late at the restaurant every night, sleep till noon, and then do it again.

January 26, 2007

I got my yellow belt! I'm so unbelievably excited! The a*djant* told the class to get there by 4:30 p.m., but then told me to be there by 4:00 p.m. I was already really nervous, anyway, and sitting at home wasn't helping my nerves, so I got there just before 4:00 and practiced and warmed up and then just talked to everyone. At about 4:45 *Adjant* Beer went through a few of the kicks and routines with all the colors as practice. Then we all got in shoot formation and waited for the master to come. I was the fourth and last of the white belts to go up there. Right away he corrected us on where to put our hands for the punches. I did the punches great (they were the easiest thing—*Adjant* never actually taught me those; I just followed the movements of the others, then remembered them). Then we did the three kicks. My side kicks still aren't the greatest because I'm not that flexible yet, but my form is good. Then we did the six-count block. I did awesome on my way up, but, coming back the last step, I was thinking too hard and did it backward. I don't know if the judge saw me or not because my back was to him, but I was beating myself up over it for the rest of the testing. I was so nervous; I was shaking after sitting down. I had no idea what to expect, and I knew that more was expected of me because I was older, so I couldn't even compare my presentation with the others.

Another thing I forgot to mention. The judge was calling the names of all the students in the class and got to mine and had the worst time stumbling over it. Then all of the judges decided to have a huge conversation about me. This made me even more nervous because I knew that I stood out and any mistakes would be easily spotted. Finally, after everyone tested, we got a lecture type talk from the master about the right kind of kicks and the right kind of blocks. I understood only about half of what he was saying, anyway. Then *Adjant* went to the front and just had everyone go up in the order we were sitting to get our yellow belts from him. I was so annoyed that it was that simple to get a yellow belt. We all did well, but I expected to get graded like the other color belts did. I'm really looking forward to testing for a green belt. We have to do a longer routine, then a walking group of kicks, and then a three kick/jump combination. Then we also have partner kick/block routines to do, I think.

This morning, I went to Ran LookThan to make food for the *farang* doctors who were visiting our hospital for a seminar. P'BaiThong was explaining it to me and then proceeded to say that it was probably about the bird flu. Nakhon Phanom has had cases of a different kind of bird flu, for which there is no vaccine. She said something about the doctors giving shots, but I don't know if by "shot" she means treatment for the victims or to vaccinate people for immunization. It's kind of scary to think about the bird flu being in my province!

I forgot to mention a fun event that happened a few weeks ago. P'Nuan came to *Piyamahalachalai* to pick me up from school a few hours early. We drove to a local grade school and met the rest of the Rotary club members who were hanging a banner and setting up two tables. We would be administering the Polio vaccination to the Kindergarten classes. Once everything was ready, the teachers led their students to the first table where the vaccination would be administered orally. I was told to stand behind the second table with one other Rotarian and call the kids over for a treat after they had received the vaccine. Handing out ice cream and other treats would have been fun had the vaccine tasted better. As soon as the first few kids received the vaccination, they began crying because it did not taste good. They refused to move over to the table I was attending for a treat. Then the kids in the back of the line started crying in anticipation of the vaccine. The Rotarians were able to help calm the children who then started enjoying an impromptu recess. It was fun to be a part of this experience.

After considerable thought, I have come to the conclusion that I have become a milkaholic. I'm not exaggerating. In America, I would estimate that I drink about a glass a day, sometimes two. Here it seems every imaginable flavor is available, including yogurt milk! They're packaged in convenient drink boxes. There's chocolate, plain, whole, strawberry, skim, green tea, lycee, chocolate malt, and these are just the flavors at school. They have this kind translated as "sour milk" in many flavors, too. I've had only the original flavor, but it's really good. Then for the yogurt milks, they have orange, mixed fruit, strawberry, and blueberry. They also have sweetened milk. It is too sweet for me, but I like the sweetened milk in a bowl with bananas. Usually at home we add sugar, but this milk is so sweet that adding sugar is not necessary. I think I drink about three or four boxes a day and then constantly go to 7-Eleven and get either a large container of yogurt milk or a cup of Ovaltine (which is cheaper and is a fountain drink, so I've been getting that a lot lately). I didn't realize until I got to school and tasted the chocolate malt milk that Ovaltine is malt. At first, I didn't really care for it, but I've gotten it so often that now I've grown to like it. We also have coffee milk at school, but I hate coffee, so I have yet to taste it. When I get home, I'm sure I'm going to have milk withdrawal. I'll just have to get the Nesquik flavor containers. I wonder if milk is more expensive than gasoline or just what the price of gasoline is. That's interesting to think about.

Baa LaWang just got her test results from the doctor. She didn't tell me anything except that he said to stop working for a number of days and that they are closing her shop on Sundays going forward so she can rest. I don't know any more about it right now.

12

AN UNEXPECTED TOUR

January 28, 2007

I went to work at the restaurant like I do after every Tae Kwon Do practice. Because of Baa LaWang's fall, she decided to take a week off and go to Bangkok. She asked me if I wanted to come along and I enthusiastically replied, "Yeah, my bags are already packed." I think the conversation started out as a joke, but when she realized that I was serious, it was for real. I called P'Nuan and asked if I could go to Bangkok the next day, but I had English camp the next Friday, so I wanted to come home, alone, which would mean riding alone on the night bus on Thursday. That was the only problem. So, she called the president of the club and then called P'BaiThong to make sure she understood what was going on. Then she said that, because of the short notice, that she had to double check with the district adviser. Finally, the club president called back and said that it was okay but be safe. He was concerned about the bombings, resulting from the political unrest in southern Thailand. Then I called Mae. After a long conversation, she was fine with it. She said at first that I have to ask P'Nuan and after I said I already did and it was okay, she seemed angry that I had asked her second. I feel as though either way I handled it would have been wrong.

January 29, 2007

I slept as late as I could and then walked around town to get all the things I would need. Around 6:00 p.m. I got to the bus station, and Baa LaWang, P'BaiThong, and I set off for Bangkok. Only at the bus station did I find out that we were just going to switch buses in Bangkok and continue on to Chantiburi. They pronounce Chantiburi differently from what I am used to hearing, so I still wasn't sure where we were going.

It was on this trip that I learned the vowels of the Thai alphabet. As I've explained earlier, the Gaw-Gai video taught me the Thai alphabet, but only the 44 consonants. There is a separate song for the 32 vowels. Baa LaWang and I had just gotten our lunch at the bus stop when she asked if I wanted to learn this new song. There are a few short phrases amongst the vowels, but this song more closely resembles the English alphabet song. Baa LaWang wrote the lyrics out, which made it a lot easier for me to memorize because Baa Thao had already taught me how to read.

January 30, 2007

After about 15 hours on the bus, we got to Chantiburi and met P'LookThan, Baa LaWang's oldest daughter, and Baa LaWang's brother's family, who we would be staying with. Once I knew where we were, I told everyone that I had friends who lived in this town. Baa LaWang's brother said, "Yes, I know Nick; he comes in here a lot." I guess everyone knows who the *farang*s are. They were having a conversation together and thought that it would be cool to surprise him, so we all got into the car and went to his school. We found out that he was on his own trip to Korat, but they knew the school where Hayley and Kelly attended, so we headed there next. The counselor called Hayley and told her that they needed her and Kelly to come to the office because there was someone there to see them. Baa LaWang told me to hide right before Kelly and Hayley arrived. They were walking in really slowly and confused because they didn't recognize Baa LaWang or her family. Then I came out from behind the bookshelf, and Hayley and Kelly were so surprised. Baa LaWang left, and I stayed to hang out with them. We ditched school and got *chai yen* (iced tea) and then went to Robinsons, which is a chain of malls in Thailand. We talked about everything all day. We finally got in touch with McKinsey by cell phone and talked to her for a little while. She already had her ticket home and is not going to Phuket (southern tour). We all yelled at her, but at least we'll see her at District Conference before she heads home. McKinsey is ending her exchange year early to prepare for college. Because she will be attending college at the United States Military Academy at West Point, she wanted some time for final preparations and physical conditioning.

I hung out with Kelly and Hayley for the rest of the day; we even went to dinner together that evening. Just after dropping Kelly off, Jason called me to say that he is leaving to go home on Sunday. I called him back and talked to him for about a half an hour that night. Jason is also cutting his exchange experience short; he says that he just needs to get on with his life and is thinking about joining the Army. I hope it's not because of me. Jason had a crush on me a while back. I really like Jason and like being around him—I just wasn't ready for a serious relationship. Not only because having a boyfriend is against the rules of Rotary Youth Exchange, but also because I want to make the most of this year. I am kind of curious as to what the trip to Phuket is going to be like now that the two people I always hung out with are leaving, but we will have some newbies there, too. So it should still be a lot of fun.

January 31, 2007

I got up at 9:30 a.m., ate brunch, and visited with Baa LaWang's family. Around 11:00 a.m. we went to get Hayley and Kelly from school and went to the Mountain Temple and Museum. The museum was actually really neat; it housed about a dozen wax statues of famous monks in Thailand. The wax figures looked amazingly realistic! We ate lunch and then came back to where I was staying and just hung out. When school ended, Kelly went home, and Hayley took me to the temple in town where there was a huge Buddha who was lying down. This statue was called Reclining Buddha and was representative of his attaining perfection, about to enter Nirvana. After that, Hayley went home, and I went *pai tiow*ing (sightseeing) with P'LookThon.

It was a lot of fun to see the town of Chantiburi. It has a small town atmosphere but is a lot bigger than Nakhon Phanom and has a lot more *farang*s who are permanent residents. Back at the house, we had Korean barbeque for dinner. That was really good! After supper, I went *pai tiow*ing at night with Baa LaWang's nephew. He is 18 years old and is the only straight Thai boy I've met that wasn't nervous and shy around me. We had a lot of fun. When we got back, we watched *Pirates of the Caribbean II*.

February 1, 2007

I got up at about 7:30 a.m. and walked to Hayley's house. She had already bought breakfast for me, and we took it to school to eat. We listened to announcements and then decided to hang out in their computer lab. We had a small computer lab in *Piyamahalachalai*, but this room is a lot nicer. It not only had nice chairs and many computers but was also air conditioned! We played around on the computers a little, and then Hayley started freaking out. Apparently, Led Zeppelin is going to do one last reunited tour next summer, and the drummer from the group (who has died) is going to be replaced by his son (who is the only other person who can play the same because he was taught everything by his dad). She was absolutely hysterical about it. I'm not really into Led Zeppelin, but it was fun watching Hayley's reaction to the news.

Around 10:00 a.m., we were picked up from school and went to Khon Chang Island with Baa LaWang and her brother. We took a ferry over and then drove to the beach. We picked up another exchange student, Brittany, whom I had not met before, since she had chosen to not go on the Rotary tours. Brittany speaks absolutely no Thai, and I'm not exaggerating. At one point she asked me if *faen* meant "boyfriend." I thought, "Are you kidding?" That was one of the first words I learned in Thailand.

Anyway, we got to the beach, and Brittany and I didn't have swimsuits, so we dropped Hayley and Kelly off and then went to buy some. I got a souvenir shirt and then shorts for bottoms. I've become so Thai that I would feel uncomfortable in a western style swimsuit here. I don't even like to have bare shoulders in public.

Oh well, I guess I've been here that long. This beach was completely filled with *farang*s. The sights on the beach were really shocking; most were wearing skimpy string bikinis, and their bodies were definitely not slender. So we just talked about them in Thai. We swam for about an hour or so and then got on the ferry to go back home.

On the ferry, there was this good looking guy leaning on the railing of the boat, just looking at the water. Baa LaWang told me to go over and see if he spoke Thai and talk to him. No one knew what to say, so we were just talking to each other and then the guy started to walk away. Baa LaWang asked him in Thai if he was seasick. He didn't hear what she had said, so he walked over to us. Once we could see his face, we knew that he wasn't Thai, so I translated for him. He is from Russia and works for a touring company and is in charge of a tour group here. He said that we speak better Thai than he does; it's cool meeting someone who is almost in the same position as we are. I got a picture with him, and then it was time to get into the car to get off the ferry. We had about a half an hour conversation about how hot he was in both Thai and English so that we could include Baa LaWang and her brother in our conversation. When we got home, I went to Hayley's house to meet her mom and visit with her host family. Later, I went out with Baa LaWang's nephew again, and then we watched *Mission Impossible III* with Baa LaWang when we got back.

February 2, 2007

I got to the bus station at 8:30 a.m. and then to Bangkok just before noon. I slept a lot on the bus but was still really tired. P'BaiThong's friend said she'd be there in an hour, and, once she came, we had to wait for another friend. It wasn't that bad though. We then toured the Grand Palace, which was really cool to see again. I feel like I missed so much of it the first time, when P'Nan took me because I had just arrived in Thailand and everything was so overwhelming. After the Grand Palace, we visited a small museum of Siam. Then we went to a tourist information center where P'BaiThong and her friend used to work. They knew the person working today, so we talked with him for a while and then invited him to eat with us. We went to a shopping street and ate lunch and then waited for a bus at a bus stop. All of a sudden, a van drove up and stopped. The door opened, and a guy in a white tuxedo got out. There was a bunch of video cameras and a sign that read, "Free Hugs" (in English on one side and in Thai on the other side). Apparently, he was a double for a famous singer, and they were filming a music video. That's so cool! I might be in a music video that will be shown all through Thailand because karaoke is so popular here. I really wanted to buy the VCD, which would play the music video of each song on the album, but I didn't know who the artist was.

Then we walked on a walking path above the city. It was really pretty looking down on the traffic at night. We took the sky train and then another bus to go back to the bus station. It was a lot of fun, but I was really tired. I got on the bus to Nakhon Phanom at 8:30 p.m., and we had two huge delays during which we were parked on the side of the road for a half an hour. I don't know what was going on, and I don't think the other passengers did either. We ate dinner at about midnight. I was eating by myself, having some *phak boong* (stir-fried vegetables). Sitting next to me were two older ladies who were talking about me, saying things like, "Look, she likes vegetables." It was amusing, but I had just woken up and was too tired to start an actual conversation. I asked them what I should do with my tray and after that went to the bathroom and got back on the bus and slept a lot more.

February 3, 2007

My dad was waiting at the bus station for me (I think for over an hour), and then we went to the hospital to visit NeungEuy. She had a sore throat and spent three days in the hospital. She had an I.V. and everything. Later that day, she gave a speech at English camp. I have to wonder just how sick she really was.

This trip was so much fun, and I definitely needed it. Every time I go on a trip with other *farangs,* I always come home wanting to increase my studying of Thai because I always think my Thai isn't good enough. People tell me that I speak the best Thai of all the exchange students, but I guess it's still not good enough for me. I think Hayley speaks about as well as I do. As of right now, I can read Thai, and I don't think any of the other exchange students can. I still want to practice more to read faster and more accurately. I feel in my head that it's like a game or a contest or something. I want to be the best, so it's probably good that I'm not. It gives me something to strive for, and I want to perfect my reading and learn more words. I guess I'm a bit of a competitor.

I got a letter from Mom; she and Dad are coming to visit in less than three months. I knew when they were coming but seeing it written out it's like, Ahhhh! I need to get studying. I should note that I am definitely forgetting English, or at least Thai is becoming my first language. Every time I open my mouth to speak, out comes Thai (especially if I'm talking to an adult). I think I have an advantage by living in a province with no other exchange students.

13

GRADUATION

February 15, 2007

HAPPY belated Valentine's Day! Valentine's Day is huge here; it's unbelievable. I gave out Valentine cards to a bunch of friends. Everyone came to school with tons of candy and flowers (mostly roses) and a bunch of stuffed animals. It was also graduation day for M6, so the celebration was even bigger. The students in M5 gave everyone in M6 a rose or two for graduation. All together I got about 14 or 15 roses and a bunch of candy. We didn't have any classes that day. We changed into our class shirts, which do look really nice. Apparently, every graduating class designs a shirt for their section. Ours were black polo shirts that read, "Piyamahalachalai 6/7" on the front, and centered in small letters on the back was, "Congratulation." I overheard one of the English teachers poking fun at the girls (including Dear and Yee) for forgetting the "s."

We then had to sit through a long lecture in the big hall. I think it was a lot of prayers and good luck wishes from important people at the school. Then there was a little dancing, but I just sat back and talked with friends. It was early in the day and really hot. I didn't want to be all sweaty the rest of the day. After lunch, we went back and got white thread bracelets from the teachers. The white threads were to symbolize luck, and the teacher who tied one around your wrist would say a prayer of luck for you. I got two and then gave

161

up because it was really crowded and really hot! Then they had a band and more dancing. We had only an hour or so left of school, so I went in the big mob of people and had a lot of fun. Afterward, Yee dropped me off at home, and I took a shower and pressed a few of my rose petals and then cut the other ones for decoration in the kitchen. They looked really nice.

I found out about my third host family today; I will be staying with Baa LaWang and Loong Thao. I was really excited when I found out, but I still have reservations about it, mostly because I was already planning some trips with P'BaiThong and I already spent a lot of time there. I don't want to get annoyed with them or them with me by living there all the time. I usually use them as a way to get out of my house now. So where will I go to get out of their house? They didn't seem nearly as excited as I was when I told them about it. P'BaiThong just said that it would be good to have someone else working, too, because Baa LaWang's not supposed to do that much. I'll be glad to help out as best I can. I'm sure it will be a lot of fun.

Apparently, there is a northern work program that Prapart offered to us so that we don't have to go back to school. If I take that, then I don't know if I will live in Nakhon Phanom and work at the restaurant or go to work elsewhere. Besides that, I'm booking my remaining schedule completely so that I can travel everywhere once I get more fluent in Thai. I keep saying that I am not that fluent in Thai, but I really am improving. I'm just not good enough to satisfy myself. My last day of school is tomorrow. I'm so nervous about what not going to school is going to do for my Thai language progress. I hate school because of how boring it is to study Thai every day, but at least that pushes me to actually study. At home, there is always something more appealing for me to do. If I go home to America and still can't speak Thai, I'm going to be very disap-pointed in myself. I know that I still have four and a half months left, but I am planning to do so much with the other exchange students that it won't force me to learn Thai. At least by living in Nakhon Phanom, I find that everyone wants me to speak Thai and tries to help in their own way.

Ever since I got here, I realized that Hardee's was very popular, but I was puzzled that I never saw one. It's probably because I live in Nakhon Phanom, and we don't have any fast food franchise restaurants here. There would be pictures or signs and people wearing red shirts with the yellow Hardee's star on it. The only thing that confused me was that it never had the Hardee's name on it or the smiley face on the star. I visited other (bigger) towns and found KFC, McDonald's, and Subway, among other fast food chains, but no Hardee's. Now I was totally confused. Then, I found out that the red background with a yellow star, centered, is the Vietnamese flag. There are a lot of Vietnamese people in Nakhon Phanom, so it seemed that everyone had one or something like it. Now every time I see the Vietnamese flag, I get a craving for a cheeseburger. Mmmmm.

February 20, 2007

Lent begins tomorrow, and I was just sitting here thinking that I have two more hours to decide on what I want to give up but couldn't come to a decision. I was debating between milk and listening to American music. Everything here is made of milk, so I thought that for the sake of my exchange, I shouldn't pick food. I was desperately trying to think of something other than my iPod because I'm going to be traveling a lot and the only thing that passes time on a bus is having music on in the background. I was still trying to think of something else when I realized that suddenly there was silence, and the CD was only half over. So yeah, God broke my iPod. It became official that I will be giving up the use of my iPod for Lent. I just hope that my iPod will work again and isn't completely broken because I paid a lot of money for it and have used it for only seven months. Of course, the death of my iPod would eventually force me to part with 200 *baht* to purchase a normal CD player and then some Thai CDs that I'm too cheap to buy. It is probably better in all cases, but I still miss my iPod.

Later that night, I was lying in my bed reading and half listening to all the night noise from outside because my room isn't the least bit soundproof. All of a sudden, I heard a clunk, kind of like a car door slamming shut but not exactly. It's not a sound I hear a lot, so I stopped reading and concentrated on hearing any voices, concentrating on Thai. I heard a girl yell, "Briow," a few times, apparently calling out to her friend. Then I heard a lot of voices talking and dogs barking in the distance. At first I thought that a dog had been struck by a car, but then how would they know its name; so then I thought that maybe someone ran into the big scooper truck (I never knew the names of construction trucks) with their motorcycle. Upon hearing more voices, I got curious enough to peek out my window, and I saw a group of about five people standing around the scooper truck talking in Thai. Then I realized that they were standing around a body of a young man, trying to wake him up. He was positioned as though he had hit his head on the truck and fell down, but they were moving him into different positions, and he was obviously unconscious (assuming that he was still alive). I was just about to waken Paw (he sleeps right next door to me) to call for an ambulance when a bunch of other motorcycles drove by and slowed down, and the girls would just say, *Mai pben rai, mai pben rai*" ("Everything's okay, don't worry about this"). I'm thinking, "What? Are you crazy? He's unconscious!" I decided not to wake Paw because obviously they thought they had everything under control. They kept talking to him and were saying, "Okay, let's go home," and other things as well, but this was all in Thai, so I understood only part of the conversation. Then, they picked him up and stuck him on the back of a motorcycle between two guys, the back one holding the injured one on, and drove off. He was probably drunk too, so I don't know if they were afraid to take him to the hospital or what, but if he goes home and sleeps, I'm not sure that he will wake up. I'm no doctor, but I do know a thing or two about medical treatment. After they left, a girl got the motorcycle out that was rammed into the side of the scooper truck. It didn't look like he hit the truck and then was flung off because of where he was positioned, but who knows if they moved him before I saw anything. It was obvious that the motorcycle ran into the scooper truck because of all the remains of a crash underneath. I would like to know how this ends. If Nakhon Phanom is anything like Ottawa,

Illinois, a report will be in the newspaper tomorrow. It doesn't matter anyway because 1) I can't read that well, and 2) I'm leaving to go to Bangkok tomorrow. A few people just came back and are making phone calls from the pay phone. Probably to get someone to pick up the rest of the motorbikes parked there. It sure keeps life exciting by living only a block away from Duck Pub.

I just found out what happened. He was driving the motorcycle, probably drunk, as I have stated before. He crashed, flipped the bike, and hit his head.

14

DISTRICT CONFERENCE

March 9, 2007

RAYONG is only about a three hour drive from Bangkok, and yet I was still the last one to arrive. At first, we went to the wrong hotel, but then finally got checked in at the right one. I met McKinsey and Steffen in my room. Steffen didn't have a room yet, so he was hanging out with us. Then I said goodbye to P'Nuan, P'Nan, and Sinwia and went to dinner. I got to see all the exchange students at dinner and catch up on everything that had happened since we last saw each other. Once we were finished eating, which didn't take long because everyone was too excited to eat, we snuck out of the banquet hall and just hung out and talked with everyone while looking around at the little shops in the lobby. Then we decided to go up to the roof and met a few other exchange students, so we decided to hang out for a while. After we returned from the roof, we decided to go out and find something to do; we ran into a bunch of people and then went to a Lotus store. We kept our tradition of getting cookie dough. Then we went to the market and bought *Step Up* and *Thank You for Not Smoking* DVDs and went back to our room and watched the second with Kelly, Brittany, and Marie. Everyone else left our room, and McKinsey and I somehow started discussing political issues. I've never really been interested in politics, but McKinsey is. She swears that the presidential election nights are more fun than Christmas because they occur just once every four years. I don't think I agree with her about that, but we had interesting discussions nonetheless. We finally stopped talking and got to bed around 2:30 a.m.

March 10, 2007

No one provided us with any type of schedule for this weekend, so we were just taking the word of all the other exchange students. We got dressed in our school uniforms and went down to breakfast at 7:45 a.m., thinking that the meetings were starting at 8:00 a.m.

Before we left the room, Pornchai, who is rooming next door to us, knocked on our door to give us an extra meal ticket. We had three people in our room and he had his own room, but the hotel provided two tickets per room. I was standing in the hallway with him and waiting for Marie and McKinsey, and he leaned over to me, obviously trying to be discrete but in such an obvious way, and asked if I want to go somewhere. He named the place, but I had never heard of it and because it didn't really matter to me, I said, "Yes," right away. Then he invited Marie and McKinsey and told us at the break of the meeting to change clothes to go. He added, of course, not to tell anyone else about it. Pornchai is the Youth Exchange Officer for Korat and because McKinsey is the only exchange student hosted by his club, he goes out of his way to do a lot of things with her.

We went down to breakfast and realized that breakfast didn't start until 8:00 a.m., so we got to talk with everyone and hang out a little. The meeting was so boring. We were supposed to walk in behind the flag of our home country, which didn't work because no one was paying attention. I think I actually walked behind the flag for Japan. Then the Rotarians showed us to the back, and we had to sit through a terribly boring meeting; I was staring at my watch the whole time, waiting for the break.

Every time Pornchai would walk by us, we would look up at him hopefully, as if he would tell us to leave right then. We still thought that we were the only three going. He came to our table and reminded us that we needed to hurry when the break arrived and to bring our cameras. He said it was almost time for the break. Then he said that we get to go because we are his kids, and he rubbed my head. I resisted the urge to fix my hair because I thought that would be impolite, considering that the head is the most sacred part of the body. McKinsey and I held our laughter until after Pornchai had returned to his seat. That has to be the funniest thing that Pornchai has ever done. I'm a little jealous of McKinsey because Pornchai lets her do a lot of different things, but I don't know if I'd like living in Korat as much as I do Nakhon Phanom.

Finally, the break came and Marie, McKinsey, and I were trying to come up with an excuse to leave to go change our clothes. We told the other exchange students that we were going to the bathroom. We decided that we should take the stairs up one floor so we weren't waiting in the open for the elevator.

As soon as we had climbed about five steps, Prapart appeared, seemingly out of nowhere, and said, "Don't go anywhere. We have a meeting in that room and anyone who isn't there can't go on the southern tour." We hung out to let most of the students walk past, so we could explain ourselves to Prapart, and then saw Pornchai at the entrance to the meeting room. Before we could say anything to him, Pornchai shoved us behind him and told us to hurry. We ran up the stairs to the fourth floor and quickly changed and brought our swimsuits along, as instructed. When we got to the lobby, another Rotarian, whom I'd never met before, shooed us out the door and told us to hurry to the bus. We went there and saw all the Korat exchange students and a bunch of *farang*s, along with some Thai people. Our group was large; we had two big charter buses packed full. I felt really special because I was the only exchange student not from Korat, and I really appreciated being included.

We stopped at an aquarium and looked around there for an hour or so and then went to lunch. Then, we got on a boat and went to an island and hung out at the beach for a few hours. That was a lot of fun! We stopped at a dried-fish processing "factory" on the way home and got back around 5:00 p.m.

We showered and changed back into our school uniforms (unfortunately) and then went down to dinner. A bunch of exchange students performed Thai-style dances and one played a Thai instrument. We managed to slip out of that after the people that we knew had finished their performances, and then McKinsey and I went to Tesco. Tesco is a large department store, where we knew we could find almost anything. We just got outside of the hotel and saw a group of about 10 or 15 Thai boys just hanging out. We had to walk past them to get to Tesco, so, as we were getting nearer, they were pushing each other toward us and would shy back. Then one "brave" Thai boy came up to us and said, "We're going to the beach," indicating his friends who were getting on the back of a truck. "Do you two want to come?" I said, "Yes," and McKinsey said, "No," at the same time. We turned to each other, deliberated for a few seconds, and decided to go with them. The Thai boy, completely taken by surprise, turned to his friends and then back to us, saying, "Just kidding, we're not going," and then got on the truck himself.

We laughed at the awkward situation and continued walking toward Tesco. We bought cookie dough again and ate it as we walked through the town. We stumbled upon a carnival, which was run down and had hardly any games. We walked by a motorcycle taxi driver, who asked us if we wanted a ride. I said, "No," but asked if there was anything to do in Rayong because we were bored. He asked, "What do you like to do?", and McKinsey suggested a discothèque. He told us that there was one right on this block, but we would have to change out of our school uniforms to get in.

We decided to head back to the hotel to change, and the taxi driver offered to give us a ride for 10 *baht*. I wasn't going to pay, so we became "cute" and got a ride to the hotel for free. I think he was going to wait for us, but, before we got to the entrance, I told him to let us walk because my dad wouldn't like us being on a motorcycle with him. We got to our room and changed. Then Hayley came in, so we hung out with her for a few hours. Hayley left for a little while, and McKinsey and I decided to watch *Step Up* with Marie. Hayley came back at the end of the movie, but we decided to hang out in the lobby because Marie had fallen asleep.

We were getting really tired, trying to stay up all night, and decided to watch *Thank You for Not Smoking* again to pass the time until 5:30 a.m. and then be obnoxiously on time to order room service when it first opened. Hayley wanted to take a 20 minute nap, and McKinsey was falling asleep. I was awake but didn't want to order the 5:30 a.m. room service. I mean, why pay for food when we got a free breakfast at 7:00 a.m.? We decided to split up and go to our rooms to actually get some real sleep. Morning would come soon enough.

March 11, 2007

I set my alarm for as late as possible and had to rush to get ready. We went to breakfast around 8:00 a.m. and ate with Kelly, Brittany, and Jeff and then sat through another horribly boring meeting. Worse than the first! This time everyone was anxious because it was our last day together, so we kept trying to sneak out, but each time we did, someone from Rotary caught us and made us go back and sit through it. Eventually, people started "going to the bathroom" in small groups and, basically, everyone left. Everyone decided to go upstairs and change, but McKinsey still wanted to ask Pornchai if the two of us could go to Pattaya, by ourselves. She had only a week left before her parents came, and then she was going home with them. If we were going to visit Pattaya, we'd have to plan it soon. Everyone was told to stand for the national anthem, which signaled the end of the meeting. All of the exchange students have this song memorized, as it is played on every TV station at 8:00 a.m. and 6:00 p.m. When it was almost over, McKinsey and I made our way to the back of the room where Pornchai was. We barely got in there in time, but as soon as we got still, Pornchai looked over and saw us there. It was too perfect!

McKinsey went to talk with some of the people from Missouri, and I went to stall Pornchai until McKinsey got back. When McKinsey came over to talk to Pornchai, I took all of our things to our room and waited. After she talked to Pornchai, McKinsey came back to the room and said that I couldn't go home with them, but we could go to Pattaya. Actually, he said that we could go anywhere we wanted, so I'm still not sure if we know where we want to go.

We finished packing and went back downstairs for lunch. Pornchai called McKinsey and me over to sit at his table and told me to ask my Rotary club if I could *pai tiow* Korat and to have them call him. He emphasized the word "Korat," too, so I still don't know if my

Rotary club knows that I'm going to Pattaya. Marie came to our table toward the end of our conversation and asked where we were going and if she could come along. Pornchai vaguely told her, "*Pai tiow*," and said that she could go. I didn't think that Pornchai wanted a lot of people going because the larger the group, the crazier it gets.

Members of my hosting Rotary club came to my table and announced that we were leaving and would eat noodles elsewhere. I left to get my bags, and Pornchai reminded me to have my Rotary club call him and then he gave me a hug, which was really weird because Asians don't usually hug, and they don't seem to know how to hug, so it's always really awkward. Actually, I think Pornchai is the only Thai person who has ever given me a hug; he gave me one on Christmas day, too.

That was basically my weekend. I had to leave lunch to go eat with a bunch of Rotarians elsewhere for about an hour and a half, and nobody talked to me. I was so annoyed because I thought that I was holding them back and that they wanted to get home more quickly, which I can completely understand, but no, the other Rotarians were at the district meeting, too, so we very well could have stayed for lunch and eaten at separate tables and enjoyed the free food provided. I was really tired from getting only about two hours of sleep the night before, so I slept on the way home. Overall, the district meeting was a lot of fun. I can't believe that the southern tour is just around the corner, but it's not going to be the same because of all the people who are going to miss it. I rushed out of there so fast that I didn't really get to say a proper goodbye to everyone. I guess that's the major reason why I'm so upset, but I wasn't thinking about it, either.

I am so excited about going to Korat tomorrow and seeing McKinsey and *pai tiow*ing! I have a feeling that Pornchai is going to take me to see the sights when I get there, so that's another province I can mark off my map. I am so excited about having a little more freedom, too. I wish McKinsey had more time, so we could go to a lot of different places but that would probably be pushing it a little bit too far.

15

TIME WITH MCKINSEY

March 28, 2007

I'M really getting bad at disciplining myself to write these entries. I just got back from spending about a week hanging out with McKinsey. We had so much fun! The plan was for us to go to Pattaya, but we didn't have enough time. We ended up hanging out in Korat and then Bangkok.

First, we had the whole ordeal about which bus to take. Rotary always puts me on the 999 bus because it's "safer." We have three levels of bus service here. They are termed 9, 99, and 999 because the number 9 is a lucky number in Thailand. The 9 bus goes only short distances at a time. It will stop whenever anyone wants to get on or off and is by far the least expensive. The 99 bus makes one stop in each province on the way to Bangkok. The 999 bus goes straight through to Bangkok, with just one stop in Korat, to allow the passengers time to eat and to let people on and off. The 99 bus has four seats to a row and an extra row or two, making it rather crowded. The 999 bus has three seats per row, and two snacks are also provided; one when boarding and another one just before reaching Bangkok. Certainly the 999 bus is the most comfortable one, but I always get an uncomfortable feeling when I have to part with my 840 *baht* to get the ticket. The 99 bus costs less than half of the 999 fare, so, naturally, that one always looks more attractive to me. For this trip, I told Paw that I wanted the 99 bus, and we had a

173

big discussion about it over dinner, but they still got me that ticket. Then P'Nuan called while I was on the bus and wasn't very happy about the fact that I was on the 99 bus, but she didn't say much about it. On the way home, Pornchai paid for a seat on the 999 bus for me. That was very sweet of Rotary. I would really be upset if they insisted that I ride the 999 bus but still made me pay for it.

Hanging out in Korat wasn't too bad. McKinsey's host sister, P'Ja, took us out at night, so we could go to the night bazaar and other places. That was pretty cool. During the day, we just *pai tiow*ed by ourselves. McKinsey's house is right next to the railroad tracks and, because Nakhon Phanom doesn't have any rail service, I acted completely *farang* and took a bunch of pictures. It was great timing, too, because a train had just come, so we were looking for something to occupy our time while we were waiting to cross. Then, we went walking on the tracks away from traffic and put some coins on the tracks. I think we lost about 28 *baht*, but we each got a nice five *baht* piece, completely flattened. We wanted a 10 *baht* coin because of the different colors, but someone stole them before a train came along. The 10 *baht* coin is about the size of an American half dollar. It is brass in the center (about the size of a dime) and a silverish color around the outside. Good thing no one saw us doing it. We could have been in serious trouble because the coin has the King's image on it, and allowing a train to run over it is considered to be very disrespectful; punishable by being fined or imprisoned. I doubt if they would have done anything except tell us to stop. We really get away with so much here. Most likely it is because we are two young white girls who happen to speak a little Thai.

This is a funny story. We were going to Wat Phra Kaeo (The Grande Palace) and Wat Pho to see if we could get in for free because we "live in Thailand." The translation for *Wat* is temple. For Thai people, there is no admission fee for temples. Much like the massive price differential that I experienced at Phu Kradung, *farang*s must pay an entrance fee. They didn't give us free admission, so we decided to just walk around Bangkok. While we were walking, a guy along one street was trying to sell us some embroidered cloth. He was really persistent, so we decided to haggle a little bit without really wanting any. He started at 500 *baht,* and we just walked away. Then he followed us, continuously offering a lower and lower price. McKinsey told me (in English, of course) that she'd bought one a while ago and had paid only 80 *baht,* so I knew about how much they should be. We had a long conversation with him about how we are sisters who live in Nakhon Phanom and about our mom who is Thai and our dad who is *farang.* The tale went on about our having been here for only seven months because we usually live in America. The guy was so impressed by all this that he ended up selling me one for 50 *baht*! Only 10 percent of what he had originally asked and probably got from most *farang*s. Now I can totally relate to what one of the rebounds told me at Grand Rapids last summer about how he bought so much stuff that he didn't even want just because the price was so unreasonably low.

On one of our free nights out, we went to Barnana, a chain of clubs in Thailand. McKinsey wanted to go dancing, and I was up for something to do. We got there around 9:30 p.m., but the place didn't open until 10:00, so we hung out at a hotel that was right next door to the bar. We tried to find the roof, but with no luck; we just hung out in a lounge on the second floor, which was empty. A little after 10:00 p.m. we went back. Normally, there is a cover charge, but we went in with a group of about 10 guys who worked there, so they waived the fee. Then, all 10 of the guys awkwardly hung around, waiting for us to order. We ordered two cokes and then sipped on them slowly, waiting for more people to come. We danced a little bit, but then people started coming around 11:00 p.m. We had to meet P'Ja a half an hour later, so we didn't get to dance all that much. That was completely fine with me because I don't even like dancing. I just went along because McKinsey wanted to go.

We drove to Bangkok with her first host family the next day. On our way, we stopped at an outlet mall. We looked around a little bit, wasting time, and then her parents said that we were eating at a steak house. That was a great meal! We got cream of mushroom soup. It was unbelievably good! We decided to each get separate entrées and then split them. We both agreed on spaghetti and a steak. Oh, it was heaven on a plate! I haven't had a steak in more than eight months! The "steaks" that are available in most restaurants are just hamburgers without the bun, but this—this was so good; I savored every bite of it! I've had dreams of getting home and going to the Texas Roadhouse or Lone Star Steakhouse and ordering jalapeno poppers with my scrumptious steak, grilled to a perfect medium. Mmm! I still have that dream. Although, I think Taco Bell tops even that. I was brainstorming with McKinsey about the first meal we were going to have when we get home. It was a tossup between Taco Bell and Subway, but I already had Subway at Chiang Mai. Okay. I'll stop with the food talk. Actually, I was just having a conversation with my host family about what a flour tortilla is and what Mexican food is made with. It's really hard to explain. They still don't completely understand it.

Hanging out in Bangkok with McKinsey was fun because we just left during the day, agreeing to come home by curfew. On our first day, we went to Chatuchak market and got a ton of stuff. I think I spent between $50 and $75, but, it was well worth it! I got a lot of CDs and some t-shirts, and we each got a nice puppet. Anyway, we still had two hours on our hands and didn't want to go home early, so we went to the mall and saw a movie, "Bridge to Terabithia." It was a really good movie, but it was more than two hours long, and we still had to get across the city to get home. We got on the bus just as it was starting to get dusk, but little did we know that we got on the wrong bus! McKinsey lives next to "The Mall" so we got on that bus, but apparently there is more than one place called "The Mall." So we got off at "The Mall" and got in a taxi to go the rest of the way home. We asked him, and he said that there about seven stops called "The Mall." Oops. We got home two hours late, but her parents had already gone somewhere for dinner, so they weren't home. They called and told us to find ourselves dinner, obviously meaning in the refrigerator. We, instead, found ourselves *som-thom* across the street and brought it back to eat while we were watching some movies.

One mall that we went to had a restaurant called The Pizza Company, which was known for having the best pizza in Thailand. We went in, and they seated us; then the waitress gave us menus and just stood there, waiting for our order. It was a bit awkward. We just looked at each other and then told her that we needed a minute. We ordered a small pizza, about the size of a personal pan pizza, and two glasses of water. They must have had about 10 waitresses for that little shop. There were only two tables that had customers seated at them. After the people at one table left, three waitresses went to clean it and to set up the napkin holder and condiments in exactly the right spots. Once we finished eating, they gave us our bill and were just standing at the end of our table, so we put down 120 *baht,* but the waitress pointed across the room to the cashier. McKinsey rolled her eyes but went up to pay and then came back and told me that they gave her the wrong change, so she had to explain that to the cashiers. The whole experience was frustrating, but the pizza was good.

We decided to visit another mall. There really is not much to do in Thailand, even in Bangkok. We decided to play Picture Check. It is played in a small booth at the shopping mall. Two pictures are shown, and the goal is to see the five differences in them before time runs out. We played twice; the last time McKinsey's contact lens was coming out, and it must have hurt really badly. We lost the game quickly, and she went to the bathroom to take them out and throw them away. It wouldn't have been any big deal, except for the fact that I didn't know what bus to take and she couldn't see properly to read the signs. We got to the curb, and I was yelling the bus numbers to her and then a gust of wind came, and I got dust in my eyes. Oh, it hurt so badly, but I had to laugh. We were just so pitiful. Luckily after a few minutes of my eyes watering, the dust was washed away, and I could see again to read the numbers. What a day!

It seems that we watched an unbelievable number of movies in Bangkok, but, because we had to be home by 6:30 p.m., there was not much else for us to do. I ended up buying the complete set of "The Lord of the Rings" movies, and we watched them all within two nights. They were really enjoyable. Now, I'd like to read the books.

Also, we came up with the idea of a scavenger hunt for "Thai things," so that we would have something to do, but we didn't get very far. More about that later.

The day that McKinsey's parents came, we went to the airport to meet them and arrived fairly early. I had hopes of finding a Subway because this was the "new airport," so I figured it would have some good eating places, but no Subway. We walked all around the section of the airport that we were permitted to go without a ticket and then settled for a shop that had sandwich meals for 100 *baht*. We learned from our Pizza Company experience (where water is 15 *baht*) to not order a beverage. So, we got one meal of three half sandwiches with chips and split it. It's good to be friends with someone as frugal as I am. To kill some time, we made friends with all the waiters and decided to come up with American names for them. Then, we made a plate face with all of our left over potato chips that would change to a different expression every time the waiter came by. I'm sure by now you've guessed that we were really bored. It wasn't like they were that anxious to see us leave, either, although the manager of the place didn't seem to like us.

They gave us our check, and we put money down and were still talking. No one came to get it for a good 10 minutes, so we decided it was time to leave and search for a drink somewhere. So, we got up to go pay, and they quickly said, "No, no, no, no. Sit down, sit down." Then, they took our money and went to the cash register. We thought about asking for a job application but talked ourselves out of it at the sight of the evil-eye coming from the manager.

We bought some milk at 7-Eleven and, having walked many times around the airport, got on one of the moving sidewalks and just walked the opposite way for a while and talked.

Finally it was about time to meet her parents, so we went to the central waiting area but forgot that we still hadn't made signs for them. We found a scrap piece of paper (the back of our scavenger hunt list) but didn't have a pen. We started back to the 7-Eleven but saw an information booth on the way, so we stopped there instead. We asked to borrow a pen, and they pointed to one we could use and then watching us, they offered us a piece of paper. We thanked them and were starting to tear it in half. When they saw us, they gave us another sheet of paper and pen. I wrote "I ♥ Ma" and McKinsey wrote "I ♥ Dad." It was cute. Then we practiced holding them up at distances to see if we could see them or if they had to be darker. The girls working at the information booth were getting a kick out of it. We thanked them and ran half way back when we realized that this would be a good photo op, so we ran back to have them take one. Well, they tried to show us the picture that they had just taken of us, and, apparently, it didn't take because the one that came up was the "non-smoking" picture of McKinsey. (I'll write that story later.) That was kind of embarrassing, but it was way more funny than embarrassing.

We had no trouble meeting up with McKinsey's parents. We all went straight to the hotel; her parents let us have our own room. While McKinsey was taking a shower, I played with all the gadgets in the room, trying to get the TV to work, and clumsily searched for the remote control. I was pulling all of the knobs to open the dresser drawers, although some of the knobs were just decorations. I discovered that by accidentally pulling the front panel off the dresser.

McKinsey came out and said, "What were you doing, making all that noise?" Of course, having "guilty" written on my face, I innocently replied, "Nothing." She started to put something on the nightstand when she saw the front sidepiece of a drawer unattached and partially sticking out, after being shoved into the "newly made" drawer. "Did you do th—" "No!" We both burst out laughing.

The "non-smoking" story. We were at yet another mall, and both of us had to go to the bathroom. When we were finished, I heard McKinsey say how she really wanted one of those signs that read, "No Smoking" in Thai. Once she mentioned it, I wanted one, too. So we worked together to peel two of them off the wall. We were standing at the sinks discussing what we could do with them because they were still sticky on the backside. Well, right in the middle of our conversation, a cleaning lady walked in. We both just turned and headed into two stalls. The cleaning lady also went into a stall. I came out and said in Thai, "Are you finished yet?" in as bored a tone as I could. McKinsey opened the door and asked,

"What did you do with yours?" knowing that I would not just put it back. I lifted up my shirt and all she could see was the No Smoking sign stuck to my belly. When she saw it she gasped, "Ah, good idea!", and she went back in her stall to stick hers on. Back at the house, we took pictures before taking them off, and those were the pictures that the girls at the airport saw.

One night, McKinsey's first host parents took us and her real parents out to dinner at a really nice place. We ordered so much food, probably trying to impress her real parents, and were completely stuffed afterward. One of the things on our scavenger hunt list was a "toothpick," so we found out how to say "toothpick" in Thai and then asked one of the waiters because there were about five of them hanging around, for one. As soon as he brought the toothpick container, we each took one and then put it in our pockets. Then we looked up and noticed the guy staring at us with an expression like, what are you doing? We laughed and had to tell everyone at our table about the scavenger hunt. Overall, we didn't do too well, but we got a few things. Maybe McKinsey was able to find some more items after I left.

March 31, 2007

I was actually rather nervous about meeting McKinsey's parents. I didn't know what it would be like to stay with *farang*s, after living away from them for eight months. Actually, the most nervous part was wondering about how I'd changed over the past eight months. I have been told that when the exchange year is over and kids go back home, their parents always comment on how much their son or daughter has changed; some good and some bad. So, when we met them at the airport, I hung back a little bit because it was so nice of them to invite me along, and I didn't want to be in the middle of their "family time." I was rather quiet on the drive home. The next day, I got to talk with them a lot, and I realized that I had been so impolite! I was speaking in English so I couldn't say "*ka*" at the end of everything, and I was completely lost. It actually crossed my mind to say "sir" at the end of sentences because my first host dad told me once that "*ka*" was like saying "sir" or "madam." Which is not true in the least, and it had stopped me from saying it in the car. I figured that I was just making too much out of it and decided to push it out of my mind for a while.

A few days later, McKinsey's parents were commenting on how McKinsey and I are so much alike and how they wanted me to stay with them longer on their trip. Then, I realized that I was just being paranoid and that I'm sure I was being completely polite the whole time, as I usually am. That was definitely the one huge "culture shock" type of thing that I noticed when staying with *farang*s. I honestly didn't know how to act around them, which makes me a little nervous to think about what it is going to be like when I go home. A little nervous but very much more excited!

16

BACK WITH MY FIRST HOST FAMILY

April 1, 2007

I just got out of the shower at my first host family's house and grabbed my towel, and it was just huge. I have been using only a hand towel at my second family's house. I had a big one there, too, but it was in the laundry that I gave to the maid, and when I got my laundry back, my towel was gone. I presume someone placed it on the wrong pile. This was about the time when my mom was telling me to do my own laundry, so I guess I was being stubborn and cheap. I didn't want to tell her about the towel theft because it would just give her another reason to tell me why I should do my own laundry. I also was too cheap to buy myself a towel, although I was looking at them in the market, but 300 *baht* for a towel is just insane. This all happened within the first or second month of my living there, so I had gotten used to using a small, hand towel, and I learned that it is so much easier to use a little towel. What's all the extra material for with the big ones, anyway? I mean, I like the fluffiness, but there are fluffy hand towels, too. I was having such a time trying to make sure the ends of the towel didn't touch the floor and get wet. After a week of living back in America, I'm sure I'll think I had gone crazy by writing this. It's so much easier to pack a hand towel for tours than a huge, normal bath towel. Luckily my next tour is Phuket, and bathing suits and shorts don't take up much space.

Sinwia was really excited to see me move back. He will be living here for the rest of the summer break, then moving to Bangkok where he will be starting school next month. Baa Thao went to Vietnam again, so that's probably another reason he is glad to see me. I really missed Sinwia. He's sweet to be around when I don't live with him all the time. I'm going to try to get myself out of the house a lot more anyway, so that shouldn't be too much trouble. It's a lot nicer to be able to communicate better with him, now that I can speak Thai. I know he was getting frustrated with me before, when I couldn't understand him, but now it's a lot easier talking with him. We were hanging out upstairs, and P'Nuan was taking a shower, and Sinwia has been glued to me ever since I came home. So, just making conversation, I pointed out a bunch of stuffed animals that P'Nuan had gotten for her birthday a while back and asked Sinwia whose they were. He said they were his, so, teasing him a little, I said, "Who gave them to you? Do you have *faen*?" And he replied, "Yeah, I do." I acted surprised and asked him what his girlfriend's name was, and he said, "P'Salee." It was so cute. I really missed him, too.

April 11, 2007

Last week I was in a parade. I don't know what the parade was about, but it had something to do with the Princess, maybe her birthday or something. Anyway, P'Nuan told me that I was going with Mae and her friends and that I was to wear a Vietnamese dress. I was pretty excited. Vietnamese outfits are all so pretty, and this family never wears the same outfit more than once. Well they actually do, but every time I went to a wedding, or somewhere where I had to dress up, they went out of their way to get me a different dress. I know that Baa Thao had a ton of dresses, so I was excited to see what color dress I would get to wear.

First, Mae does my makeup and hair. Halfway through doing my hair, the electricity goes out (meaning the fans, too). I was already in so much pain because she wanted my hair tight so that it wouldn't fall out, but now her hands were sweating, too, which made it hurt even more. It brought back childhood memories of getting my hair done for dance recitals. I never said that it hurt because, even if I did, it wouldn't matter. Besides, I'd rather just get it over with as quickly as possible. After that was done, P'Nuan handed me my outfit. At first I thought she was joking. Then she went on to say that it was Mae's dress. Now, Mae is the smallest Thai person that I know. She is very petite and short, reaching only to about my shoulders, which is really short considering that I'm only about 163 cm tall.

This outfit. Well, it had a purple skirt (that actually was about the right length) and a fuzzy, red halter top with gold sequins on it. Then there was a coat type of thing that was white velvet on the top half and red velvet on the bottom half. There was a blue silk belt to hold the coat closed and a pink Vietnamese hat with sequins, too. Then, they added jewelry that, to me, completely didn't match the outfit or the other jewelry. I could very well have worn this as a joker costume for Halloween. Everyone else going with me looked the same way, so I wore it proudly.

I keep thinking about how my life is going to be so different when I get back to the U.S. I can't believe that I am going to college in just four and a half months! I'm really glad that I applied, got accepted, and deferred, before coming on youth exchange. I will attend Washington & Jefferson College, located in Washington, Pennsylvania. It is a small, liberal arts college, and I think I will be happy, studying there.

Some of my friends are trying to get applications for college started from Thailand, and they were stressed about everything. What's worse than that is that some of my Thai friends still don't know what college they will be attending, and it starts next month! I definitely couldn't do that. Anyway, I still have some paperwork to do here that needs to be returned by May or June. It's not that bad though, and, thankfully, my parents are helping a lot with that from home. One of the forms I had to fill out was for housing next year. I'm really excited about that, but this form was ridiculous.

Example: "Check as many as you wish that describe your personality."

- ❏ Outgoing
- ❏ Shy
- ❏ Neat
- ❏ Messy

I was obviously outgoing enough to come to Thailand on youth exchange, but everyone here says that I'm shy. I like my room neat and organized, but right now it's really messy. I "wished" to check none of the choices. I hate stupid forms.

April 14, 2007

Today, I went with my second host mom to her hair stylist, and she was afraid that I would be bored, so she was going to have them wash my hair, too. One thing led to another, and now my hair is permanently straightened and I have an Asian haircut. I'll know in a week or so if my hair stays straight. As for the Asian haircut—it's definitely not my thing, but my hair looks a lot thinner now, so I guess I can pull it back better. It's just a really drastic "V" shape in the back. My hair is so long anyway (I haven't gotten it cut since I've been here) so the longest part is at the low part of my back, and the shortest is cut a little bit longer than my shoulders. I figured that I would let them cut it however they wanted because I could still just cut it all short in a straight line, and it would still be long enough to satisfy me. This whole process took more than five hours. I really trust that it will be okay because Thai people always like to make sure that everything is perfect.

17

SONGKRAN FESTIVAL

April 16, 2007

SONGKRAN. What an event! It is definitely the best holiday in Thailand. It is officially called the Water Festival, and everyone in Thailand will get wet at least once during the festivities. The best way to describe it is a four-day water fight, involving the entire country. Well, no one played on Thursday, so on Friday, Yee picked me up by motorcycle, and we drove to Joe's house, which is pretty close to mine. I got wet on the way there; it was so unexpected, Yee slowed down just a little because the turn was coming up, and someone threw a bucket of water out that got me straight on. I didn't know what I expected Songkran to be, but not that. Anyway, we were waiting for more people to meet us for lunch, so Yee decided to take me for a ride through town because they were running late. It was so much fun! She took me down all the streets around town, and there was a ton of people out that had the big bath buckets filled with water and bowls for everyone to scoop water out and throw on people. In about two minutes, I was completely soaked. Some stations had kids that were about my age or a little older standing in the middle of the road, dancing or lying across it to make the motorcycles and cars stop. Then they poured bowls of water directly over Yee and me.

Some had baby powder or bowls with baby powder mixed with a little bit of water and would smear it on our cheeks. The boys

187

usually had the powder, used as a way of flirting a little, or for just making a statement like, "Oh, you're cute" or something like that. When they saw me, everyone attacked our car, and then there were hands everywhere, but I couldn't see anything because, even if I tried to open my eyes, someone was continuously pouring water from above our heads. It's crazy, but a ton of fun. We went to eat, but I was too excited to really eat anything. Then, we drove around a little bit more. I couldn't imagine that anything else would be as fun as that.

We saw other friends that were filling their bath buckets and had them on the back of a truck. We stopped and parked and then got on the back of their truck. That was fun, too, being able to throw water back at them. It's a lot easier to stop a truck than to stop a motorcycle, so we stopped a lot, and people would jump on the truck, too, and put the powder on us. They also have huge blocks of ice that people would buy for only about 60 *baht*. Then they could pour ice water on everyone. It was so unbelievably cold! It's fun because I never knew if the water would be luke-warm or ice-cold. We drove around a lot and then got in line to drive through the Songkran Road. About two city blocks were blocked off for the festival, and inside were three stages and a lot of beverage stands. There was an entrance for cars, but just two lanes because there were so many people walking. The cars would have to stop a lot and go really slowly. The line to get in was long and moved slowly, so we hopped off the back of the truck and walked in. I can't even describe what it was like. As we were walking in, people in the cars were pouring water on us. The entrance to the Songkran festival was amazing. It was a short tunnel, only about three car lengths long, and had sprinklers on the walls and ceiling. Once we got through the entrance, we were more soaked than before, if that is possible.

Inside, I saw a massive number of people dancing everywhere. We walked through at a rather fast pace but got stopped every five seconds for people to put more powder on our faces and for a more thorough soaking. Sometimes the water had coloring in it or diluted flavored syrup. Yee was a good bodyguard for me. There were three stages inside, and at each one there were a lot of drunk guys, so we tried to sneak by them. If we got caught, Yee would just lead the way out, and I'd hold on to her waist. Actually, being attacked with water was the most fun. I know that she liked it, too, because we walked in the street a lot where we were most vulnerable.

The first day of Songkran was the best, mostly because I didn't know what to expect. When we were still on the truck and in line to get in, one lady came over and gave me a lei of flowers. They were really pretty but really heavy. I never wanted to wash my face during Songkran because I liked having the powder on it, but everyone kept insisting I wash it off all the time. Before we left to go home, I washed my face really well, but, on the way home, a group of guys stopped us and poured ice water all over us and put really clumpy powder goo all over our faces. I loved all of it, but even after my long (10 minute) luke-warm shower, I was still freezing.

Saturday was a ton of fun, too. I thought we were going to leave at 10:00 a.m. to play in Mukdahan province, but no one came for me until noon. I ran some errands with Dear and Mee Pooh until about 1:00 p.m. A lot of friends came over to Mee Pooh's house, and we played there. Mee Pooh is a nickname that our friends gave to Bow. It literally translates as "Pooh bear." They chose this name for her because she is cute and likes Winnie the Pooh. Similarly, our friends gave Ging a teasing nickname of "Sing Tho," meaning lion. They poke fun at her for having hair with more volume than most Thai girls. Ging pretends not to like the name but laughs along with everyone else.

Mee Pooh lives in front of the big Vietnamese Memorial Clock Tower on the same road as Songkran, so we had a lot of people drive by. It started raining in the late afternoon but that just made it even more fun and wet. We went to play on the road and then camped out near one of the stages. I liked walking better, but this was fine, too.

Part of the way through, Yee told me that the guy on stage was giving out water guns and asked me if I wanted one. Of course I did. So, she just went with me to the front of the stage and asked the guy about it. He made me get up on stage along with two cross-dressers (guys dressed as girls) and another girl. He went down the line with the whole name thing and then told us that we had to dance first. I was so embarrassed! First of all, I can't dance well at all, and I was up on stage with at least a hundred people watching and dancing, too. I danced a little bit with the only motivation being the water gun, and, if I didn't get it, I would freak out. After the song was over, the guy went down the line again and the whole crowd judged by clapping. During that song, I determined that Songkran was a big wet t-shirt contest, as well. Well, hardly anyone clapped for the cross-dressers, but the two of us girls got about the same amount of applause. She got a lot because she was pretty and danced really well. I got just as much as her because I was white, period. They gave everyone water guns anyway, but I think I appreciated mine the most because of the amount of humiliation I had to endure to get it. Don't get me wrong; I'm glad Yee pushed me to do it, but I pretended to yell at her about it for the rest of the day.

Sunday was the last day of Songkran. I was really disappointed about that, so I wanted to play as early as possible and as long as I could. I tried calling Yee at 11:00 a.m., like she told me to, but she said she would be going out at about 1:00 p.m., so I got dropped off at Mee Pooh's house around 1:30 p.m. (I'll write more about that later) and played there. Everyone else was eating, but I wanted to play as much as I could, so different people would come over and play with me for about an hour or so. I drove around with Yee a little bit, and then we all decided to park and play on the side of the road. It was a lot of fun playing there and seeing a bunch of people that I knew. A ton of people in cars were yelling my name to get my attention, so I would go over and let them put powder on my face. The ones that yelled "Ashley" or "Anchalie" were kids, I assumed to be from *Piyamahalachalai* School, and they are really sweet. A lot of people were yelling "Salee," too. I think part of that was that they recognized me from being on stage on Saturday. It was a lot of fun, all in all. I really liked getting all the attention, too. I really hated to quit playing, but I was so wet for so long, I started looking like a raisin; I was freezing, too.

I hung out with my family and friends of family from Bangkok every night and was sharing my bedroom with P'Ja, so I didn't sleep that much during Songkran. It didn't help that I was so excited for the next day of Songkran that I couldn't calm down to sleep. Sunday night I was so exhausted, I lied down while the other two people sharing my room were still getting ready for bed. I woke up only once, in the middle of the night, to find the room dark and everyone asleep. I was so tired. I got up around 8:00 a.m. because I wanted to say goodbye to everyone, and I knew that I wouldn't be able to sleep tonight if I slept in really late this afternoon. I wish Songkran wasn't over and lasted more than three days, but then again, it was a ton of fun; I might have gotten bored if it lasted longer. I doubt it, but I'm trying to look on the bright side.

April 18, 2007

I had my first "bad day" in Thailand yesterday. Well, "bad morning" anyway. It is impossible to have a bad day during Songkran with friends. It started out with my second host parents saying that they were going to pick me up to go to an Open House celebration for my host uncle at 6:00 a.m. When they told me about it I half-heartedly complained, whining, "Oh, that's so early." I felt like that was the response that I was expected to give. They said that I didn't have to go, but they knew that I wanted to. So on Sunday I woke up on my own about 5:00 a.m., and at 5:15 a.m. figured that I'd just get up. That way my alarm wouldn't wake P'Ja. I didn't sleep well, anyway, because of sharing my bed and also because of being excited about Songkran. I took my time getting ready and went outside about 5:50 a.m. to wait for my ride. Soon, well actually "soon" would not be the best word to use, 6:45 a.m. rolled around, and they still had not come to pick me up. I decided to call them. It seems all cell phones were turned off, so I took a shot in the dark and called "Home," not remembering which house I had given that label to. Paw answered and said that he would be there in just a minute to pick me up. I felt a little less anxious now because part of me thought that maybe they had forgotten about me. Well, soon it was 7:30 a.m., and still no one had come to get me. Now I started to get annoyed. I ended up calling again at 7:45 a.m.

and, hoping that no one would answer, Paw picked up and almost sounded annoyed that I kept calling. Well, I thought, if you hadn't told me that you were coming at 6:00 a.m., maybe I'd be okay with waiting. They finally came at 8:15 a.m., and, when I started to get in the car, Mae told me that I couldn't wear black and had to dress up a little bit. I was dressed to play Songkran. I ran back inside and put on jeans and a King shirt, I was frustrated and probably could have looked a little nicer, but was also concerned with Songkran.

When we got there, I sat at the kid's table, with NeungEuy and her cousins, one of whom I had met before. The cousins were from Sakhon Nakhon. Well, the food came and, although I'm quite capable of getting my own food, NeungEuy took my plate and started dishing things onto it. This happened all the time when I first came to Thailand, but since I've been here for eight months already, most people have trusted me to get my own food. Feeling a little idiotic that my 15 year-old sister was feeding me, I tolerated it and told her when there was enough on my plate, but she didn't listen and just smiled as she continued filling the plate. I just stayed decidedly quiet because it is more Thai to do that than to express true feelings. I rebelled in my own way by making sure I left a huge portion of everything on my plate untouched. I think NeungEuy got the hint. Some other mom that was sitting at our table kept treating me like a deaf mute who was five years old and kept pointing to dishes and gesturing for me to put it on my plate, and I gave her a look back like, "Yes, I understood," but really meaning, "No kidding; I'm not stupid." Then, thinking that I didn't understand or something, she takes NeungEuy's job and starts dishing out food for me, even though she is sitting directly opposite me at the round table. Again, I just didn't eat. If people here were not so pushy with food, I would probably be getting really fat, but I rebel by just not eating. To me it's a natural reaction. The best meals that I've had are those that I've eaten by myself.

Then, Paw's sister-in-law from Sakhon Nakhon came to sit with us, too. I learned that she is an English teacher. Great. So she started talking to me in baby English. I replied in Thai, thinking that she would get the hint. No, she just thought it was cute of me to try to speak Thai. I just sat there, being quiet and reliving my frustrations of the day, and she asked if I was lonely. I replied that I was not lonely, just tired, but really I was mainly frustrated, annoyed, and basically angry. Then, my American personality surfaced as I put in a jab about how I thought Mae was coming for me at 6:00 a.m. but did not get there until closer to 8:30 a.m. She said, "Oh, so you got up at 5:00 a.m.?" I nodded. "Have you ever gotten up early?" What kind of question is that? No, in 19 and a half years I've never gotten up early! I tried to hold back my facial expressions and just said, "Yes." Then later Mae came over and commented (as usual), about how I ate basically nothing. Although, (also as usual), she wouldn't have known, because from where she was seated, she couldn't see me. Then the sister-in-law said that I was tired, and Mae replied, "Oh well, she has never gotten up early, before." I was beyond frustrated! I excused myself to go to the bathroom.

When I moved in with my second host family, I got up at my usual time, around eight or nine, and went downstairs. Nobody was up. I tried to occupy myself with reading or something (I wanted to go for a walk, but this was my first day there). Around noon, Mae finally came downstairs. From then on, I made sure that I got to bed around 1:00 a.m., so that I would wake up later. I have always gotten up early.

My day got a little better after that. I told them that I was going to "go for a walk" meaning leave, but they wouldn't let me go alone. I guess it wouldn't be good for me to walk the streets alone, but I didn't know what else to do. Everyone was beginning to get drunk, and Yee wouldn't pick up her phone. Finally around noon, I was allowed to walk to the end of the street and play Songkran with their neighbors. I left a voicemail for Yee around 1:30 p.m. to ask her to come and get me, so we could do something together. Suddenly, there was my family, riding by on the back of a pickup truck. They stopped and insisted that I go with them. I thought that that could be fun too, so I got on. I figured that Yee would just call me, and I could tell her what I was doing then. I got on the back of the truck, and they grabbed my cell phone out of my hands and told someone to put it inside the front of the car, even though I told them I was waiting for a friend to call and I had it safely wrapped in a plastic bag. Well, riding on the truck was far from fun. I was right next to one of the aunts, who was completely drunk. The people driving thought it was funny to slam on the brakes, which was dangerous considering the number of people that were on the truck. When the driver hit the brakes, the aunt would grab on to me for support so that she wouldn't fall off the truck, but she wouldn't sit down. I'm glad she grabbed on rather than fell, but honestly.

Every time we got to a station where people were playing, she'd scream and just act like a drunken idiot. I was embarrassed for her, and I don't even know her. Luckily, we got in line to go in Songkran Road, which went right past Mee Pooh's house. I asked if I could get off here to play Songkran with my friends. They stopped and gave me back my cell phone (three missed calls in less than five minutes), and I said goodbye—very fake, but like they would notice.

When Yee asked me if I had fun, I just rolled by eyes and said that everyone was drunk. Then, I realized that the truck hadn't left yet. Oops! I'm not sure if they understood me or not, but, then again, I didn't really care. I am probably only this frustrated because I am so tired. It was very nice of my second host family to include me in their plans for the day. I wish they would have told me the correct time to be ready this morning, but I understand that everything here is *sa-bai*. I have always hated being late for appointments because I feel badly for those people who would have to wait for me. It is hard for me remember that I am the one that is different minded and that this is another cultural difference.

18

SOUTHERN TOUR

May 23, 2007

I just returned from traveling almost everywhere in Thailand during the past month. The first "tour" was to southern Thailand, which started April 21st, and then my parents visited and traveled with me for two weeks. I'll start with the southern tour.

April 21, 2007

My alarm didn't go off, so I woke up late and got myself ready in 15 minutes; luckily I had completed packing the night before. We were meeting at a hotel in Korat and leaving for the southern tour from there. When I arrived at the hotel, however, no one was there. Apparently, they all decided to go to the mall. Having no choice, I hung out at the hotel and talked to Gui until other people showed up. It seemed that everyone had done something crazy with his or her hair. They were all different, either dyed, shaved, or cut in some bizarre fashion. Anyway, we had a short ceremony during which they handed out our certificates for completing youth exchange. Then we ate and got on the bus for an all-night ride. I sat with Kelly. We talked and talked and hardly slept at all that night.

April 22, 2007

We stopped for breakfast at a truck stop, but we were also able to take showers, brush our teeth, and clean up a little. We still had three more hours on the bus until we got to our hotel, and even then we just dropped our suitcases off and proceeded by boat to a cave. This cave was really awesome. I was in a boat with five other exchange students, as well as our two boat drivers. We walked around inside the cave and then got back on the boat to leave. Toward the end of the boat trip, the driver told us to take off our shoes and lay down. We were so confused but did it anyway. Then, we went through a passage so narrow with water so high that our boat kept hitting the walls on either side of us, and I was pushing my upper body down in between the seats so that I didn't hit the ceiling. It was so much fun! That was a great opener for the southern tour. There was really nothing else to do for the rest of the day. We walked to the night market and then just wandered around.

Later that night, I played Egyptian Rat Screw with a bunch of exchange students in Marie and my room. At about 1:30 a.m., a Rotarian came in our room, freaked out, and made everyone leave. He freaked out about the noise, but said absolutely nothing about us having three guys in our room. We ended up talking to Jeff and Kelly, who came in afterward, and stayed until it was really late.

April 23, 2007

We ate breakfast and then boarded our boat. The boat stopped occasionally, so that we could get off and swim around or snorkel. Jennifer can't swim and is actually quite afraid of the water, but we got her into the water with a life jacket as tight as possible and because she is so small, the jacket lifted her whole upper body out of the water. In addition, she was holding on to a life ring. We all were required to wear life jackets. It's impossible to snorkel in a life jacket, so I put mine inside the life ring and became Jennifer's taxi driver. She seemed to be having a good time, and I was having a lot of fun, too. Then we went to a cave. We had to swim through it to get to the small island inside. They took Jennifer through first along with our cameras, and we all followed them. We had a big string of exchange students who were each holding on to the life jacket of the person in front of them. I was holding on to Kelly and trying to swim, but I kept kicking the guy that was behind me, so I stopped. I'm light anyway, so they pulled me along.

The inside of the cave was really cool. We took pictures of us all together, and then Gui said that we could stay there for an hour. After taking a bunch of pictures, I followed Kelly down a short path where there were some caves. Kelly went back to the beach because she said she couldn't climb the rocks as well as we could, so basically it was Evan, three other exchange students, and me who climbed all through the caves. It was a lot of fun. They were going to try to explore the third cave when I decided I'd go back. I walked back to the beach and called to some exchange students who were swimming, asking where the camera box was. It seemed that someone moved it to some other place, and I couldn't go swimming until I found a place to put my camera. As it turned out, the people that I yelled to were just random *farang*s, so I embarrassingly apologized and went to ask a real exchange student. Only then did I realize that everyone else had left without us. I ran back to the caves and told everyone that they had all left and took our life jackets, too. They followed me back to the beach, and everyone decided that we could swim back because it was not that far. Everyone, that is except for Evan and me, who were both holding cameras.

We were trying to figure out what to do, quite loudly actually, when another guy, apparently a guide of some sort, came to help us. He had a small bag in which we could put our cameras, and he had two extra life jackets. Henrietta and Evan put them on, and he helped us swim back. At the mouth of the cave, someone yelled at us for not having life jackets and mentioned something about a 2,500 *baht* fine. It was ironic that it was a *farang* who yelled. I held on to Evan most of the way, and then some random Thai guy grabbed my hand and pulled me the rest of the way. That cave was so cool. That definitely was the highlight of the southern tour thus far.

We had lunch on the boat, and we stopped at another inlet for snorkeling and jumping off the boat. They were all trying to get me to jump off the second level of our boat (after it had taken me at least 10 minutes to get enough nerve to jump off the bottom level). It took all of 15 minutes, but I did it, and it was so exhilarating!

I loved everything about it: the fear and then relief after I hit the water and how everyone was so supportive. I screamed the whole jump, too. It was right before I jumped that I realized just how much we have really become a family. Sure we may fight occasionally, but everyone was being so supportive of me, helping me to get past my fears and then celebrating with me afterward. Then, they told me to do it again, and I was like, "No way!" I'm really glad I did it one time, though. We really didn't do much the rest of the day. Everyone ended up hanging out in my room again, and we talked until pretty late, but we were all really tired from spending the whole day in the sun.

It was on this trip that we learned about Katie's dad dying. As I understand it, he had been fighting cancer for a little while prior to the start of Katie's exchange year. He unexpectedly took a turn for the worse and passed rather quickly. Katie found out about the situation before he died, but knew that she would be unable to get home to Canada in time. She went home, anyway, in time for the funeral service and then stayed for a week or so before returning to Thailand. It was a bit awkward for me because Katie has been rather cold toward me since Jason started spending more time with McKinsey and me. Still, I feel really badly about her loss and would like to let her know. Maybe on this trip there will be a chance for us to talk about it. I don't know what I would do if I were faced with that issue. I have a large extended family, and accidents can also happen. I am so lucky to have not only my parents, but all of my grandparents, as well. I also have several great aunts and uncles that I am very close to. All of my grandparents, plus Aunt Ginny, Aunt Florence, and Uncle Joe are at or past 80 years of age. With the normal human aging process being what it is, it is very possible that I could receive some very bad news during this year. Before I left America, I discussed this possibility with my parents. I decided that if someone died, I wanted to know about it. I wasn't sure if I would come home for the services or not. I would decide that when I had to. Nevertheless, I wanted to know about it.

April 24, 2007

I missed breakfast because I had to go buy a small bag to take with me to the Similan Islands. Then, we spent all morning on the bus, stopping only for lunch. Lunch was embarrassing. They put us in our own room because exchange students are known to be noisy, but then some exchange students started throwing rice and dripping water on everyone saying, "Happy Songkran." It was just too much, even for exchange students. So, I got up and left, as did a few people sitting close to me. We walked to a nearby shop and just hung out. That behavior is just not acceptable for anyone in a public restaurant. After a short while, the rest of the exchange students joined us at the local shops. Apparently, a Rotarian had gone into their dining area, yelled at them about their behavior, and told them to leave. I'm glad I wasn't there for the discipline. I think Rotary allows me to do more because they know that I don't usually get into trouble.

After lunch, we got back on the bus and drove to a boat dock where our tour guide had booked a boat tour. It was really pretty. We saw James Bond Island, and I explored the caves with Jeff and Alex, a newbie from South Africa. It was a pretty awesome cave, but we cut it short because I didn't want to get left behind again. Actually, we were washing our hands off in the water when one of the tour guides yelled at us to get going because everyone was back on the boat. We hurried back, stopping only long enough to buy a shirt. On the way back from the boat tour, we stopped at an island type shop, which was a lot like Chatuchak market in Bangkok, only smaller. When stepping into the strip, a monkey was thrust into my arms, and I didn't even have my camera. Jeff said he got a picture though, and, shortly afterward, a hand was held out. She wanted 20 *baht*, but I had already gotten the picture, so she wasn't in much of a bargaining position. I decided to give her 10 *baht,* anyway. On this tour we had to make our own fun, so everyone decided to have a pool party that night. I showed up just to be a good sport, although I had one arm tightly around Jennifer and was saying that she can't swim, repeatedly to ensure that they wouldn't throw me into the water. We listened to a Southern CD while everyone drank and smoked. The Southern CDs were made by all the exchange students while we were on the southern tour. The Southern CDs were a collection of popular Thai songs during our exchange year, as well as *farang* songs that had memories associated with them from our trip.

April 25, 2007

We had breakfast and then got on the boat for our three-hour ride to the islands. We didn't really do much when we got there. We went swimming for a little while and then did some hiking. We stayed on this island for three nights in tents. Have I ever mentioned how much I dislike camping? I guess it's not really the "camping" aspect that I don't care for but more the common bathing areas and the sand sticking to everything. I've never been camping before, so it was a fun, one-time experience.

April 26, 2007

We got on the boat and went to another part of the islands, to a place called Ship Rock. I love hiking, but I hate heights, and this rock formation was huge. It was a lot of fun to climb up, but, once I got to the top, I was terrified. I think part of it was that all of my friends were dangling their legs off the side of the rock, and I was scared for them. Anyway, I wouldn't touch anyone and was terrified to try to go back down, so I was just hanging out. Evan came over, and we started talking about something. He brought up a topic that we agreed upon and held his hand out to shake. I figured he was just being Evan, so I smiled and shook his hand. Then he said, "See, you just touched someone." I went back down with him and a few other people but would only let Evan help me down. I'm really going to miss that kid.

I didn't really do much the rest of the day. I went hiking by myself to an overlook (but forgot my camera). Apparently, people were looking for me, but I think it was just Gui, which was part of the reason for me going off anyway. It's obvious to everyone that Gui has a crush on me. Some of the exchange students prodded me to start dating him, but I think Gui had some part in that. Either way, I wasn't interested. Not only is dating against the rules of Rotary youth exchange, but Gui is just not my type.

The previous night, we had a huge downpour, and Alex and

Brittany's tent collapsed, soaking everything. I felt so badly for them. Marie and I told them that they could sleep in our tent, but the Rotarians were already getting them a new one.

The rest of this day was wasted by traveling. We left the island early and had our three-hour boat ride and then another really long bus ride to Phuket. In the evening, we stopped and did some shopping and watched the sun set. Then we ate dinner and went back to the hotel, which was about 20 minutes away from downtown. I think Prapart has us staying in a hotel away from downtown because he doesn't trust us. I wasn't surprised at the lack of trust because we have been scolded numerous times for getting too loud or people getting too drunk at clubs.

Marie and I did laundry in our hotel bathtub, and then everyone got together to pay for a van to take us to the night bazaar. Half of the kids wanted to go dancing, too, so we had a lot of people in the van. It was cheaper that way. The night bazaar wasn't all that good, and I was kind of shopped out, anyway. When we got back, Pornchai called me over to his table, where he was sitting with all the other Rotary supervisors, who were all pretty drunk. He told all of my friends to go back up to their rooms but motioned for me to stay there. Then he asked me where we went (shopping) and what I bought (not much of anything), and then said that I was a good girl and gave me a big hug and let me go up to my room. I think part of the reason that he called me over was to brag to the other Rotarians about my fluency in Thai. I also think that it was partly because McKinsey had gone back to America, and, while visiting her in Korat, Pornchai spent a day with us, and we grew closer. Anyway, when I got upstairs, Marie pounced on me for what he wanted and everyone sent text messages for information. Marie summed it up with one text message "It was just Pornchai being drunk." Everyone loves Pornchai!

I previously mentioned the Four Ds: drinking, driving, dating, and drugs. And then the unofficial fifth D: disfigurement. It seems that it was the social "goal" for the exchange students to see how many of the Ds they could break. Driving was really the only D rule that I broke. Nearly all of the vehicles have standard transmissions, and, because most of the other exchange students didn't know how to drive cars with a manual shift, few, if any, broke that rule. It is a bit of a stretch, but it can be said that I broke three. I probably had a sip or two of beer, and I did spend an entire day with one of my guy friends from school, so I counted that as dating. I had no interest in doing drugs in Thailand. I mean, I don't do drugs in America, so why do something that I don't even want to do, just because I'm in Thailand?

April 27, 2007

We drove to a jewelry shop, and then Rotary announced that everyone would have to take a Breathalyzer test before they got off the bus to go shop because so many students had gone out the night before. I was so excited! I've never been breathalyzed before, and it was just too funny that they would give it to me, of all people. I told Kelly that she had to take my picture when we went down to take it. When our group was called down, Kelly went first, and I got her picture. Then Pornchai asked, "Who is next?" I giddily sat in the seat, and Pornchai said, "No, you're my daughter. You don't have to take it." I told him that I wanted to take it, and he still said that I didn't have to. Finally, I explained to him that I wanted a picture, so we agreed on Pornchai and me posing for a picture of me taking it, but that I really wouldn't take it. Maybe there is a cost to giving the test. Apparently, I was the only one who went out "clubbing" the night before that didn't have to take the Breathalyzer test.

The jewelry shop was nothing but a time-waster. Then we moved on to an aquarium. That was fun; actually, it was better than the one in Rayong, but aquariums are about the same everywhere with different fish, but fish nonetheless. After that, we went to a restaurant and had *som-thom* and *kao nio*. I was sitting at a table with all girls, mostly from Korat, plus Evan. He didn't feel awkward at all talking to all of the girls until the conversation turned toward "torpedoes," something one of the girls said that she needed to buy. Evan and I were the only two who were lost with the code word "torpedoes." Once we figured out that this was a discussion about a feminine hygiene item, Evan decided to go talk with the people at another table, while we left to go to a nearby shop so that the girl could buy some.

After lunch, we drove back to the hotel and changed for the FantaSea Show. I was late to get on the bus because I was catching up on what we did every day and lost track of time. When we returned from the Similan Islands, my entire suitcase (which I kept on the bus) was soaked. Everything stank from being wet, and I had no clean clothes, so I needed to do laundry.

I got on the bus and saw that everyone had really dressed up for the show. It was a lot of fun. On the way, Jeff asked me why I never do anything with my hair. He decided to braid it in little braids, but I was afraid that he wouldn't finish in time, so I had five people braiding my hair, and Jeff finished only one braid because he was so slow. Then everyone was complimenting Jeff on how great my hair looked, which was ironic because he really didn't do much at all. My hair did look really nice, though.

Once we got to the show, we had some time before dinner, so we shopped and then went in the game room and played some games. I just watched, but Jennifer was getting good at the basketball game, and she gave me a stuffed pig the second time she won. Since this was the Year of the Pig in the Chinese zodiac, there are images of pigs everywhere. When it was about time to eat, we went in and saw a huge buffet. They had so much food, Thai and *farang*, and such a variety of dishes. I was too excited to just eat, though, so I walked around with Jennifer and took some pictures, eating as we walked. They had bread! I have not had a slice of bread since the first week I arrived in Thailand. Because Thailand's food base consists mostly of rice, bread is never served in restaurants and is not commonly stocked in smaller grocery stores. We had a little extra time before the show started, so Jennifer and I decided to go back and play some more games. Finally, it was time to go see the show. I was really excited because I've always wanted to see "Siam Niramet" in Bangkok but never had the chance, and this was supposed to be along the same lines. It wasn't bad, but it doesn't compare to "Wicked", which I saw in Chicago prior to going on exchange. They did have a bunch of elephants on stage, though, and for the most part it was cool. When we got back to the hotel, it was rather late, and everyone was tired.

Earlier in the day, we stopped along some coastline to go shopping. I decided to walk around, and Alex wanted to come, too. We walked in the city a little bit and found a daily market with clothes and other things. We started looking at the first shop and talking with the guy in Thai. As we were walking back, people would yell at us to look in their shops. Right before we would get to the next booth, the people before them would yell ahead and say that we spoke Thai. It was a crazy feeling because we weren't even stopping to browse in any shop. We were just walking ahead, and yet we seemed to be on a red carpet. Everyone seemed to know us and was calling out to us, and we couldn't get away from it, not that I would have wanted to. It was fun getting all of this attention.

April 29, 2007

Our trip was basically over by this point. Today and tomorrow were scheduled to be traveling days. We were told that our hotel for the night was about an hour away from Bangkok. Upon hearing the news of our hotel accommodations, many exchange students began planning ways of traveling to Bangkok to go out to the clubs. I think the Rotarians heard about the pending plans of the exchange students because we ended up stopping at a hotel about three hours outside the city. Like I said, our trip was basically over. We didn't do anything but drive this day.

April 30, 2007

Another driving day. When we got to Korat, Pornchai said that I would be spending the night with Marie (it turned out to be with Alex). I was supposed to be staying for just one night, but, because Alex's host mom seems to have a hobby of collecting exchange students, she wouldn't let me leave. I had planned to return to Nakhon Phanom but ended up going straight from Korat to Bangkok to meet my parents, who were arriving from Illinois for a two-week visit.

It was on this trip that we learned that Jennifer's parents had divorced. This news shocked and upset Jennifer immensely. As I understood it, she read the news in an e-mail from her dad, who stated matter-of-factly that, "Your mother and my divorce is now final." It seemed to me that Jennifer's parents were completing the legal documentation that was necessary to end something that emotionally had ended years earlier. The problem was that Jennifer believed what she had shared with me at the Youth Exchange Conference in Grand Rapids last summer that her parents were having some problems and that her mom had moved out of their house. Her dad also went on to say that he had a girlfriend (another shock) and that she had moved in with him (total shock). Then, most shocking of all, he had attached a picture of himself with his girlfriend. When Jennifer opened that attached photo, she angrily exclaimed amid sobs, "She's wearing my shirt!" I felt so badly for her.

Jennifer says that she is not going home. She doesn't want to live with either of her parents and will stay in Thailand. During my parents' visit, I told them this story. My dad said that he wasn't sure that extending her stay was possible. He reminded me that I had a student visa, valid for up to 364 days in Thailand. He said that he believed that overstaying my visa would result in the police arresting me, then escorting me to the airport and putting me on a plane back to America. I don't know. I just feel really bad for Jennifer. I guess we'll see.

19

MY PARENT'S VISIT

May 4-19, 2007

HANGING out with my parents was fun, I suppose, although at times I wanted to strangle them. They seemed to want to know everything I was saying to every Thai person, even if it was insignificant. At first it was really neat being able to show off my Thai skills, but, after a tiring few days, the constant need for translations seemed to be unnecessary.

We traveled a lot, even visiting some places that I'd never been to before. It was really nice to be given a little freedom and responsibility, too. How much I miss that! I can't remember everything that we did and saw. The schedule of events turned out to be a bit more than was possible, but they wanted to see as much of the country as they could in two weeks. This was what was originally planned:

Friday

11:55 p.m.	Meet at airport and take shuttle car to Boonsiri Place Hotel. (Grab some noodles if hungry).

Saturday

8:00 a.m.	Breakfast at hotel.
8:45 a.m.	Proceed to Wat Phra Kaeo (the Grande Palace).
12:00 a.m.	Eat at random street restaurant.
12:30 p.m.	Proceed to National Museum.

2:00 p.m.	Take a tuk-tuk to Wat Pho.
3:30 p.m.	Take the boat taxi to Wat Arun.
4:30 p.m.	Take taxi to Vimanmek (Largest Teak Wood Mansion).
7:00 p.m.	Take taxi to Siam Niramit.
8:00 p.m.	See show.
9:30 p.m.	Have dinner at random street restaurant.
10:15 p.m.	Overnight at hotel.

Sunday

6:00 a.m.	Breakfast at hotel.
6:30 a.m.	Leave hotel and visit Damnoen Saduak Floating Market.
8:00 a.m.	Arrive at Market and enjoy walking around.
10:00 a.m.	Go back to hotel.
11:30 a.m.	Taxi to BTS Sky Train.
12:00 a.m.	Shopping at Chatuchak Market (Lunch there).
6:00 p.m.	Drop purchases off at hotel.
7:00 p.m.	Dinner with P'Nan and friends.
8:30 p.m.	Boat ride down the Chao Phraya River.
9:30 p.m.	Go to see Lady-Man show / weekend market.
11:00 p.m.	Overnight at hotel.

Monday

8:30 a.m.	Breakfast at hotel.
9:30 a.m.	Go to Ayutthaya.
10:30 a.m.	Arrive and visit the ruins.
12:00 a.m.	Lunch at restaurant in Ayutthaya.
1:30 p.m.	Back to hotel (free time).
4:00 p.m.	Shopping on Khao San Road.
6:00 p.m.	Have dinner somewhere.
7:00 p.m.	Free time.
9:30 p.m.	Overnight at hotel.

Tuesday

7:30 a.m.	Breakfast at hotel.
8:00 a.m.	Check out of hotel and take bus to Korat.
12:00 a.m.	Meet Mr. Pornchai and have lunch with him.
1:00 p.m.	Proceed to Wat Maha Viharn.
2:30 p.m.	Go to silk shop.
4:00 p.m.	Check in at hotel and proceed to Suranaree Monument.
5:00 p.m.	Continue touring with Mr. Pornchai.
7:00 p.m.	Dinner with friends and family.

9:00 p.m.	Enjoy walking through the city's nightlife.
10:00 p.m.	Overnight at Sima Thani Hotel.

Wednesday

8:00 a.m.	Breakfast at hotel.
9:00 a.m.	Leave hotel and go to airport.
11:30 a.m.	Arrive in Chiang Mai and rent car; proceed to Lanna Palace 2004 Hotel.
12:30 p.m.	Lunch at nearby restaurant.
1:00 p.m.	Taxi to San Kamphaeng (Thai handicraft villagers) and Bor Sang (parasol makers).
6:00 p.m.	Back to hotel with purchases and dinner near hotel.
7:30 p.m.	Free for shopping at night bazaar.
9:30 p.m.	Overnight at hotel.

Thursday

7:00 a.m.	Breakfast at hotel.
7:30 a.m.	Leave for Mae Sa Valley Elephant Site.
9:00 a.m.	Arrive and get seats for the elephant show.
9:40 a.m.	Enjoy watching the elephants playing and working.
10:15 a.m.	Pictures and feeding the elephants.
10:30 a.m.	Experience elephant riding.
11:30 a.m.	Visit the elephants on break; visit gift shop.
12:15 p.m.	Lunch somewhere.
12:45 p.m.	Proceed to the Monkey Centre.
1:15 p.m.	Take a look around Chateau Kumone Art Museum (across from the Monkey Centre).
2:15 p.m.	Enjoy the Monkey show.
4:30 p.m.	Back to hotel (free time).
5:30 p.m.	Thai dinner at some nice restaurant.
7:00 p.m.	Free for shopping at the Night Bazaar.
10:00 p.m.	Overnight at the hotel.

Friday

8:00 a.m.	Breakfast at the hotel; check-out.
8:45 a.m.	Leave for Chiang Rai.
10:00 a.m.	Taste the food made by people on the sides of the road for snacks.
12:00 a.m.	Stop at Wat Rong Khun (The White Temple).
1:00 p.m.	Eat som-thom near the temple for a light lunch.
1:45 p.m.	Continue on to the Golden Triangle Paradise Resort.

3:00 p.m.	Check-in and then proceed to the Golden Triangle.
5:00 p.m.	Enjoy a Thai-style dinner at a restaurant that I have yet to find.
7:30 p.m.	Go for a drive; see the different parts of Chiang Rai.
9:30 p.m.	Overnight at hotel.

Saturday

8:00 a.m.	Breakfast at hotel.
9:00 a.m.	Drive to the Hill Tribes.
11:00 a.m.	Drive to the Princess Mother's Royal Palace, Doi Tung.
12:00 a.m.	Arrive and have lunch at the cafeteria.
3:30 p.m.	Drive back to the hotel.
4:30 p.m.	Free time.
7:00 p.m.	Grab dinner somewhere.
8:00 p.m.	Free for shopping at the Night Bazaar.
10:00 p.m.	Overnight at the hotel.

Sunday

8:00 a.m.	Breakfast at the hotel; check-out.
8:45 a.m.	Go to airport and return car.
12:00 a.m.	Arrive at Nakhon Phanom; shuttle to River View Hotel.
1:00 p.m.	Vietnamese lunch at restaurant.
1:45 p.m.	Go to Lotus and buy food for the monks.
2:30 p.m.	Visit with 2nd host family.
6:30 p.m.	Fish Dinner at 2nd host family's house with teachers.
9:30 p.m.	Overnight at hotel.

Monday

6:00 a.m.	Give food to the monks.
6:45 a.m.	Back to hotel for breakfast.
8:00 a.m.	Leave for Phra That Phanom.
10:00 a.m.	Arrive and sight-see.
11:00 a.m.	Leave for Mukdahan Province.
12:00 a.m.	Lunch there and free for shopping.
4:00 p.m.	Tour around in car.
5:30 p.m.	Come back to Nakhon Phanom.
8:00 p.m.	Meet friends and family at Korean BBQ.
10:30 p.m.	Overnight at hotel.

Tuesday

8:30 a.m.	Breakfast at hotel.
9:30 a.m.	Visit the food market.
10:15 a.m.	Walk to 1st host family's house and visit.
12:00 a.m.	Som-thom, sticky rice, chicken, etc., with 1st host family.
4:00 p.m.	Go to the Mekong River and walk the promenade.
5:00 p.m.	Aerobics at the promenade.
5:45 p.m.	Walk to main street and eat noodles.
6:15 p.m.	Walk to Baa LaWang's restaurant and visit.
8:30 p.m.	Walk to the night market and get juice and a snack.
9:15 p.m.	Walk around town and then get a tuk-tuk to hotel.
10:00 p.m.	Overnight at hotel.

Wednesday

7:00 a.m.	Breakfast at hotel.
7:45 a.m.	Tuk-tuk to Piyamahalachalai School.
8:00 a.m.	Watch students line up for morning announcements.
8:30 a.m.	Visit my teachers and get a tour of the school.
10:00 a.m.	Back home and pack my things in parents' suitcases.
12:00 a.m.	Eat lunch somewhere.
1:00 p.m.	Visit more with family and friends.
3:00 p.m.	Go to temple and have palms read by a monk.
7:00 p.m.	Plane to Bangkok.
8:30 p.m.	Arrive in Bangkok and shuttle to Holiday Mansion.
9:00 p.m.	Dinner somewhere near hotel.
10:00 p.m.	Overnight at hotel.

Thursday

8:00 a.m.	Breakfast at hotel.
8:45 a.m.	Get a taxi and visit the Ancient City (museum).
3:00 p.m.	Back to hotel and move onward to Siam Center.
3:45 p.m.	Get a traditional Thai massage.
5:30 p.m.	Make way to Sky Tower.
6:30 p.m.	Dinner at Sky Tower.
8:00 p.m.	Taxi to Suan Lum Night Bazaar.
8:30 p.m.	Enjoy viewing the city from a gigantic ferris wheel.
10:00 p.m.	Overnight at hotel.

Friday

7:00 a.m.	Breakfast at hotel; check out.
7:45 a.m.	Leave for Dream World.
6:00 p.m.	Meet P'Nan and family for dinner somewhere.
8:00 p.m.	Go see a late night Thai movie at the mall.
10:15 p.m.	Make our way to the airport.
11:15 p.m.	Say last goodbyes.

Although we didn't follow the plan exactly, we covered most of Thailand. It was nice to be able to travel around the country on my own. When my parents arrived, I met them, along with P'Nan and P'Kip.

It seemed to take us a long time to find our hotel because Bangkok is a very large city. P'Kip drove, and, because no one was familiar with the exact location, P'Nan would occasionally get out of the car to ask directions. Once during the trip, P'Nan engaged me in conversation in Thai, which consisted of about five minutes of casual dialog. Afterward, she commented to my parents that, "Ashley has become Thai; she is no longer American." Some may not appreciate the huge compliment. Thais are a very proud people. To tell a *farang* that they have become Thai is the ultimate compliment.

During one of P'Nan's direction-finding exits from the car, I explained to my parents that P'Kip was not really my host brother. My dad commented that it was puzzling to him when P'Kip was introduced as my brother because my parents understood that I had only one host brother (P'Pond) and that he lived in Nakhon Phanom, not Bangkok. I explained that P'Kip was not only not my host brother, but that "he" is actually female. P'Kip's outward appearance was masculine. P'Kip was dressed as a man, wore a man's style eyeglasses, and had a male hairstyle. With loosely fitted men's clothing, few could tell that P'Kip was a girl. In fact, for several days I thought P'Kip was a guy. Then, one morning, "he" came out of the shower and walked to the bedroom wearing only a towel. A guy would have just wrapped the towel around his waist. P'Kip had the towel wrapped high, like a girl covering her breasts.

I explained that Thai women do not date in high school, and most do not date in college. Only after college, when they have established themselves in their careers, do they seek to match up with a partner. Thai women are expected to wait until they are in their mid-twenties to become "involved" with a partner. Any potential suitor must meet the approval of the girl's parents, and this could possibly delay the courting process. In the interim, because many Thai women are emotionally and physically "ready," they find a girlfriend to fill the void. My dad, seemingly more open to the subject than I ever thought possible, asked, "So, is P'Nan gay?" I said that right now she is bisexual. She told me that someday she will meet a man whom she will marry and have a family. Right now she is just having fun. P'Kip, however, is gay and wants a long-term relationship with P'Nan. It will be interesting to know how it all works out.

Another funny story. During their visit, I wanted my mom to experience a Thai foot massage. We went into a massage place in Bangkok, and they took us right in. Mom and I sat next to each other, and two young men came over, sat down in front of us, and began to massage our feet. The one massaging Mom's feet looked at the other young man and said in Thai, "So why do you get the cute one?" When I started laughing, he looked at me and asked, "Do you speak Thai?" I nodded and said in Thai, "Yes. I speak Thai." He didn't say anything but turned beet red.

After my parents' visit, I was a lot less excited about going back to America, which seemed to be the consensus among all of the exchange students. I'd just forgotten, to put it bluntly, how to be an American. I hadn't realized quite how Thai I'd become until I could compare myself with my parents. They are total *farang*s, but I supposed that going back to America wouldn't be so bad. I did expect it to be different (at least to me) from the America I left last year, but I'd adjust. Besides, I missed my dog.

I really didn't want to go to *Piyamahalachalai* School anymore. I mean, I had learned the language and culture, and there is nothing in any of the classes that would be new to me. I can't just stay home, either, because I am on a student visa. Considering the age and maturity levels of the oldest students at *Piyamahalachalai* School, I would gain nothing by returning there.

During my parent's visit, my dad asked me if I was considered to be an adult in Thai society. I answered that Thai women never really attain adult status. Their fathers take care of them until they leave home. They generally leave home because they get married, and then their husbands take care of them. I learned very early on that Thai society is male-dominated. When I learned the language, I also learned Thai culture. So, when I spoke Thai, I became Thai. I became the shy little girl that the Thais expect. When I spoke English, I was an American adult.

After my parents returned to America, I began thinking about what I wanted to accomplish before my exchange year was over. Because I did not want to return to *Piyamahalachalai* School, I was brainstorming about just what to do with my remaining time in Thailand. I decided to ask my host family if I could instead go to temple to continue my studies as a Buddhist nun. When P'Nuan heard this she said, "Oh, you are such a good girl!" I think that she believed that I wanted to become Buddhist, which is not the case. I really wanted to go to temple by myself for a whole month. I wasn't sure if they would let me do that because doing things on one's own is not the Thai way. Thai's assume that no one wants to be left alone or even do anything without the company of others. I would find out soon enough.

May 31, 2007

Today is the birthday and death day of Buddha. We were planning to go to the festival tonight, but there was a big storm, so we decided not to go. Speaking of the storm, I just realized how very differently we Americans view things in comparison to the way Thais view things. For example, I was playing on the computer (my brother wasn't home), and the electricity flickered off and then right back on. I quickly turned the computer off, but they didn't understand why I would do that. In America, we would always shut down the computer during a thunderstorm because the lightening could cause a power surge. Later that night, I went to take a shower, and, while there, I remembered that at home Mom would beat on the bathroom door yelling, "Ashley, I'm serious, you need to hurry up!" Her actions were based on the possibility of being electrocuted by being in the shower during a thunderstorm. Afterward, I was watching the storm when P'Nuan strolled into the bathroom for a shower, taking her time.

I realized the other day (actually this was about a month or so ago, but I'm really behind on writing) that I was just picturing coming home to the United States for the first time in a year: walking into the garage, kitchen, living room. Then...wait a minute—I couldn't remember what the living room looked like. Mom moves the furniture around so often that I couldn't remember where everything was placed before I came on exchange. That just made me laugh. I'm sure it will all be moved around again by the time I get back home. During my parent's visit, Mom told me that my little Christmas tree in my room at home is still up, with my presents under it, waiting for me to open them. I can't wait!

20

MORE CULTURAL DIFFERENCES

June 2, 2007

I haven't written about bathrooms before because I wanted to see all of the different types. The ones in Thailand are very different from anything I had previously experienced.

First, showers. Bathtubs are less commonplace than in America, although all hotels had them to accommodate *farang*s. In the downstairs bathroom of my first family, there was a shower-head fastened to the wall and a drain beneath it. Every time I used that shower, everything in the bathroom would become soaked, but because the entire interior of the bathroom was made of marble, everything getting wet really didn't matter. In my host sister's house in Bangkok, P'Neui and her husband P'Sia had a bucket shower. Basically, it was a large bucket, almost like a trashcan. The showerhead was used to fill it with water. Then a bowl that floated on the water would be used to pour water over the body to wash. It was a good way to conserve water and was actually quite efficient. I didn't mind the bucket showers.

Second, the toilets. Most of the homes that I visited had regular Western-style porcelain toilets, although some had just a hose for personal cleaning, rather than toilet paper. If toilet paper was available, it was not to be flushed down the toilet after use but was, instead, to be placed in a trash container nearby. Because foreigners are not used to this form of disposal, this can lead to embarrassing situations. One exchange student told me a story that occurred shortly after he had moved into his first host family's house. He explained that he needed to use the bathroom and flushed the toilet paper after he was finished. Unknown to him the toilet tank contained just enough water to flush the waste but nothing else, so the toilet clogged. He could not find a plunger and, being out of options, awkwardly tried to explain the situation to his host parents. Because most Thai people are very relaxed and do not get upset easily, they calmly came to help. He stood outside the bathroom with his host mom while his host dad remedied the situation. About 10 minutes later, his host dad came out of the bathroom with his hand over his nose, telling them that everything was fixed, then went on to show him where the trash can was to dispose of the used toilet paper. Everyone laughed at the situation.

Public restrooms were a different story. Every public restroom I entered, including the ones at school, had squat toilets. To use those, a person would walk in and, facing the back wall, straddle the porcelain edges of the toilet and squat low. A girl learned quickly, no matter how badly she needed to pee, to control the force. To the side of the squatter, there would be a container of water and a floating bowl for cleaning oneself afterward. Sometimes the public bathrooms would have a faucet on the outside of the building to be used for hand washing.

21

*PAI TIOW*ING BANGKOK

⚜

June 4, 2007

P'NEUI came to visit, and she asked, "Do you want to *pai tiow* Bangkok?" Obviously, I said, "Yes," although, at the time, I thought that she was just joking with me. A few days later, P'Nuan said that she purchased a bus ticket for me and asked if I had finished packing. I had no idea how long I would be there, as usual, so I packed all my clean clothes that I could fit into the suitcase. Good thing, too. When I arrived in Bangkok, she said that she had to work every day, so she couldn't take me anywhere but said, that if I wanted to, I could walk around by myself. She didn't have to ask me twice! As soon as I woke up the first day, I got my purse and said goodbye for the day. P'Neui and P'Sia were laid back about it, but all of the other workers at their shop were completely surprised that I'd go off on my own. Hey, I'd been here for 10 months already! It was about time I had a little freedom.

P'Neui gave me 1,000 *baht* in case I got stuck and her cell phone number and P'Sia's cell phone number and then let me go. Well, I wasn't about to get lost on my first day of actual freedom, so I started off the day by walking in circles around where they lived and looking for land marks and places to remember so I could find my way back as long as I got within a few blocks of my house. Once I felt comfortable, I found the closest main road and then walked down it. I knew I wouldn't get lost if I went in a straight line.

As it turned out, the street that I chose led directly to the MBK shopping center. I walked into the mall because I was so hot from the hour and a half of walking around, although I told myself that I wasn't going to buy much more for two reasons. First of all, I didn't want anything else, and, secondly, I knew already that it was going to be difficult to get my suitcases packed under the weight limit. I looked around for quite a while and ended up stopping for my one weakness: pirated DVDs. Just $2.50 for a DVD; I could maybe rent one for that price in America. I bought a bunch of them, walked around a little bit more, and then walked back home. I wasn't gone that long, but I was really tired because it was extremely hot.

June 9, 2007

The next day, I went back to MBK, got bored after 10 minutes, and then kept walking down the street. There was nothing there but shopping! I turned down a side street to waste time and stumbled across the Arnoma Hotel. I wish I would have known it was this close when my parents and I were staying there. Then I went to see "Pirates of the Caribbean III" in a theater (even though it cost 120 *baht* to see it, and I had already bought the DVD for just 100 *baht* the previous day). I needed something to do to get out of the house. It was a good movie, though; well worth the $3.00 ticket price. The next day, I decided to go down a different main street. The street was leading nowhere when my friend, Fam, from *Piyamahalachalai* School, called me and asked what I was doing. He said that he was at a college in Bangkok, but that school had not yet started and asked me if I wanted to hang out. Of course I did, so I went to MBK, which has a sky train stop to wait for him. An Indian pop group just happened to be shooting a music video right outside MBK that morning, so I stopped and watched them for a long time.

I had been talking with two business men, who stopped to watch for a little while, about what was going on there, and then one of the camera men came over and talked to me. He asked me where I was from, and I told him that I lived in Thailand and could speak Thai. He then asked me to help him find his hotel and gave me the name of it, though I don't remember what it was. I said that

I lived in Nakhon Phanom and was just visiting Bangkok and asked him how long they were staying. He said that the group would be there for four days and then he asked, "How about you come back to my hotel with me?" I was thinking, "I thought you didn't know where your hotel was." I just laughed and said that I couldn't. After I denied about three times, he shook my hand and said that it was nice to meet me, he hoped to see me again, and wished me luck.

By then, Fam had arrived, and we took the sky train to the Bangkok Zoo. That was fun but expensive for me because I'm white. After we left the zoo, he gave me a tour of his college, and we tried to find a friend of his. With traffic congestion and missed communications, we never found him. With all of the places we went, time flew by, and I didn't realize that it was 7:00 p.m. until P'Nan called. She told me that she and P'Neui's family were going out to eat at 7:30 p.m. and asked if I would be there. I said yes because there's no traffic on the sky train. Getting to the sky train, however, was another issue. Fam insisted on accompanying me all the way back, which was really sweet, though unnecessary.

I arrived at the restaurant around 8:00 p.m., and P'Nan didn't say or ask anything except for inquiring about what I wanted to eat. During dinner, P'Nan asked me what I had done that day. I replied that I had gone to the zoo. She just gave me this shocked look. When I said the province where it was located, she jumped back and continued with the shocked expression. I said that I went with a Thai friend, and, instantly, she was fine with it. It's crazy because I thought that she would be more worried because first, she didn't know who I was with, second, she thought that all of my Thai friends were in Nakhon Phanom, and third, she would have a fit if she knew that my friend is a boy. Then again, maybe not, because everyone wants me to get a Thai boyfriend. They don't even seem to care who he is.

When I woke up, P'Nan said to take a shower and pack necessities because we were all going to temple to stay for three days. I learned enough in my 10 months in Thailand to pack for 10 days, just in case. I shot off a quick e-mail to Mom and Dad, saying that I was finally going to temple. I mentioned that P'Nan said we could not stay more than a few days because she had to go back to work. I decided that I would learn as much as I could in the three days, then whine to see if I could stay longer. It's amazing that I had starting thinking like Thai kids because I've never been a whiner.

22

LIVING IN TEMPLE

Day 1, June 9, 2007, 5:15 p.m.

I arrived at temple a couple of hours ago. As soon as we arrived, we sat and listened to the Head Monk talk to us for over an hour. I really liked him. He is around 40 years old, and, when he was talking, the conversation was very laid back. He would go off on tangents and then catch himself and turn to me and see if I had understood what he had said, which I never did. Then he would say some of it again with hand motions, while talking very slowly and easily so that I could understand him better. After that, we were shown to our rooms, where we showered and changed into our nun clothes. As Buddhist nuns, we were required to wear white clothes. They are light fabric pants and blouse. The monks wear a wrap that is a burnt orange color. We had free time, so I took the opportunity to just get away from everyone and explore this new world in which I was living.

This wasn't really the temple that I had pictured living in. First, it wasn't beautiful; no sparkles or color on the buildings. It seemed rather small, but maybe it was actually larger than it appeared. I wasn't really sure what was off limits to nuns and girls, so I stayed mostly in the main areas. I've seen so many monks here, and their living quarters are huge, but I have yet to see one nun—not a real one, anyway. I think there are supposed to be 10 of us "trainee-nuns," but the people who showed us around said that they had just arrived here, too. I have seen pictures of devout nuns with their heads shaved, as the monks must do. The women staying in this temple seem to have arrived just a few days before us and don't know the rules or have the experience that a woman who devoted her life to being a nun would have. I came here with my three older sisters and their friends, P'A and P'Big. Just before we arrived, we went to Lotus and bought boxes of milk, water, juice, and some snacks to *thak baht* (to give food or goods to the monks to gain merit for the afterlife).

I appreciated them taking me to do this, but I really wanted to do this alone. I figured that if the temple didn't have something that I was used to having, then I would just live without it while I was there. Maybe I was being too finicky. It just felt as though they were looking at the experience in temple far differently from the way that I viewed it. I had really hoped that I would be permitted to stay longer, after my sisters left, but time was running out before I had to go home, so I didn't know if that would be possible. Then again, if there aren't any nuns who actually live here, it might not be possible for me to stay alone, anyway.

I also really wanted to go to a strict temple. Here I saw monks smoking cigarettes, listening to iPods, and talking on their cell phones. I guess it's just not what I expected. I'll adapt.

Day 1, June 9, 2007, 10:30 p.m.

P'Nan and P'Nuan took me aside and explained a few things to me, but it was not much more than I already knew. Apparently, the iPods only have recordings of other monks chanting or praying. I don't fully understand why monks have more than 200 rules to live by, the nuns have only eight, and ordinary citizens have just five. I asked because I've heard of other rules that nuns had that weren't included in the eight that P'Nan had explained to me. Then she said that if they really want to become a more devout Buddhist nun, then they would follow the rules of the monks. Even though a lot of the nuns do that, it's not required. I knew the basic rules – that I can never touch a monk or even touch something that he is touching. I also knew that my head must always be lower than a monk's head whenever I am in one's presence. From going to temple with my family, I knew the proper way to bow to Buddha, as well. This is done by kneeling before the Buddha image and placing the hands in the *wai* position. The hands are raised to the forehead (thumbs touching between the eyes). The hands are then placed on the floor, and the head bowed until the forehead is touching the floor. Then the worshiper returns to the original position. The bow is repeated two more times, for a total of three.

I asked about the whole rebirth thing because I didn't fully understand it. Apparently, until one reaches Nirvana, he or she is just continually reborn, lives another life, dies, and is then reborn again. I thought that, if people went to hell, they got out of that cycle but apparently not. If people do something bad enough to actually go to hell, they have to spend like 10 million years there before they're reborn again. Similarly, if they get into heaven, they stay there only long enough to be compensated for all the good things that they have done during their lifetimes. I like the Christian theory better in that when we get into heaven, we're there, period. Same with the hell aspect.

I also asked about the killing of living things. Apparently, the larger the living thing is that is killed, the worse the sin. They also believe that if someone kills a person, in a future life-to-come that person will kill them. This didn't make any sense to me. If I killed a person (who was a good person) and I spent 10 million years in hell and was born again, then the person (who was a good person) killed me, wouldn't that person have to go to hell for 10 million years? P'Nan's explanation for that was that maybe the person was a great person in 95 percent of the time, but, in the lifetime during which that person killed you they were bad. A better explanation could be that maybe in the next lifetime the person was reborn as a dog and that you accidentally ran over the dog and killed it, but that's just an explanation I came up with off the top of my head, so I'm not sure if it is correct.

Day 2, June 10, 2007, 10:30 a.m.

There really isn't much to do in temple. Last night, we had

meditation in the main hall. Some other people who live close by came to worship. During meditation, the Head Monk (I was wrong before; the other monk, who I thought was the head monk, is actually 3rd in seniority) told all the kids to sit in the front row and then taught them by telling stories. I, not being able to understand everything, just sat there sitting Indian-style for over an hour. After 10 minutes, one of my feet went to sleep; I had to readjust myself. The kids did a lot better at meditating than I did. By the end of the session, my back was in pain, and my legs were sore. I don't enjoy sitting cross-legged normally, let alone for an hour. My friends at school always teased me about being "so proper" because I sit with my legs to one side, when everyone else is sitting cross-legged while listening to the morning announcements before classes. After the hour-long meditation and sermon, we had meditative walking. Everyone left the *sala* except for us nuns. The *sala* in many temples is an open-sided building that is used for ceremonies and other religious purposes. In my temple, the *sala* has sliding glass doors and air conditioning. The meditative walking was a whole lot better tonight. Actually, by this time, I was looking forward to sleeping on my mat on the floor. We just walked back and forth for about 20 minutes and then went to bed.

Oh, I nearly forgot. Before everyone started meditation, the monks and nuns had to read and chant prayers. I was annoyed during the first part because P'Nuan told me what we were going to chant and then told everyone to say it slower so I could follow a little bit better. The Head Monk started slowly, but when it came time for us to repeat, P'Nuan would race through, and everyone else would scramble to keep up with her. I was so upset with her because that was just seconds after I had asked her to speak slowly. Not obnoxiously slow, but at least she could have mimicked the speed of the monk. After the first set of prayers, the monk stopped and told me to read it alone, out loud. I was nervous because I always am when speaking in public, but I had already practiced it a bunch of times. It was a really short line, and we were supposed to say it three times. I read through it, and he was really impressed. Others tried to explain to him what an exchange student is, but he just couldn't seem to grasp the concept. It was cute, though, because he finally got it, and this morning he was telling everyone who came to *thak baht* (give alms to the monks) at temple that I can speak and read Thai, but I'm not Thai, I lived here for only 10 months and am going back next month. He was so proud of himself for being knowledgeable enough to tell other people who I was. Actually, it was rather embarrassing this morning to sit through that with everyone staring at me. But hey, I've gotten used to it.

Last night, I was horribly uncomfortable. It wasn't so much sleeping on a mat on the floor; I just felt like I had bugs all over me all night, and the fan didn't help my paranoia. We were wakened at about 4:30 a.m., which was extremely late! I was quite annoyed because they were constantly rushing everyone, and I would have been perfectly fine with getting up at 3:00 a.m. like we were supposed to. We got to the main hall, and everyone else was already there. It was all of the other nuns, our Head Monk, and some other mini-monks.

The time that a young man would spend being a monk could range from a few days or weeks to several years. At some point, the mini-monks must decide whether to devote their lives to temple and to be a monk for the remainder of their lives or leave the temple and return to civilian life. Because many boys and young men become monks for a short time, I started calling them mini-monks. Buddhists believe that when a man's parents die, they are able to hold onto their son's robes and ascend into heaven. I think that is why most parents have their sons study at temple, even if it is for a short period of time. The Head Monk and the Teacher Monk are monks who have dedicated their lives to Buddha. They will remain Buddhist monks for the rest of their lives.

We prayed and did our morning chanting and then meditated. After meditation, we walked while the monks went to collect alms (food). Every morning, the monks walk through the local neighborhood areas to collect alms. After we had walked enough, we went to the kitchen and made more food to eat. The monks came back, a bunch of villagers came with more food, and we meditated and listened to the Head Monk talk to us. Afterward, we watched all the monks take the food that they wanted; then the Head Monk said a prayer over the food, and we were permitted to eat.

P'Nan said that the reason that we *thak baht* is to keep the monks alive so they can teach us. Then she said that the reason that they put all their food into the bucket to eat is because it doesn't have to look beautiful to provide nutrition, and, either way that it is eaten, it does the same thing. What I don't understand is why monks don't eat only rice. If the food is not meant to satisfy a craving or taste, why don't they just eat plain rice? Instead, they have food enough for three buffets to choose from. I'm sure the answer to that would be something along the lines of no one would want to be a monk, then, if he can't eat real food, but isn't that part of what monks are supposed to be working toward? In order to get to Nirvana, one must realize that nothing is real that is around them. Sometimes I feel that the monks are simply putting forth a 50-percent effort and ignoring the rest. Monks aren't supposed to smoke, so why don't they realize that and take the steps needed to stop? Instead, they just overlook that rule and focus on another one that they can follow.

I also don't completely agree with the way that Buddhists view the world. They look at it and figure they'll be back here—they're not leaving, basically. Because Nirvana is the ultimate best place, why doesn't every Buddhist stop living a normal civilian life and just live in the temple meditating? They must really be content with being on earth because it seems like they are in a never ending cycle that they can't escape.

I've learned that Buddha had at least 550 lives before he reached Nirvana. If Buddha had to go through that many lives, how many would a normal person have to go through? Maybe people like to believe in this because they are afraid of the unknown or, put more bluntly, afraid of death. If they know that they will end up back on earth, then they know what to expect, right?

Another question: If Buddhists believe that a person can be reborn as an animal, why aren't the monks vegetarian? It can't be said that they eat what they are given because, if all monks were vegetarian, no one would give them meat. It's not like they don't have enough nonmeat dishes to choose from.

I have learned that calling a Thai person a monkey is a horrible insult yet, Buddha was a monkey in a past life, and he seemed quite content with that.

I don't mean to be negative in all of my journal entries, but I really question a lot of things that I've seen and heard. We seem to have a lot of those "I'm right and that's just how it is" back and forth arguments that no one can win.

My favorite part about studying here is the chanting. I've been practicing about three short chants and am so excited to be able to do them tonight. P'Nuan said that she was going to help me find a book (like the one we chant from) so that I can have it to study. I want to get a CD of the chants, too, before I go back to America. One of the chants that we say is our eight rules that we have to follow. I wonder if the monks have to chant their 200 plus rules.

Day 3, June 11, 2007, 3:30 p.m.

P'Nan and P'Nuan left about an hour ago. I whined a lot, so they agreed to let me stay three more days. There are not many nuns living here, only about three or four, besides me. I just got finished doing my laundry by hand. Actually, I quite enjoyed it because it took a fair amount of time and it was something to do.

Last night after meditation, the Head Monk called me to the front (after talking to me for quite a while in front of everyone) and gave me a little Buddha book. I've read the first chapter, and it's actually a really good book. It's just a few sermons translated into bad English, but I like how it gives me a better idea of what I'm missing when we are meditating and when the monk is talking. Our Teacher Monk wasn't there for the meditation, so afterward, when everyone left, we walked with the Head Monk. Then, halfway through, our teacher came in and continued walking with us and then made us sit down for another meditation session.

This was my first full day as a nun—with five broken hours of sleep the night before on a thin mat, on a hardwood floor without air conditioning, and no daytime nap. While I was looking forward to going to bed at our usual time, around 11:00 p.m., the Teacher Monk made us sit through another session of meditation. It's not like a class or anything that we know how long it's going to last, so I just assumed that it was going to be just as long as the other two night ones that we've had: an hour plus.

4:00 a.m. was not a very appealing time to wake up the next morning, but the meditation this morning was actually really good. I didn't get sore at all because I was too tired. I guess I really am getting the hang of it. It's scary to say this, but I was actually disappointed when it ended after 35 minutes. I guess I wanted to prove to myself that I could handle the hurt. I slept like a rock when I got to bed last night, waking up just two times during the night. I was really upset when I woke up this morning because I was late. It was 4:45 a.m. P'Big and P'A were the only ones still in our sleeping quarters, and they didn't even wake me — I did on my own. We have to be meditating at 5:00 a.m., so I scrambled to get ready. We made it, though, just in time.

I don't really mind staying at temple. At first, I wasn't sure if I liked it but that was because I didn't understand what was going on. Now I understand it a lot better. My favorite part of the day is eating. Oh, it's so much fun! (Not to mention the fact that I haven't eaten anything for 24 hours). First, a lot of people from the surrounding neighborhoods visit temple to *thak baht,* and they bring tons of food. Then we all sit and watch the monks, who are always served first, in order of their rank and seniority. The first dish served is rice. Each monk will scoop a big spoonful into his bowl, then dump some of it back, until the amount that they want remains in their bowl. This is a ritual and is a symbolic *thak baht.*

Then, the monks go back to their seats, and the food trays are pushed through the line. We watch them take whatever they want to eat and put a scoop of it in their bowl. When it reaches the end, people take the trays down to our kitchen area and set it up for all the other people to eat. I love it because watching the food go slowly through the line is like a preview of a buffet, one tray at a time. There is so much food, too, that usually it takes about a half hour to get all the food through the line. Then, after all of the monks have their food, the Head Monk will pray, saying that all the food that he eats will pass through him and go to our dead relatives. He usually prays for another half hour or so, which I hate having to sit through.

Today, there were so many people that we gave up our seats and went to help in the kitchen. That's what P'Nuan said, but I think that she had the same intentions as I: first dibs! The buffet looks scrumptious when it's filled, and no one is there. We dished out our portions and then went back and sat at a table to listen to the rest of the prayer on the loud speaker because we couldn't eat until it is over.

Actually, while I was dishing food into my bowl, the Head Monk called for me. Oops! He was probably going to make an example of me because everyone thinks that I want to become Buddhist, and I'm naturally quiet, so being a nun isn't all that difficult. We decided not to go up to see him because we had to talk with him, anyway, after we ate. Once he concluded the prayer, we dug into our huge feast. I love it because I don't have to worry about how much I eat, like every other Thai person. I eat until I can't eat anymore, and then my feast is over for the day.

What I don't understand is why the monks get first choice, and then it's a free-for-all. I mean, shouldn't the nuns be allowed to at least eat before the common people? I won't get started on the gender issue. I'm not going to ruin the feast. Because we are normally really hungry, the feast looks 10 times more scrumptious. The only bad thing is that after finishing, I know that I won't get to eat anything else until the next day, but that's okay.

My favorite part of the day is between 7:30 p.m. and 10:30 p.m. I'm around a lot of people, and I really like being with people, I guess. The rest of the time is spent alone.

Some of my feelings about this experience have changed. In fact, my experience completely changed after my sisters left. Now, all the other nuns willingly approach me and are teaching me more about what to do and what is expected of me. Now I feel that I'm starting to learn something. For example, you can't stand and eat something, you have to sit; you can't go to the *sala* alone (even then you don't talk to the lower class monks).

These were just some of the things that I was doing wrong. Everyone told me that it's okay to drink milk; we bought 10 packs of it before we came! I, however, found out that it is okay to drink milk only before noon. Well, no kidding! We can have anything before noon. I found out that I don't have to wear the sarong unless I'm going to the *sala*. I guess I'm grateful that my experience has turned out like this. I got to understand the meditation and Buddhist part from my host sisters, and now I would get to study the nun part from people who are staying in temple for an extended amount of time. I can't be upset that my host sisters didn't tell me what I was doing wrong because they're not really nuns and they might not have known what they were doing wrong, either.

I like how everything is so laid back at my temple. The monks who are in charge don't even pretend that it's normal that I'm staying here, being a *farang* and all, and they play with the miscommunication issues. Usually they talk to me when there is a big group listening, but, even if there isn't, they still make me feel special. I said that I wanted the experience to be normal, but actually this is more like what I wanted. I want to have the same rules to follow and expectations to meet (at an understandable level that would make it possible for me to meet them), and, yet, with the jokes and normal conversation, it takes the edge off and helps me to relax. I guess relaxation is the main part of Buddhism. I really like the two Head Monks. Did I mention that my Teacher Monk got promoted to 2nd position? I don't know what happened to the other monk. He probably was just visiting or moved to another temple.

The Head Monk is so cute. He can't hear very well, so whenever he talks to me during meditation, he says, "What?" or "Huh?" every time that I respond to him. I normally speak quietly, even more quietly when there are a lot of people listening, and even quieter yet after someone asks me what I said. I then get overly conscious about my Thai and just assume that I'm not saying it right, and I don't want to say it loudly again because everyone will make fun of me. The Head Monk always walks around with a white hand towel folded in half on his head; that makes him look even cuter. The towel is damp and is used to keep him cool. I wish I had a picture, but he always takes it off for photos.

Then there's my Teacher Monk. He could be doing anything, but when he makes eye contact with me, sees me looking at him, Buddha, or just spacing out, known to Buddhists as pondering, he'll start a conversation with me. During meditation or before a sermon, he'll yell my name, "Salee," and then everyone will quiet down to listen or look at me, when, of course, I just smile back. Sometimes he'll follow that with "Ashley," and actually he says my name very well. A lot of Thai people can't pronounce it, but I have to give him credit. He likes the fact that I smile all the time.

One night or morning—I can't remember—people were late in arriving for meditation in the previous session, so he was disciplining us, saying how even the little kids who come for the evening sessions sit better than we do. I didn't catch it all, but I'd sit and stare at him intently so as to try to catch as many words as I could and to understand better. Everyone else would be looking at the floor because we were being scolded. Then, he'd run his eyes through everyone and stop at me, the only one looking back. Naturally, I smile when I make eye contact with someone, so he'd just chuckle, lose his train of thought, and then start up either a conversation with me or about me.

He likes the fact that I tend to surprise him a lot. First, I came to temple: surprise! I could speak a decent amount of Thai: surprise! I could read Thai: big surprise! Then I spent the whole afternoon practicing parts of the evening's chants and could follow along fairly well: another big surprise!

One time, we were all chanting, some of which I had practiced earlier. I was stumbling along, but loudly, so it was a bit noticeable. Most of the nuns-in-training can't chant, so I thought I was being rather discreet but, at the same time, outgoing. So, I was following the first two lines of the chant and practicing the third line in my head, so, when we got to it, I would be able to chant it, too. I had all the words of the third line in my head, and they are about to finish the second line. I confidently said the first two words of the third line into dead silence. Everyone had paused to take a breath, and I was so confident that it came out even louder than my usual tone. Everyone's face broke from their meditation straight into a really big smile, but they acted as though they hadn't heard me and continued chanting without falter. I was trying to keep myself from laughing while continuing to chant. They all made me feel at home as soon as I came, so it wasn't really embarrassing at all, just funny. To them, it was the kind of thing that was expected. I think they like having a *farang* living here. The two Head Monks always tell me to stay in temple and not leave or to stay until I go home to America. All of the nuns invited me to come back and visit next time I come to Thailand. I love these people.

Day 4, June 12, 2007, 10:45 a.m.

Apparently, it is a rule that we have to wake up on our own every morning. I don't know if that's true, and no one has told me, but no one seems to wake me up. I'm always late, but they are never mad at me. I was getting upset with them because I thought that they didn't bother waking me up, but, because it's happened every morning that I've been here, I assume it's a rule.

Yesterday, I was talking to another girl who is a little older than me, asking her about places in the temple that are off limits to nuns. Then I asked about the *sala*. The *sala* has four floors, with the main part being the second floor. I wasn't sure about the first floor or the upper two. She said that she's never been to the top two, but we are allowed to go to the first floor if we are with someone. She said that she would take me later. We went and discovered that it was where the Second Monk, who did not move to another temple, resides. He had gone to the doctor's office for a check-up the other day. We brought him iced coffee and then sat and talked to him for a little while. He's a nice guy and seemed really interested in talking with me. He'd ask me a quick question and, after I replied, go on to preach about how Buddhism affected my answer. He would then ask me if I understood and laugh at me when I answered honestly. Then he would continue talking to some of the other people in the room until I was caught up and then go back to talking to me.

Maybe it's normal to have meditation twice every night because that happened again last night. Usually the second time is shorter, so it's not that bad. I don't really mind meditation all that much, anyway.

I forgot to mention that I'm sick again today. I have the same symptoms as I had the week before coming to temple, so I think it was just in remission for those three days. My throat is really sore, worse than before. We didn't have any antibiotic pills in the medicine cabinet, so we had to go ask the monk for some. That was cool, but I had to wait in the kitchen and didn't get to go along. Now I just don't feel well and there is nothing to do besides read and think. I just took a shower and did laundry. I would sleep, but I'm afraid that I won't be able to sleep tonight if I sleep now. Of course, that might be good considering that I would more likely wake up on time in the morning. I want to practice chanting, but I can't speak, so I think that's out of the question. I hate being sick.

Day 4, June 12, 2007, 5:45 p.m.

Earlier today, I went to visit the monk who is second in command—I really should learn their names—and sat and talked with him for a long while. I guess that nuns eat only one meal per day, but monks (or at least the Head Monks) eat two because we brought him food for his lunch. I really don't see the reason for two meals within two and a half hours. One is plenty satisfying, but no one is permitted to eat anything after noon.

I learned that today is the six-year anniversary of the Second Monk's kidney transplant. At first, I thought that six years was quite a random occasion to celebrate but have learned since that the number six is highly significant in the Buddhist faith, reflecting the six means of perfection of a Buddhist: patience, charity, energy, wisdom, contemplation, and purity.

To help him celebrate, we brought him an ice cream cake from Swensen's packed in dry ice with six candles. After he finished his meal, another monk placed the cake in front of him with a big butcher knife and a fork. Then the Second Monk started eating the cake. He didn't even cut out a slice; he cut out individual bites and ate them. I want to do that the next time I have a birthday cake. He ate about a third of it, too!

I took a nap late this afternoon and feel a lot better now; the medicine has finally started to kick in. This was the first day that I've taken a nap since being here. Actually, I learned a lot while sleeping, too, which surprised me. First, I was just going to lie down on my back. I'm not sure when I fell asleep because I was just thinking about Buddhism and reflecting on what I've learned since I've been here. Then I heard myself snoring because I'm sick; I'm confident that I don't normally snore. Anyway, I'd never before been that aware of my surroundings while being asleep. I enjoyed it, actually. I felt refreshed, but, at the same time, I wanted to sleep longer. I think it's a type of sleep that you have to get used to because I like normal, deep sleep better, but I woke up feeling the same as though I'd slept deeply. Hopefully, I will be able to sleep like that for the rest of the time that I'm here and not be late for meditation in the morning.

I'm getting to know the Second Monk very well. He's the only monk whom we ever visit; I really don't understand why. He invited me to go to a temple in ChonBuri next Monday for the whole day, with some of the common people also going along. I want to go, but I'm supposedly leaving temple on Wednesday, so I'm not sure if I will be able to or not. I would just ask P'Nan if I could stay at temple until next Tuesday, but my time in Thailand is running out, and there are many things that I want to do before I go home. I wish I could have come into temple earlier like I had wanted to do originally.

One rule for nuns: we must squat or be seated when eating or drinking something. I always forget that rule, especially whenever I want a drink of water, which is all the time. It's not the Thai way for them to correct me, so only on occasion do I remember what is expected. I try to think about it because I want to follow all of the rules while I am here.

Because I had a stuffy head and sore throat this morning, I barely touched my breakfast. It just didn't taste good; my stomach rejected it. All that I have been eating today has been flavored water, bottled water, and an occasional chocolate square. Apparently, dark chocolate is okay to eat after noon because it is considered medicinal. I didn't understand the whole conversation, but the other nun put such an emphasis on dark chocolate and not milk chocolate. I'm not sure why. It is also okay to eat coffee-flavored lozenges. I don't know if every flavor is okay because this is the only one that they had. It was black coffee, though, so maybe there is a rule about being able to eat black things. We can also eat prune candies, which are also considered medicinal for well known reasons. I haven't figured out if there was anything else that is allowed. With the chocolate and flavored water, I feel like I have been eating all day and am not hungry at all, although I could go for some of that cake!

I have begun reading *The Teachings of Buddha*. It is a really good book: a quick read, informative, and interesting. I find it amusing that a lot of stories are about elephants. I thought that the stories were very Thai, and I think that elephants are a big part of Buddhism. I learned that if a person owns or finds a white elephant, it must be presented to the King because white elephants are considered to be royalty. Buddha's mother had a dream about a white elephant walking around her three times and then walking into her, which she perceived to mean (with the help of priests) that a great hero was going to be born. Soon after, she learned that she was pregnant. Because it is a requirement for the King to be Buddhist, it's probably the reason that white elephants have to be presented to the King.

I walked in to the *sala* for the night's meditation and walked to the center of the floor to *wai* Buddha. I couldn't read any more of my book because it was dark outside, so I went into the *sala* a half hour early. There was a mini-monk already inside who didn't seem to know what to do when I walked in. Then another one came in while I was doing my initial *wai*ing to Buddha. He told the other one to turn on the lights and the air conditioning. They were talking back and forth while the second one rolled out the mats, so I moved and sat in the back at the table, then he yelled at the first monk to turn the lights on in the back. It's cute that I'm getting all this special treatment, but I feel bad at the same time. It's not natural for a nun to be treated special. I'm sure that it's because I am a *farang*. Oh well!

Day 4, June 12, 2007, 9:55 p.m.

There are only two of us nuns left. I think we are getting newbies tomorrow, though. It was a lot of fun tonight. I was reading a Thai children's book until it was time for chanting, but I wasn't watching the clock because I was so into the book, so everyone was just about ready to start when I looked up. I sat next to the other nun. She helped me locate the page we were chanting from a few times, but she really got into the service, which forced me to find the correct pages myself. I sometimes feel like I'm a burden for her, but then she does something really sweet. She's kind of like Baa Thao.

One of the nights when we were chanting, I couldn't find the page, and she didn't know where it was either. So, she just closed her eyes to meditate. I looked a little bit longer and then decided to watch the monks chant. I looked over at one of the monks; I wasn't sure if he was a mini-monk or not. He looked a little older than me and he was sitting next to a white monk, i.e. a monk dressed in a white robe, as opposed to wearing the burnt orange colored robes that is the more typical monk attire. I think we have two white monks. They are here to study but don't have as many rules as the mini-monks. I think they have the nun rules plus two more, for a total of 10, but I'm not sure. They are always at the end of the food line, and they *wai* with the common people and us nuns, instead of with the monks and mini-monks. I now understand how long each man has been monk by his seated position. At the end of the line are the newbies, but the white monks are always last.

Anyway, so that monk looked right at me and mouthed, "*Ha-sip see,*" while he put up five fingers and then four. It was really sweet and something that was completely unexpected because he was telling me that the chants are found on page 54. The reason why I think that he is not a mini-monk is because he talked to me, and the mini-monks are not allowed to. I really appreciated it, though. I turned my book to the correct page, and I started listening to the chant and found where they were. As soon as I found the line that we were on, everyone stopped and changed chants. I turned the page because a lot of the chants are in order, but it wasn't there. I looked up at the monk, and he was flipping through the white monk's book. Then the white monk pointed it out to the monk who looked back at me and said, "*Hok-sip,*" as he put up six fingers and then indicated zero. That time he actually said it out loud, and I could hear the page number. I hope he didn't get in trouble for that. From then on, I referred to the nun for the page numbers.

During meditation that night, only a few local people attended. One boy, who was about 10 years old, comes every night and seems to have a lot of nervous energy. He has a difficult time sitting still every night. The Head Monk was going on with his sermon and then told the boy to stand to meditate because he couldn't sit still. The boy stood for about 10 minutes and then inched his way toward the back of the *sala* so that he could lean on the post. With every step he took, the hardwood floor creaked. The Master Monk would open his eyes and look at him and then close them again.

It seems that every night during the sermon, the Master Monk always calls on me, asking me how my meditation is, among other things. It's the fourth night already, and I've used up all my answers: "It's good," "My heart is relaxed," which I've used twice already. Tonight I used, "It's better." I'm having fun meditating, but now he's starting to ask me why it's good, and I have no idea what to say. I'm getting better at meditating because I am so tired and too lazy to fidget. Finally, he moved on to talk about something else, and I was off the hook.

Toward the end of the sermon, the boy was sitting with both of his legs to one side. I heard snoring coming from behind me, and I tried not to laugh. The Master Monk didn't do anything for a while, but then he opened his eyes. I didn't get a chance to look back because I didn't want to be noticed. Then, the snoring stopped, and the Master Monk continued preaching. Later, the boy decided to recline his body, still in the position that he started in (2 legs to one side). So, the boy was lying down, and the Master Monk hadn't seemed to notice. About 20 minutes later, the Master Monk opened his eyes and noticed the kid sleeping. He chuckled and threw his box of milk to the boy, but the boy didn't wake up, regardless of the loud noise the milk box made when it landed on the floor a few feet away from him. The Master Monk continued talking about him, and, finally, the boy's dad, from the back row, crawled up to the boy and shook him gently but hard enough to waken him while saying his name. The boy awoke without opening his eyes, straightened his back, placed his hands in the meditation position and sat "meditating." It was so funny, and everyone laughed. It was a nice ending to the session.

Day 5, June 13, 2007, 4:15 a.m.

I was determined to be on time this morning. I was so nervous about getting up on time that, as soon as I heard a creak that woke me up, I jumped out of bed (well, off my mat) and went to the bathroom and then looked at the clock. I probably could have slept a little longer, but I'm afraid I won't wake up in time, so writing this is a better use of time, especially at this hour.

It's funny to me when watching the monks as they are meditating. A lot of them either fall into a light or deep sleep. I'd heard that in the moments before people fall asleep, they are the most relaxed, experiencing a feeling of euphoria. I have come to the conclusion that this euphoric state must be what Enlightenment is. It seems to me that to reach Enlightenment, people must train themselves to stay in that moment for as long as they wish and to have the ability to reach that state whenever they wish. That makes perfect sense to me. In that state of mind, one loses the sense of "self" and is in a euphoric state of mind. Hence, all monks and nuns get only four or five hours of sleep a day. They are in perfect condition to go to sleep again, but they restrain themselves from that (most of the time) and try to get to or stay at the "high" stage.

I think that Buddha was very intelligent about nature and knowing about oneself, but I don't see that as any reason to worship him. He did good things during his lifetime; he helped people to relax and to contemplate the world around them. He went away from home when he was just a boy and preached that people never actually die, but are continually reborn and continually have chances to perfect their lives. Buddha has died because he has reached Nirvana which means that people will not be looking for him here on Earth, and no one can take his spotlight as the next Buddha. I remember playing with the idea of rebirth when I was younger. I think that he might have continued on with that idea and made a religion based upon it. It fits in great with Thai society because it seems that no one wants to grow up.

It seems to me that there is a lot of double talk in Buddhism. For instance, in my book it says how nothing is discriminated against before we discriminate, such as who decides what's right and wrong. We decide on our own—our own discrimination. That discrimination is a physical and worldly thing, and we should let go of all worldly things. Didn't Buddha come up with the Five Laws, similar to the Ten Commandments of Christianity? He preached to make merit by doing good deeds. Isn't that discrimination? Who decides what's good and evil?

The book has a section on why Buddhism is better than Christianity. It doesn't mention the word "Christianity," but it is obvious what it is referring to. Do we, as Christians, do that? Compare our religion to others? Maybe we do, and I'm just ignorant of that fact.

Day 5, June 13, 2007, 11:35 a.m.

Today has been very emotional. I went to meditation this morning, as usual, and the Master Monk told me to sit in the front row. A retired English teacher attended worship, and the Master Monk asked her to sit next to me to translate. He asks everyone to translate for me; I think he likes to hear them speaking English with me. She began translating, and then she asked me if I believe. Well, I couldn't lie to her, so I confessed that I am really Christian (which I've been telling people openly, but they hear it and then a minute later think that I have converted) and that I just came here to study Buddhism, but not to become Buddhist. She was really taken aback, and then the Master Monk asked what I had said. Seeing the look on her face as she translated it, I was thinking, "Oh, boy!" She translated for the Master Monk, even though I spoke Thai to her. I looked at the walls, ceiling, floor, anywhere but toward the front of the room. After she finished the translation, there was dead silence. Oh, I wished I could have melted. Then he went on to say, "Regardless of whether you are Muslim or Christian, as long as you believe in doing good, it's okay." Then he asked me if I understood hot, cold, happiness, troublesome. I answered yes after each one (except the last one; I learned a new word today), and then he went on to say that we all feel like that and that I should become Buddhist. We both laughed at the ending.

Then, thankfully, he prayed, and we were allowed to eat. After I finished eating, I was walking down the stairs from our sleeping quarters, and someone said that the Master Monk wanted to see me. I heard that little voice in the back of my head saying, "Ooh, you're in trouble, now!" I went to the *sala,* and the Master Monk was talking with some people, so I waited. Then he called to me and told me to sit in the front. He talked for a few minutes and then asked if I have any questions for him, now that we had a translator. I told him that I did not have any at the moment, and then he went into another speech. He was really stuck on the speech about our bodies being dirty like clothes: even when we wash them, they get dirty again, but we have to try to cleanse our minds. It's a really good sermon, but I'd already heard it for three days. I thought of a few questions to ask. I asked about what happens to people who don't believe in Buddhism when they die: are they reborn? If there are two people, one good and one bad, and neither are Buddhist, do they suffer the same consequences in hell?

I'm not sure if he directly answered me or not; he kept going on about having happiness in heaven with Buddhism. My mind has been wandering back to a month ago when my parents visited. It had never occurred to me that they were getting old, but, after not talking to them for nine and a half months and then meeting them again, I felt older, and they looked older. Dad was having trouble catching his breath when we were walking up a stupa in Ayuttaya, and Mom was getting lightheaded from the heat. I just realized that we're all moving on to new stages of our lives. Then I asked him a hypothetical question. If I became Buddhist and my mom died (this is where I got teary because I haven't coped with the inevitable yet), then I died and went to heaven, how could I be happy knowing that my mom was suffering in hell? The Master Monk threw me a tissue box and told me how I should try to convert my mom before she dies and asked me if I thought I could do that. I told him that I couldn't do that because I'm not Buddhist either, but, again, I think he forgot that I had not converted.

I explained how I've lived in Thailand for a year and have so many friends and family here and just as many friends and family in America. How could I possibly be happy knowing that half of the people I love are going to suffer? This is actually true because more than half of my friends in America have not accepted Christ as their Lord and Savior. Then I got to thinking about how I'd be leaving in a month and probably wouldn't ever again see most of the people whom I have grown to love in Thailand. While I was explaining that to the English teacher, I noticed that she had tears in her eyes, too. Then she passed the information on to the Master Monk. He laughed at me and said that I'm not as worried so much about myself as I am other people. Well, I can't help it; that's just the kind of person that I am. It was quite a moving moment for everyone, and now I'm fairly sure that they all think that I've converted. I can't help that, though. The Master Monk told me that he thinks I was born in the wrong country and that I'm naturally Thai. I told him that everyone says that, and many also think that I was Thai in a previous life. I'm glad that I've been able to fit in so well here.

After a little while, I came back and helped two ladies put flowers in vases and then went back up to the *sala* to present them to Buddha. My Teacher Monk was there and joked with me, saying if I stayed there alone that I would cry. Wiping the last tear from my eyes, I said that I never cry, smiling at him. He laughed at me, and the lady who was with me said, "She misses her mom." We started to leave, but the Teacher Monk told me to stay and walk. I had to compose myself first, so I excused myself by saying that I wanted to take a shower. Which was true; I have to do laundry in the morning hours so it will be dry for me to wear the next day. Because I have only two sets of nun clothes, I have to alternate them.

Now I have to go walk or study or something. I really wish I could have one of the chanting books, but I'll just copy down our chants and then buy a CD or something. This was such an emotional morning, possibly heightened by my getting only four hours of sleep last night. Oh, well—I can sleep when I get home. It's less than a month away!

Day 5, June 13, 2007, 1:35 p.m.

I walked into the *sala,* and the Teacher Monk was pacing in front of the doorway. Then he stopped a good distance away to let me pass. I placed my book on the table and then *wai*ed Buddha. All this time, the Teacher Monk stopped walking and just watched me with a puzzled look, as though he were trying to understand me. I wanted to do everything perfectly because he was watching me. So I *wai*ed Buddha nicely, and, the last time I bowed, I hit my forehead on the hardwood floor loud enough to be heard. I was trying to be very polite, keeping my face emotionless and especially not laugh. Then I got up and started walking, not looking at the Teacher Monk, and staying a good distance away from him.

Day 5, June 13, 2007, 5:00 p.m.

I was walking for a while, but then some people came to make merit by giving food to the monks, so I sat down to read while they talked. As usual, the Teacher Monk was telling them about me, and I just smiled and then went back to reading my book when their conversation turned to a different topic.

After they left, the Teacher Monk, a mini-monk, and I were the only people left in the *sala.* The Teacher Monk asked me what I was reading, but I didn't know how to say it in Thai, so I approached him and handed him my book to look at. The mini-monk read the title and then translated it into Thai. Then the Teacher Monk asked, "What is it about?" I replied with a very short comment about the content. Then he said, "Talk to me about it. I want to talk to you." So we had a nice little conversation. Between my Thai and the mini-monk's English, it was a fun conversation. Finally, the Teacher Monk said, "Okay let's clean the *sala,*" but, instead of using the words, "*Tam kwam sa-at,*" he said only, "*Tam,*" and I was confused because he didn't say the rest of the phrase that I was used to hearing. So, he taught me a little more Thai, and then we started to clean.

The mini-monk left to get more mini-monks to help, and the Teacher Monk showed me a floor buffer and asked me if I'd ever used one before. I had not, so he showed me how to steer by pulling the handle up to go right and pushing it down to go left. It was a large, industrial-type buffer that most certainly outweighed me. I took hold of it and pushed down and tried to go right. I didn't quite understand the steering part, and I wasn't doing very well. So, the Teacher Monk stopped me and again showed me how to run the buffer. This time I pulled the handle up really high. The machine just took off and started circling around the *sala* while dragging me along behind it. I was trying to keep from laughing at my inability to use this machine, and the mini-monk who was cleaning the floor with brushes made from coconut shells was laughing at me, too. The Teacher Monk came over to me, and I asked, "Can I just clean with the coconuts?" The mini-monk was laughing really hard, and the Teacher Monk, while trying to stop laughing, said, "No, you can do this. Try it again." I finally got the hang of it with a little practice and was doing pretty well. Then the Teacher Monk told me to go to the other side of the room because more mini-monks were coming in to clean. I finally made my way over there, even though the machine seemed to want to go a different direction. Every time I took a step backward, I had to keep looking over my shoulder to make sure I wouldn't stumble over a monk.

After we finished cleaning, I grabbed a broom and followed a mini-monk to the closet to put it away. On the way, the mini-monk picked up a dustpan and asked, "What is this called in—" and then stopped to think, and I said, "English?" and he nodded, so I told him. Trying to practice his English with me was really cute, although I didn't think that they were allowed to talk idly with me or any girls. He's just a mini-monk, so it might be okay. Monks are not permitted to have an emotional attraction toward any female in particular, so whoever told me not to talk to them and for them not to talk to me was probably just telling me that to be on the safe side.

While I was talking to the Teacher Monk, he kept insisting that I stay longer at temple. He said that P'Nan called him last night to ask how I was doing. I told him that she had given me a cell phone, but that I kept it turned off. I didn't have a charge cord with me, so I figured that I'd turn it on only if I needed to call someone. He kept telling me to stay for just two more days to make a full week and that I could write to the King and tell him how I stayed at temple for a week. They have never had a *farang* come to stay at temple. I think they might have had a *farang* boy come once, but I don't know if he stayed. They certainly haven't had a nun come alone and stay, Thai or *farang*.

I really like my temple. It took a few days for me to settle in and understand the people and get to know them. Now that I have, I wish I had the time to stay the full month like I wanted to. I just called P'Nan, though, and she said I could stay until Friday when she, P'Big, and P'Neui were going to come and get me in the evening. I wouldn't mind coming back here for a day before I leave Thailand, just to say goodbye, and I would have them pray for me and wish me luck. I'm really going to miss these people.

Day 6, June 14, 2007, 4:35 a.m.

Meditation last night was so painful. My back still hurt from it this morning. Sometime during Day 4, the Teacher Monk had us meditate again after walking, and he told me to sit cross-legged with each foot on top the opposite leg, like the Buddha image. I sat that way for the 15 minute session that followed. Then after that session, he said that I should sit that way for the next evening session, as well. Usually he doesn't come to the evening meditation sessions, but last night he did. Hoping he didn't remember, I sat down in the normal cross-legged style. When we were getting ready to start, he put his foot up, so I followed. I have to go to meditation now, so I'll have to finish this story later.

Day 6, June 14, 2007, 6:15 a.m.

Back to my story about the meditation session. So, I had to follow suit. I figured I could sit that way for at least 20 minutes.

After 35 minutes, I was starting to feel the pain in my leg. That pain exaggerated the pain in my back, but I wanted to see how much I could endure. After 45 minutes, I figured that I had only 15 minutes left, so I could do it. The last 15 minutes was torture; I kept closing my eyes and then opening them to look at the clock. I was in so much pain that I didn't realize that I wasn't being discreet, and every time I opened my eyes, the Master Monk saw me do it. I felt kind of bad about that, but I made it for the full hour. Whenever the Master Monk said that we were finished, my leg didn't seem to hurt as much. I'm sure it was because I knew I'd be allowed to move soon. So, I just stayed in that position for a few more seconds, waiting until the Teacher Monk put his leg down. I could tell that he was in a lot of pain, too. He first opened his eyes and looked at me. I smiled, still sitting in the Buddha position. He then put his leg down, and I followed suit, trying to make it look as though I wasn't in any pain. It actually wasn't too hard, considering that both of my legs were asleep. It felt so good to move out of that position. I slept with a blanket under the arch of my back last night. That helped a little.

Day 6, June 14, 2007, 10:50 a.m.

Whenever I talk to a monk or see the Teacher Monk, I have to *wai* three times before and after I speak to them and hold the *wai* position while I am talking. So much respect is protocol, yet they don't use polite endings when they are speaking to me. Thai men will usually say *ka* at the end of a statement when they are talking to me, but it seems that the monks never do. Although boys end their sentences with *krub*, older men would say *ka* at the end of sentences when speaking to me, as if to encourage me to say *ka* at the end of my sentences, as well. When talking to Sinwia, I would say *krub* occasionally to emphasize that he should use that ending. When I was talking to the Teacher Monk and he wanted me to stay a bit longer, instead of saying *ka* at the end of his sentence he said *"jao ka"*, which is being extra polite and very respectful. I didn't know that he was trying to teach me and was so taken aback that he'd be so proper to me because monks never end their sentences with even *krub*. It seems that the nuns usually get little or no respect from any of the monks. I can remember only one time when we were doing dishes, and I went to take more dishes to the drying rack, and someone's husband was helping us. He actually stopped and let me pass before he went in the opposite direction because he knew that as a nun I was not permitted to touch any male person, and there was room for only one person at a time to pass. That was the first and only time that I was given respect. I was so excited that the Teacher Monk said "*ka*" to me, even if it was purely educational.

Day 6, June 14, 2007, 2:55 p.m.

I just spent the last four hours sleeping. I was so unbelievably tired, and I felt like I had the same cold symptoms. Now that I'm awake, I still feel that way, plus I have a headache. I'm going to take some of the medicine that I have, but I have only enough for tonight. I don't think I'll be feeling much better tomorrow. We'll see. I really don't want to leave temple early, but they are telling me I can stay for only two more days, so, cold symptoms or not, I can tough it out.

Day 7, June 15, 2007, 10:40 a.m.

Meditation is either completely silent or someone is giving a sermon. The purpose of meditation is to block everything out and lose your body completely, which is easy for me to do because I tend to tune people out. I really struggle to pay attention because I'm constantly trying to keep up with Thai conversation, which drains my strength. At the end of meditation, whoever is in charge of it will clear his throat obnoxiously loud, so as to wake everyone up. It makes me laugh because usually that is what lecturers will do to wake people up when they are boring them to sleep.

This morning we had a very small group for chanting. There were only two of us nuns, a white monk, and our Teacher Monk. After chanting, we sat for meditation, and, 10 minutes later, the Teacher Monk started coughing. I'm thinking, "What are you doing? It's been only 10 minutes." The other nun who was with me just ignored it and was still meditating until the second episode of his throat clearing. I found out later that the monks were traveling to another temple and had to leave soon. So the Master Monk and the Teacher Monk, along with a handful of mini monks, went to a temple in Ubon today. Apparently, they will be back tonight.

I can't believe that today is my last full day here. This morning everyone was asking me when I would be leaving and if I was going to come back to visit.

Day 7, June 15, 2007, 12:40 p.m.

I woke up from another nap this afternoon, and my watch showed 2:55 p.m. I was really upset with myself for taking a four-hour nap again when I was going to be here for only one more day. Not that there is anything to do during the day, but I still would rather be awake so that I wouldn't miss anything. I walked into the *sala* and looked at a clock, which read 12:40 p.m. All of the temple clocks seemed to be dead; no one ever seems to change the batteries. There are at least five clocks in the *sala*, so I checked another one to verify that 12:40 p.m. was the correct time. So the clock wasn't dead, after all. I'm happy that I slept only for a little over an hour, but annoyed that my Doremon watch broke so soon. Doremon is a Japanese anime series, that is incredibly popular in Thailand. I'm sure I'll be able to find a replacement battery in the States.

Back to the rules of Buddhism. There is a rule against killing any living thing, especially another human, and committing suicide is the ultimate sin. There is a story about a prince observing a famished tigress and her cubs in a pit. The tigress is contemplating eating her cubs to satisfy her hunger. So, to save the cubs, the prince climbed a tree and threw himself into the pit so that the tigress would eat him instead of the cubs. "This action by Prince Satlua shows the true determination to gain Enlightenment."[1] Okay, the prince saved the cubs—merit, but he committed suicide in the process—sin. Again, I'm confused.

Rust grows from iron and destroys it, so evil grows from the mind of man and destroys him. What? What in the world do those two statements have in common? It seems to me that someone just

---

1. Quote from "The Teaching of Buddha," by Bukkyo Dendo Kyokai.

came up with a topic he wanted to preach about and then found a nature-like example to support it.

Day 8, June 16, 2007, 10:10 a.m.

There have been a lot of events that I need to write about, but I always seem to forget them by the time I have a chance to write them down. Yesterday, when we were cleaning up in the kitchen, a nun told me to dump the bags of rice with holes into the big bucket of rice. I was pouring the rice when suddenly a decomposed furry thing came out of the bag, too, covered with dozens of maggots. I was freaking out, so she came over and got rid of the mouse corpse. Then she turned to me and asked if I could pick the bugs out or if I was too scared. I just looked at her. I do not deal well with bugs, especially the kind that live off animal corpses. She said that it was okay if I didn't want to do it and asked me to just wash the bucket out, which had more bugs in it. Eww!

We cleaned the floor of the *sala* again yesterday. They clean that floor so often. Then again, what else is there to do here? I couldn't even count how many times I've put my head on that floor while *wai*ing the image of Buddha. There weren't that many people helping to clean because they were all helping with the construction project. We are building a new main hall and another building next to the nuns' quarters. I'm not sure what the second building is going to be.

Yesterday, we had a lot of people come to meditation, at least a lot for a weekday. I was talking to a few adults before we went to the *sala* when two boys and a girl started walking toward me. The two boys had their heads shaved but were wearing street clothes. So I think they recently were mini-monks in another temple. One boy walked over to me and very confidently said, "Hello, Salee." I said, "Hey," back, and he was absolutely beaming that he was talking to me in English. I'm pretty confident that boys are not permitted to talk to nuns when they are monks, even mini-monks. The reason that I think this is true is because one of the mini-monks from my temple was helping the Teacher Monk to tell me something during one session, but, whatever he would normally say to me, he instead said it to the Teacher Monk. It was an awkward way to converse, but he didn't break the rules.

Yesterday, there was a young boy here who is the son of the English teacher that I was talking with earlier. The boy spoke English very well. We talked for a little while, and he told me that, if I asked the Master Monk, he would give me some of his hair. Apparently, he keeps it in a little ball; it's supposed to bring good luck. Then his mom cut in and said, "But you're Christian, so you don't believe in that." I replied that, just because I don't believe in it, that doesn't mean I can't partake in it. I *wai*ed Buddha many times this last week, but that doesn't mean that I have been worshipping him. The hair thing is kind of gross, but it would still be cool to have some. Then some mini-monks walked by, and the boy ran off to talk with them until meditation.

It seems that, as each day here passes, I am more respected. People make sure I get the best of the food and the most they can put on my plate before I make a fuss. All of the men watch out not to bump into me. Last night, I was sitting near the kitchen, visiting with some people who had come for evening meditation. I was offered a bottle of orange juice, and the ladies preparing the drinks were going to let a little boy that I was talking with give it to me because he was the closest, but then they instead gave it to the little girl, acknowledging the rule that a nun should not touch an object at the same time that a boy is touching it. So, she came over and gave it to me. It was really sweet.

Later, the same women were making lemon smoothies in the kitchen and I was pacing back and forth, waiting for the other nun to come downstairs so we could go to the *sala* together. I always go with her so I can sit next to her because I never know what page we are on when we are chanting. The people making the smoothies saw me waiting and gave me a glass of it. When making the smoothies, they used the soda syrup and some cheese because these are medicinal foods that we are permitted to eat after noon. I assumed they were making the smoothies for the boys, but I don't know when they gave them to the boys because it was almost time for meditation when they gave some to me.

During meditation, the Master Monk asked how much longer I would be staying in Thailand. After I said that it was only one more month, he told me to stay here in temple until I go home. He said that I could study Thai by reading it from the chanting books. It was sweet of him to ask me to stay, but I think some of it had to do with him wanting more time to convert me to Buddhism. That's okay, though. I guess I take that as a compliment that he likes me enough to want the best for me after I die. I really like the whole respect thing. I get the normal respect of a human being, then the respect of being young and female, topped off with the nun respect. I like it.

When we began our meditation, I was watching the Teacher Monk as he sat cross-legged and then put his right foot up on top of his left knee. I followed him by putting my foot up. Then, I closed my eyes for a while and then got a bit bored. I was looking around when I saw it; his foot was back on the floor. I was thinking, "Hey, you're cheating," but I kept my foot up. He is fun to watch because, during meditation, he sways as though he is going to fall over, but then catches himself. Then, suddenly, his one eye popped open, looking directly at me. It was just so odd because usually I am tired during meditation, and I always have to open my eyes slowly to let them adjust again. Not the Teacher Monk; his eye just popped open, looking directly at me. I smiled, avoiding laughter, and closed my eyes again.

I have no idea why people choose to meditate twice at night. Some people opt to stay for a longer meditation even after we are dismissed. I mean, the second meditation is over by 10:00 or 10:30 p.m., and we have to get up at 4:00 a.m. I don't know about anyone else, but I am tired. I go up to our room and 15 minutes later I am on my mat with the lights out and relaxing. I mean, if a person wanted to meditate more or something, why not save it for the afternoon when there's absolutely nothing to do?

I like taking my showers in the afternoon so I can sleep in my clothes and wake up wearing what I'm going to wear for the morning of the next day. It makes getting ready for the day so much easier. In the mornings, I always wake up as soon as P'Ang, the only other nun-trainee staying in temple, gets in the bathroom because

I hear the door and see the lights. I'm always afraid that I'm going to get up late, too, so usually during the night, I wake up a few times to check the clock. I didn't realize that we were supposed to have a flashlight. I feel so stupid when my face is just inches away from the huge clock on the wall. I'm sure I look stupid, but at least I can laugh at myself. Whenever P'Ang gets in the shower, I usually complain silently and procrastinate for a good 15 minutes and then get in the other bathroom and just do the basics: contacts, teeth, face. Fifteen minutes later, I go back to my mat and just lie there waiting for her to finish getting ready, after which we walk over to the *sala* together.

I think I'm starting to get closer to P'Ang. She always gets me a book if she gets to the *sala* before I do, and she makes herself soup for breakfast every day; because I've been here and sit with her, she'll give me a bowl of it. I like her. She'll always give me a job if I'm just standing around in the kitchen because I don't know what there is for me to do.

I'm not one for the sitting and meditating for an hour, but I really like the walking meditation. I could do that for several hours at a time. It gives me time to reflect upon my life here in Thailand and daydream about what life is going to be like when I get back home to America. Usually I dream about the winters at home, Christmas time and baking cookies; all the things I really miss about home. Lately, I've been stuck on daydreaming about baking cookies, and it always ends up with a song coming to my head. Then I have to control myself because singing is not permitted in temple. It is really hard for me to follow that rule. I always sing in my head when I'm walking. I try to compensate for it by reciting a part of one of the chants that we do every day because those are a lot like songs, but again, songs are not allowed in temple. It's not all that hard to comply because I like the chants.

I don't really mind living here, but it dawned on me today that I have not heard one bit of information about what is going on in the world or in Thailand since I've been here. I have not listened to a radio, watched TV, or even read one newspaper article. Living in temple really cuts a person off from the world. I cannot understand a religion that is primarily focused on stopping life as it is outside of temple. At the end of our Christian church services at home, Pastor John would always say something similar to, "Now go out into the world and show others Christ, through you." It just seems that we are doing the exact opposite by secluding ourselves in temple, but I think I have a biased view of Buddhism because I am Christian.

Day 9, June 17, 2007, 11:25 a.m.

Yesterday was so much fun. I was being lazy and getting everything ready to go, and P'Nan stopped by to tell me that she had meetings scheduled for the entire weekend and asked if I minded staying in temple for a few more days. I was fine with that. I just don't want to miss out on doing something because of my staying here. I have only 20 days left in my exchange year. It has gone by so fast!

Something was going on at 5:00 a.m. in the *sala*. I was talking to another nun around 4:30, waiting for P'Ang to come down. I intended to sit with her for the meditation, as I normally do. Then, the Teacher Monk stepped out onto the *sala* balcony and motioned for me to go there. He does it like he's in charge of everyone, but I can tell that he's just teasing. The mini-monks had set everything up for the morning service, and then, just as P'Ang came in, they started taking everything back down. The Teacher Monk said that the Master Monk is working, so we had to wait until 9:00 a.m. to set up. P'Ang and I just looked at each other and started to laugh. Working? He's a monk. All he does is sit around.

Then the Teacher Monk asked me if I want to *pai tiow*, and I said, "Yeah, I always want to." P'Ang said she wanted to go, too, but the Teacher Monk said that she had to stay and look after the temple. I started walking back to our building, thinking that he was just teasing me, and he said, "Salee, *baa* (meaning, let's go)." I was so excited; I had to hurry to get ready. We were on our way to Wat Arun, a temple that was an hour or so driving distance away. We drove there in a van that belongs to the temple. It was so cool. As we were driving along, I was thinking that I once again found myself in a situation that was just unbelievable. Here I was, a Buddhist nun, *pai tiow*ing in rural Thailand with two monks. I mean, how cool is that?

When we arrived, we took some pictures in front of the temple and then met a couple there. I knew them already because they come to temple often. We walked with them for a little while, and the woman started telling me that we were going to see her father and that he had died there. I assumed that we were going to pour water on his grave because I've done that before. In the Buddhist faith, if a person is buried at a temple, his or her remains are cremated and then buried on the temple grounds. Then, a tree or flowers are planted at that spot. We turned the corner to find a ton of chairs set up with four other monks sitting at the front. I suddenly realized that her dad had just recently died; this was his funeral.

The couple led the two monks that I was traveling with to big sofa chairs on the stage and told me to sit behind them. I was overwhelmed; was I important enough to be on stage during his funeral celebration? Crazy! They brought us orange juice to drink because it was past noon and, therefore, we were not allowed to eat anything. Because the service wasn't ready to start yet, the Teacher Monk told me to look around at the preparations for a Chinese Buddhist funeral. I went across the way and looked at all the stuff that had been made for the funeral. There seemed to be millions of little gold papers. There was also a huge two-story house, complete with a lawn, a car, a bed with pillows, refrigerator, microwave, fan, closet, shower, sofa, chair, TV, and a whole bunch of other things. All of it was made out of paper! All of the compartments that were open were filled with the golden paper. It was so cool to see. I helped fold some of the golden papers. All of these items would be burned, and Buddhists believe that the smoke would take the things to heaven. The person who died would then be able to use these items in the afterlife. The gold paper represented gold, so the person would be rich in heaven.

The funeral was about to start, so I went back and took my seat. The service consisted of a lot of chanting from the four other monks on stage. We were not required to do anything. At one point, there were at least 20 men standing around me. The women wouldn't come near because of the monks. It seemed that the men forgot that, as a nun, I'm not allowed to come in physical contact with them, so I jumped from one seat to the next to keep my distance. Finally, I took three empty chairs and blocked myself in, so they couldn't get near me. The monks kept getting all this special attention, and I was stuck in the back. Then someone came around with wet wipes and gave them to the monks but didn't even acknowledge that I was there. I was a little disappointed that I wasn't even noticed. A few minutes later, the Teacher Monk turned his head and said, "Uhm, Salee," and then threw a wet wipe behind his head toward me. I felt so loved. He likes to act like he doesn't care about others, but he really does care. As the funeral was ending, the oldest son of the deceased approached the monks to thank them for holding the service. Before leaving, he turned to me and he *wai*ed me. I was so moved by that. I mean he didn't have to do that, considering that I am younger than he, female, and *farang*.

As we were getting ready to leave, the Teacher Monk opened the van door and said, "Oh, Salee," and motioned for me to get in. I *wai*ed the people whose father had died, then turned to get into the van. I had a big smile on my face as I was thinking, "You're holding the door for me!" I got in the back of the van, and then the two monks got in. Then he turned around and said, "Salee, are you in yet?" just to show that he wasn't being so nice for holding the door for me, but I was thinking, "Nope, too late, you already did it." It was so much fun hanging out with them.

When we got back to our temple, it was just 9:00 p.m. I was glad that we missed meditation but sorry that I missed chanting. I found a seat as they were getting started with the event that had been scheduled to take place earlier. One of the younger monks was sitting in a chair in the center with all the other monks and mini-monks around him, all *wai*ing. The monk in the center had made the commitment to be a monk for the rest of his life, and this was his initiation ceremony. He had 45 minutes to recite all 227 rules that monks have to follow. He was talking about as fast as an auctioneer, and one of the other younger monks was checking off the rules from a special book to make sure he didn't skip any. He finished with about three minutes to spare. It was really neat to see, but it was really long, too. We got out of walking last night and went to bed. That was such a fun day. I didn't realize it until we got back, but, even just riding in the van and going to Wat Arun, I was having reverse culture shock. It is going to be such a change going back into the real world. I'm talking about just the real world of Thailand. It seems crazy; I've been in temple only a little more than a week! I can't even imagine what it will be like trying to adjust to life in America.

A typical day during my time at temple consisted of:

4:00 a.m.	Get up/get ready.
5:00 a.m.	Chant.
5:30 a.m.	Meditation.
6:00 a.m.	Walking.
6:45 a.m.	Finish walking and start preparing the food.
8:00 a.m.	Thak baht/finish making food/sit inside the sala.
8:15 a.m.	Listen to prayers.
8:45 a.m.	Eat/dishes/clean-up.
10:00 a.m.	Shower.
10:30 a.m.	Do my laundry.
11:00 a.m.	Write in my journal/sleep/read/or whatever.
3:00 p.m.	Help with cleaning the sala.
3:30 p.m.	Make drinks for monks and for nuns.
5:30 p.m.	Walking.
6:45 p.m.	Hang out downstairs/reading/talking.
7:30 p.m.	Evening chanting.
8:00 p.m.	Meditation.
9:00 p.m.	Walking.
9:45 p.m.	Meditation.
10:15 p.m.	Wash my face/get ready for bed.
10:30 p.m.	Bed.
11:15 p.m.	Wait for the other nuns to come back. Sleep.

It's strange, I'm not doing anything all day long, yet time flies. It's crazy how just thinking takes up the time.

This year the King will be 80 years old. All year people are making merit by staying at temple or by doing good deeds to give to the King, as if he doesn't have enough merit already just by being

King. I'm signing a paper and mailing it to the King so he can have all the merit that I'm getting by staying here. I hope he enjoys it!

Day 10, June 18, 2007, 11:15 a.m.

Yesterday we had storms during the evening meditation, and I love listening to them, so meditation wasn't all that bad, but this morning my clothes were still damp. Oh, well. It is so hot here, anyway, that it actually feels kind of refreshing.

I forgot to write down before that, when P'Nan came to visit, I had just woken up from a short nap, and I was all sweaty and gross, so I was in the shower when she came. Then she talked to me about staying a few days longer, and, while we were walking over to the *sala* to talk with the Teacher Monk, she said, "Your face. You look so refreshed," and I was thinking, "Yeah, I just got out of the shower."

I really don't mind the meditation and walking because I like daydreaming, and this gives me an hour at a time to do it. The only thing is, I'm starting to run out of things to think about. Recently, I've been stressing about all of the things I still want to do or buy before I go home. My Thai dress should be ready when I leave temple. I hope it fits because I'm not going to be in Nakhon Phanom long enough to have the tailor alter it. I'm sure it will be fine; she took my measurements before I left for temple. I also want to buy the accessories for it before I go back to Nakhon Phanom and then have professional pictures taken there because it should be cheaper than in Bangkok. I don't know how quickly the pictures can be processed and ready. I can always have P'Nan bring them to me, assuming she's going back to Bangkok again before I leave.

I'm excited about saying goodbye to everyone because good-byes are just like welcoming parties. Everyone will wish me luck and say how much they loved having me stay here and how much they will miss me. I guess it's something out of the ordinary, and I like change. I'm also really excited about reading everything on the plane, my Friendship Book from *Piyamahalachalai* School, my Friendship Book from the southern tour with all the exchange students' comments, and this journal. I can't wait to get started on my scrapbook when I get home. These next three months are going to be so much fun and so busy, but I'm sure there will be times when I will be bored, too.

Did I write about how terrible the mosquitoes are here? It's so bad, especially in the kitchen or in the evenings. Luckily, they aren't as bad in our sleeping quarters. I can't believe how many bites I have on my feet and ankles. Nun rules forbid me from killing them, even while they are biting me. I am supposed to just shoo them away. They, however, are not stupid; they just fly in a circle and find another place to land on me. Normally, I would just ignore the rule and kill as many of them that I could, but there are always people around who would see me do it, and I *am* trying to follow the rules. I think I'm doing rather well, too. I would really like to see a temple in America to compare with this temple.

Oh, so I was filling out that sheet to give my merit to the King, and some of the informational questions were so weird. I mean I can understand asking about gender, age, purpose of visiting Thailand and address, but, then it asked for an emergency contact, blood type, and a passport number, which I didn't give. What is that for? Is the King going to call my host sister if I am hospitalized? How would he know? I gave my contact information, though. Maybe they have letters already printed out that they send people who give merit to the King. That would be cool.

Day 10, June 18, 2007, 4:10 p.m.

Staying at temple is so much fun. When I tell everyone that I'm Christian they ask, "Why are you here?" I say, "I came to Thailand to study not only the Thai language, but Thai people and their culture, as well. Most people in Thailand are Buddhist, so I wanted to study meditation."

I get complimented all the time on how great I am at doing meditation. These last few days, people have been giving me all sorts of things. I've gotten four books, so far, and about six or seven CDs, two of which are still sealed. I appreciate all the gifts and am really glad I have the CDs to listen to in Thai, but I make it quite clear that I'm not Buddhist and not planning to convert to Buddhism. The subject matter of all the books is quite similar, but each has a slightly different spin. I guess they see me reading all the time here, but in part that's because there is nothing else to do.

Everyone is warm and friendly. Every morning when we all come together to eat breakfast, it reminds me a lot of the 8:00 a.m. service in my church at home. It consists of a group of people that I grew up knowing and who come to church almost every Sunday, talking and visiting with me.

Day 10, June 18, 2007, 6:45 p.m.

Today, I was invited to a temple in another province. We will be going tomorrow. I've been telling everyone that I'm going home tomorrow and then, when I got invited, I changed my answer to the day after tomorrow. We are leaving around noon and getting back around six, which is right before evening session, so I don't know if I'm spending the night or not. I honestly don't know when I'm going home. That's okay—I like spontaneity.

Day 11, June 19, 2007, 4:35 a.m.

Last night I went walking where I usually do, outside our sleeping area on the balcony, but I went later than usual, so I had to stop sooner because of the bugs. I decided to go to the *sala* early and wait for the service to start, even though I was very early. Around 7:00 p.m., a mini-monk started to come in but stopped because of the rule that a monk and a girl cannot be alone together in the same room. So, he went back out and got the Teacher Monk, and they came in together.

Then, the Teacher Monk called me over to sit right in front of him and talk. I like the mini-monk that was there because he can speak English, even if it is not completely grammatically correct. He knows more English than most boys do, anyway. The conversation started out with the Teacher Monk asking me if I had cried that day. He likes to poke fun at me for that. I said, "No," and he asked, "So you don't miss your mom, today?" I replied, "Well, yes, but I'm going home in 16 days, and I don't want to leave Thailand." He went on talking about how my mom is inside my heart and so on. Then the subject came around, once again, to him asking me if I had a temple near where I lived. I said that I wasn't sure, but that it really didn't matter because I'm Christian, not Buddhist. Then he said, "I don't see Christian anywhere. I see eyes, nose, mouth, ears, arms. Nope, no Christian." I just had to laugh.

He then asked why I came to temple, thinking that it would be against my religion to be here. I said that I am studying, so it is okay; when I *wai* Buddha, I'm not worshiping him because I don't believe. I think that sentence got a little misconstrued in the translation because they both looked offended when I said I didn't believe. I went on to say that I think that Buddha was a good person and taught well, but I don't think he is God. I also said that I believe in some of the things he taught but not everything. Then the conversation really got good because we both started explaining our religions and beliefs more thoroughly. He said, "We are not necessarily supposed to believe everything that Buddha taught, rather we are to try it out for ourselves by meditation, and then you will actually believe." I moved the conversation forward by saying that I didn't believe in being born again. He replied with an example of a mango seed.

Day 11, June 19, 2007, 9:40 a.m.

The Teacher Monk was saying that, when a mango seed is planted, it forms a tree with branches and grows other mangos that can, in turn, make more mango trees. I agreed with that but went on to say that when the tree dies, it doesn't come back to life; it's dead. I think we agreed to disagree on that subject. Then he asked what the incentive would be for Christian people to be good. I told him that we believed in a heaven and a hell, but not that we would come back to earth again. Then he explained about the Buddhist's belief in heaven, hell, and Nirvana. I explained that as a Christian I believed that heaven is the highest and that there is no Nirvana; that nothing is better than heaven.

He then asked me if we believed in killing animals. I had to think about how to word my answer, but basically said, yes, and that it is fine to kill them. He told me that Buddhists do not believe in killing animals. I asked him if people would be reborn as people, and he said that people can be reborn as people, animals, or even insects.

"Then why are monks allowed to eat meat?" I asked. He answered that they could eat meat but were not permitted to kill the animal that provided the meat. I said, "Someone had to kill it in order for you to eat it." He replied that they eat only what people give them. I stated that if all the monks weren't allowed to eat meat, then everyone would know that, and no one would give meat to them. Then, all the mini-monks started laughing, and I looked over, suddenly realizing that there were a lot of other people listening. He said that the other people buy the meat at the market and then, chuckling, he said that they aren't allowed to eat people. I laughed but insisted that the meat that he was eating was once a live animal. He said that he wouldn't be allowed to go to market and say, "I want to eat that cow" and then have someone butcher it for him. He went on to say that he didn't know the animal that he was eating. I insisted that, although he didn't know that particular animal that he was eating, he still knew that it was an animal and that it once had life. Then I asked, "What if a person is Buddhist, but he works as a butcher?" He said, as though the answer should be obvious, that that person would go to hell. I asked why a person would want to be Buddhist if he knew he would be going to hell because of his occupation. He chuckled (another agree to disagree ending) and told me that that was enough and to go back and sit down. So I *wai*ed him and went back to sit with P'Ang.

I looked at the clock and realized that it was 7:35 p.m., so we had no choice but to stop talking. We chanted, and then the Master Monk came in. The Teacher Monk told him that I wanted to know why monks are allowed to eat meat if they believe that a person can be reborn as an animal. Actually, I think that he was asking for his own benefit, as well. The Master Monk talked about the subject for about 10 minutes, but I didn't really understand most of it. I figured that I would ask the Teacher Monk for a better explanation the next time I talk with him.

After meditation, everyone left except us nuns, the Teacher Monk, and the mini-monk, who was helping translate earlier. While we were meditating, a person who had attended the earlier service came back to *thak baht* and then left. The Teacher Monk got up to turn the lights on low but then sat back down again, while the other two nuns started their walking meditation. Usually, I walk in a line right in front of where the Teacher Monk's seat is, so I moved over to the other side, so it wouldn't be awkward. I had only just started walking when the Teacher Monk called my name. I went over and sat down where I had been sitting before while we were having our long discussion, and he asked, "What do you want?" I was being cute and asked, "Why are you not walking, too?" The words for the meditative walking and normal walking are different, but I can never remember the word for meditative walking, so I just used the other word, which probably made my sentence even cuter. The mini-monk chuckled, and the Teacher Monk laughed and threw something toward me. It is proper for Thai people and, especially kids, to thank a gift giver before actually receiving the gift. In America, if someone were to give me a present, I would take the gift and then thank them for it. When I first arrived in Thailand, I was scolded for my lack of respect. Now, it has become second nature for me to thank the gift giver initially and take the present afterward. So, I *wai*ed and thanked the Teacher Monk and then got closer; it was a huge chocolate bar. I *wai*ed again and took it back to my seat, while he and the mini-monk walked to the door. The Teacher Monk said that he had work to do tonight and told us to walk for an hour on our own before we go to bed. I think that he was going to contemplate our earlier discussion, but I don't know for sure.

This morning we didn't have that many people come to worship. At about 7:45 a.m., I brought a plate of food to the *sala* and, instead of going back down to help in the kitchen, took a seat in the back of the *sala*. During this time, the Teacher Monk was staring at me while meditating; I'm sure he was trying to figure out my perspective. I tried to keep busy looking at other things, but it's hard pretending not to notice someone staring at you. Luckily, a baby was brought in, and I made faces at her until it was time for us to pray.

The food began going on the trays in front of the line of monks, and I was really excited and had been waiting all night to watch this. I wanted to see if the Teacher Monk took any meat. I watched as best I could without being obvious. I know he took a lot of fish and vegetables, but I didn't see him take any meat. I was quite proud of myself for having had such an effect on him the night before. This proved to me that he at least understood what I was saying and was taking his time to develop his opinions. The monk next to him leaned over and started talking to the Teacher Monk. I assumed that he was commenting on the fact that the Teacher Monk hadn't taken any meat because he pointed to his bowl and the tray a few times within their long, whispered conversation. I busied myself with looking at other things so that I wouldn't have to watch their looking at me.

I'm quite proud of myself, actually. I got a lot of my questions answered, as well. It just surprised me that he knew so little about Christianity; although, I guess I didn't know much about Buddhism until I came here. I was really looking forward to our evening session tonight. I just hope that P'Nan doesn't come for me today because it's always so much more fun talking with the language barrier. I just wish that people would let me stand on my own two feet sometimes instead of taking over and translating everything.

Day 12, June 20, 2007, 4:30 a.m.

Yesterday wasn't all that much fun, after all. I visited a temple about an hour and a half away, near Chantiburi, with two women who attend services at temple regularly, the monk who is second in command, and his assistant. It started out badly, though, because the woman who drove, P'Gai, is a very poor driver. The whole hour and a half, it felt as though she was pulsating the accelerator; I was starting to get sick. Not only that, but I was hungry and thirsty, and the roads weren't smooth. It was just a combination of everything. I was tired, too, so my attempt to sleep probably was the worst decision I could have made. We arrived at the temple, went inside, and *wai*ed for 10 or 15 minutes. There were a lot of people there for a weekday. Apparently, it is so crowded on the weekends that it is impossible to get inside the door. We went to look at the disgustingly polluted river next to the temple, and then we drove back. I'm glad we went because it gave me an opportunity to stay in temple longer, but it wasn't the greatest day. I also didn't like how the two women treated the monks—like they were gods or something. We would be walking and, if a monk stopped to ask something, P'Gai would slip off her shoes really fast, kneel to the ground, and *wai* before answering. I thought, "Are you kidding me?" So, whenever they yelled at me to kneel, I followed, but I didn't do it by my own choice. That's just too much.

Yesterday afternoon, the Master Monk had a bunch of people come to temple. I think he went with them to a province, fairly far away, to help with another funeral. So, he wasn't here last night when we got out of meditation. I don't know when he's coming back, though. I'm guessing that I'll be leaving temple before he returns, but then who knows?

Day 12, June 20, 2007, 9:55 a.m.

The Master Monk was here this morning, so he must have gotten back last night after 8:00 p.m. or he was just too tired to make the trip.

I forgot to write a story that happened yesterday morning. I was assembling the fruit on trays, as usual, and I recalled, from watching different people bring the fruit to the *sala*, that the deliverer is required to say a short prayer after being prompted by a mini-monk. While saying it, one of the pieces of fruit must be broken open. It is a symbolic blessing for the whole tray of fruit. I wanted to try to do it today, so I told P'Ang about it, and she taught me how to say the phrase and how to open the lychee, which was the fruit on the tray that I would take to the *sala*. I went there to give the fruit to the mini-monk, who happened to be the mini-monk who could speak some English. I just looked at him and excitedly waited for him to prompt me to say my memorized line. He said his part, and then I must have mispronounced mine because he made me repeat it two more times until I got it right. I went back to the kitchen, and everyone was talking about how well I could say it. They then handed me another tray of fruit to go back. This time, I got the prayer right on the second try, but the lychee I picked wasn't cut well, so I couldn't open it. I started to pick another one, and the mini-monk said that I had to open the first one that I grabbed. He made me say the prayer again, and my lychee kind of squished as I tried to open it, but it worked. I went three or four times to the sala with fruit trays that day.

Today, I was cutting fruit, and someone asked me to take the tray to the sala. I just replied, "No, that's okay. I've made enough merit with the fruit yesterday."

Day 12, June 20, 2007, 4:00 p.m.

I took a short nap this morning, but I have just two weeks left in Thailand, so I'm trying not to sleep that much. I went outside on the balcony of the nun's quarters to start walking, and somebody who was walking on the balcony outside temple told me to come to the sala. I went there thinking that P'Nan had come to get me already. There were two ladies there who told me that the Teacher Monk wanted to talk to me. I approached him, and he gave me another Buddhist book to read. I thanked him, again, and we took some pictures. The Teacher Monk went to get a white monk to come sit with us because he can't be alone with women, and then the five of us just sat and talked.

We talked for about three hours, after which we cleaned the floor. We would talk about nothing of importance for a while and then would return to discussing religion. I know I am forgetting a lot about the discussions I've been having, but they're all so detailed and seemingly unimportant at the time. We talked about eating animals, again, and he said that there were 10 animals that monks couldn't eat: dog, horse, elephant, lion, three different species of tiger, snake, bear, and people. He said that if they ate these creatures, their bodies would give off an odor, which is dangerous. I responded by asking, "So the only reason that you don't eat them, then, is because you are afraid?" He corrected me, saying that it is dangerous. I brought up the topic that we had discussed the other day regarding the consumption of meat. I, again, stated that if a person can be reborn as an animal, then, when eating the meat of animals, we could be consuming one of our ancestors. He said that once the animal died, the life has gone out of it; it is just food.

He said that there were a lot of vegetarians in Thailand, like me. I corrected him and said that I was not vegetarian and that I ate meat. He laughed, as if to ask why I was preaching vegetarianism to him. I said that if I believed that a person could be reborn again as an animal, then I would never eat meat. This was another agree-to-disagree topic. Then he started asking me about my religion and where I am from. It was a good conversation. I'm really excited about tonight's session, if I am still here.

Another subject that I broached was a bit daring, considering the gender inequalities in Thailand, but now I understood the separation of mind and body in the Buddhist faith, acknowledging that they believe that our bodies are not real and that people will be reborn after death. I asked, "Since a man can be reborn as a woman in his next life, then why can't women become monks? I understand that women are Buddhist monks in some locations, but not in Thailand. Why?"

He told me about the five commandments of Buddhism; one of them was "No Adultery." His reply didn't fully answer my question, but I went on with another. I asked if it was wrong to have a boyfriend or girlfriend of the same sex, considering that there are a lot of them in Thailand. He said that he didn't know and that no one had ever asked him that before. He said that he would ask the Master Monk tonight. I liked how I asked him questions that even he didn't know the answers to. It made me feel a little more intelligent about the topics being discussed.

Living in temple has really forced me to be a more responsible person. For instance, I have to wake up every morning on my own and be ready and waiting in the *sala* at 5:00 a.m.—no alarm clock, no wake-up call, nothing. I confess that I wake up only because I hear P'Ang in the bathroom or I see the bathroom lights. Everyone uses flashlights and tiptoes in the morning, so I really am required to wake up on my own. No one in temple forces me to eat anything. I eat as much as I want, and that's my meal. I miss that about America. All day long I can do whatever I want, whenever I want.

If I'm expected to be somewhere at a certain time, I have to get myself there on time. Whenever I run out of clean clothes, I have to make sure I do laundry well enough in advance to give it time to dry, although usually it takes all day. That is the same as in Nakhon Phanom, except here I do laundry by hand.

Something else that I asked the Teacher Monk: if a baby dies, since it hadn't had time to do any good or bad deeds, does it go to heaven or hell and for how long? He said that then it depends upon the previous life of the baby. So if the baby came from hell, it has to go back right away. This religion is so bizarre.

Day 13, June 21, 2007, 11:00 a.m.

I woke up at 3:00 a.m. today. I'm so tired. P'Ang said that the batteries in the clock were dead, which is why she got up so early. I just got ready and then dozed until she was ready to leave.

It was raining hard this morning; I love storms. P'Ang and I were laughing at the fact that all the monks had to go walk for alms in the rain today. Last night, the Teacher Monk gave me a chocolate bar to give to P'Ang because the night that he gave me one, she begged him for the other one, but he wouldn't give it to her. At meditation, she came in and thanked the Teacher Monk for the chocolate bar by *wai*ing three times, and I laughed to myself. The Teacher Monk just walked away while she was *wai*ing, but then he turned to look at me with a smile on his face. Those two are the funniest together.

After everyone ate and we washed the dishes, I went with a few people, including an English teacher, to talk to the Master Monk. I asked him if it was a sin for two people of the same sex to be together, and he said yes. He reminded me about his recent sermons about the body being unclean, and I replied that I believed that God didn't mind that our bodies got dirty. I believed that He gave us our bodies to use here on Earth to do good works in clean places and in dirty places, as well. When we die, we leave our dirty bodies on Earth and ascend into heaven. I was a little nervous about how he would perceive my point of view, but he said that I was thinking correctly. He waited a few seconds before going on a long talk that ended with everyone laughing. I was completely lost, mainly because I was shocked that the Master Monk actually agreed with me, so the English teacher asked me if I understood and then explained a bit of it. The Master Monk had said something similar to, "It's funny that we are teaching kids for so long, and then they turn around and teach us." That was a nice compliment.

I was talking to the English teacher's husband, who had been to America before, about Buddhism and several other topics. He said that when he went to America, he didn't think that we had any angels, but he said now he knows he was wrong. I thought that was really sweet of him. I am really going to miss Thailand.

Day 13, June 21, 2007, 12:55 p.m.

P'Ang left already with all her luggage. I already am bored and not really sure what to do. It is difficult enough to have to go everywhere with another girl, but now I am the only girl here. That's okay; I'm tough.

Day 13, June 21, 2007, 2:35 p.m.

A little while ago, P'Nan called and said she was coming to pick me up tomorrow afternoon. I'll believe it when I see it. After I went downstairs, I ran into two new monks and a real nun. They came for the big ceremony that we are going to have on Saturday. Apparently, a lot of people are going to come and donate money, and there will be a lot of food. The English teacher really wanted me to come. She said something similar to, "Everyone is coming to give big donations, but, even if you give a little one, it's okay, too." I interpreted that to mean, "Please come to the festival and give a lot of money because you're a *farang,* and we know that all *farang*s are completely rich." I really dislike English teachers here. They all seem to have the same air about themselves, and they treat me more like a *farang* than anyone else does. I'm hoping to be busy on Saturday and skip the celebration. I'll probably be in Nakhon Phanom, anyway.

Day 13, June 21, 2007, 6:15 p.m.

The nun that came to stay here is so quiet. She hardly ever

speaks and is so submissive. I can't even imagine living my life like that. I'm really grateful for my experience here. P'Ang helped me out a lot and helped me to understand everything. I met a real nun, too. Basically, I had the experience that I wanted. I'm happy.

Day 14, June 22, 2007, 3:40 a.m.

Last night during meditation and prayers, I sat next to the nun. She refers to herself as *Mae Chee*, which literally translates as "nun", so I don't even know her real name. She is a really sweet girl. She's 29 and has been a nun for five years already. When we were chanting, she helped me find the correct page and place. My first impressions of people are never accurate. I kind of like that, though —always surprising.

Last night, the Teacher Monk invited me to go to another temple, which is the one that the nun came from. Supposedly, it's really pretty and in the mountains. He's going there for three days and asked me if I wanted to go, too. Of course, I said yes, even though P'Nan said she was coming today to get me. I figured that I would just stay a few more days in temple. Besides, she was supposed to pick me up three hours ago and still hasn't come. If she doesn't come today, I will definitely be going to the other temple tomorrow. That will be fun.

Day 14, June 22, 2007, 9:30 p.m.

This morning I got roped into folding paper money to make money flower arrangements. They're pretty, but I would have chosen washing dishes over making billions of these. These are used to encourage donations to the temple. It was fun for a while, though. Then my fingers hurt, so I sat in the meditation position with my back slouched against the wall. I must have fallen asleep because everyone was talking, and, the next thing I knew, there was dead silence. I opened my eyes, then everyone turned to me, and someone told me to go in the other room and rest. I wasn't going to make her say it again.

Later that day, I went to the *sala* to walk, but the Teacher Monk and another lady were meditating, so I just followed suit. Once she left, I talked, once again, to the Teacher Monk and the English-speaking mini-monk. At one point a group of people came to visit, so the Teacher Monk had to go do something with them and left the room, so it was just me and the mini-monk in the *sala*, which isn't allowed. I expected him to leave, but when he stayed, we got to talk for about five minutes before the Teacher Monk came back and we refocused our topic. The mini-monk, who I thought was about 16 years old, was actually 22 and was a college student, majoring in science. He preached to me about how I should become Buddhist. Basically, he's a science major, and Buddhism teaches a lot about nature and science. I asked him how long he was going to continue being a monk and if he was going to stay for life. He said that he wasn't sure yet.

Then the Teacher Monk came back into the *sala*. We had already discussed so many things that there really wasn't much left to talk about, so the topic turned to my life plan. I told him that I couldn't stay at temple forever because I want to have a family and have kids. I elaborated by stating how I couldn't spend a whole year in temple because, by the time I finish college, I will be in the prime of my life. I'll be 24 or 25, ready to be in a lasting relationship headed toward marriage. Then we got into a very long discussion about why I would want to get married and how my *faen* would find another girl, and I'd cry and be sad.

He said how life is so much better in temple because, "...you are always happy." I feel like I was always content in temple but never happy. I was cut off from the world, from living. True, I was never depressed or sad, but I was never anxious or excited either. I was cut off from all emotion, which is partially what Buddhism seems to teach. He kept referring to me crying in life, but I see nothing wrong with crying. Whenever something is upsetting me, I have a heavy heart until I just cry and let it all out. Then I'm done, it's over, and I move on. I don't go on being depressed for weeks. He asked me why I wanted to have a family and how many kids I wanted. I asked him if he liked kids, and he said that they just puke, although, I could tell that he was joking. I answered that I don't know how many kids I want and that I would have to talk with my husband first. Then he asked why I wanted kids, and I said that I wanted to be a mom. He replied that, when that happened, I would always be tired because I would work and then come home and then cook and clean. He kept looking from me to the clock, and I knew that it was getting close to 3:00 p.m. Then I just laughed, and got up. He seemed surprised and asked, "Where are you going?" I didn't answer, but grabbed the floor sweeper, and he said, "Oh, she knows what happens at 3:00 p.m." So they both got coconut brushes, too.

We also talked about girls versus guys in society and in the temple. It was a dead conversation before it began. I should have known never talk to Thai men about women's rights, especially when I don't have full command of the language. After my attempt at an argument, he asked if I wanted to be a monk, and I replied, "Well, yeah," obviously accenting my tone. They both laughed at me, along with another monk who was there. Then, the Teacher Monk said, "You will have to shave your head." I told him that I would eagerly shave my head if I got to wear a toga, gesturing toward the burnt orange one that he was wearing. He just laughed while walking away. While I was getting set up to clean the floor, he returned with a toga wrap in his hand, and he acted like he was going to give it to me. "Okay, let's go shave your head." I put down my floor cleaner and skipped over to him all giddy and said, "*Baa.*" They laughed, and he said that he was going to tell the Master Monk that I wanted to shave my head. I wish I could have been there for the evening's meditation session.

After cleaning the floor, I took a shower and did my laundry, not knowing when P'Nan was going to come for me, and then went outside to sit and do some writing. There were two other ladies reading and meditating, so we talked for a long time.

Suddenly, P'Nan pulled up in her car, and, within five minutes, I was loading all my stuff into it. Then, we were running around, trying to find the Master Monk so that I could tell him goodbye. I wished that I would have been allowed to leave at a slower pace so that I also could say goodbye to the Teacher Monk and sit and talk for a while in the *sala*. I had gotten use to the slow paced style of living in temple, but reality hits hard.

From then on my life was a blur. I felt the same way as I did when I first got off the plane in Bangkok nearly 11 months ago. P'Nan is naturally stressed and late, so we just jumped from one thing to another. I did miss being in the real world, but I missed being in temple, too. Those days went by so quickly, but I look back on them and realize that I did basically nothing there. Every day was essentially the same, but I made a lot of friends and really hope I can go back to visit.

June 25, 2007

After leaving temple on June 22nd, I went to P'Nan's apartment and hung out with her for two days. Then, on Sunday, we and P'Kip went to the airport to pick up NeungNoo, who was returning from her youth exchange in America. I recognized her right away, before P'Nan did. That was probably because I was looking first for the Rotary blazer and then for her face. It was nice having her back. We stayed in Bangkok for about four days. I really liked hanging out with her and speaking to someone who was basically a *farang* because she had just gotten back. I had spent some time with her before she left for America, as well. I was able to converse with her in English before she started her exchange year, but her vocabulary was limited. Upon her return, I noticed that her English skills had vastly improved. Now, she was speaking very clearly and quickly, as well as using slang typical of Americans. It was neat to be able to observe her improvement; I hoped that my language skills would be just as impressive when I returned home.

23

SAYING GOODBYE

⁂

June 27, 2007

TODAY P'Kip, P'Nan, NeungNoo, and I drove home to Nakhon Phanom. Paw was waiting outside holding Nadia, while Sinwia was jumping up and down with excitement. It was pouring rain, so we got all our bags under the roof, and Sinwia gave NeungNoo a huge hug and then ran over to hug me and then ran back to hug P'Nan and P'Kip. Once he finished hugging everyone, he ran right back to me, took my hand, and said, "Okay, let's go," and started leading me into the house. I told him to go ahead because I had to get my bags, but he insisted on "helping" me carry one of the bags. We did it together because the bag was too heavy for him to carry alone, making our way through the shop and into the living room. I retired early that night to pack my bags a little more and to let NeungNoo have a little bit of family time.

While I was still packing, Baa Thao came in and asked me why I was packing right now, so I replied that I was going back to Bangkok with P'Nan in four days. She asked why I was leaving so soon, and I said that I had to go back to America. My year was over. She came over and gave me a big hug. I'm really going to miss her. The next two days would go by really fast.

June 28, 2007

Today, I went to get my hair permanently straightened. Then, I

275

went to pick up my Thai dress. I tried it on right at her house, which was also where she does tailoring, because we were waiting for her to return from the market so that I could pay. The strapless top wouldn't stay up because of all the weight I had lost in temple, but, luckily, I had a halter-top made to go with it. I expected the outfit to be a little better made. For example, there were no cups in the two tops she had made and there was no inside liner. My skirt wasn't made the greatest either, with or without the weight loss, but it was only 3,600 *baht*, so I shouldn't complain. It really is pretty! All I will have to do is put a few safety pins in the back, and I can wear it just fine. I was shocked with how much weight I had lost in temple; there was a noticeable change in my measurements.

I went from there to get professional pictures taken of me in my new dress at the photo shop in the market, which lasted all morning. The pictures turned out really well. Not only did I get professional pictures taken in a studio, but P'Nuan's friend, who is also a Rotarian at my hosting club, is learning to become a professional photographer. She was so excited to expand her portfolio and took me all over Nakhon Phanom to get outdoor shots.

That night, we had a Welcome Home/Farewell Party for NeungNoo and me. We had two cakes, and all of our relatives came over to celebrate. It was a very nice last family gathering for me.

June 29, 2007

I got to pick what we were having for lunch as my last meal, so I picked a Vietnamese lunch. It wasn't the food that I tried to describe to them, but I loved what we had, anyway. It's a tortilla type wrap with greens and a piece of meat with pepper, garlic, or star fruit inside, topped off with a peanut sauce. It was really good!

That night I went to a big Rotary dinner. It was another Welcome Home/Farewell Party for NeungNoo and me. That made it a lot of fun. I spent a lot of the dinner talking, in both Thai and English, so it was a lot better than usual. P'Lek gave me two more Buddha books. I would say how many I have in total, but I can't count that high. It was really sweet at the time, but then P'Nan let it slip in one of her comments that Rotary always gives a gift before the exchange student goes back. I guess it's still sweet, but they know I'm not Buddhist—why do they keep pushing it on me? After dinner, I told P'Nuan that I wanted to go to see Baa LaWang to say goodbye. She and NeungNoo accompanied me there.

It was a nice visit. A group of M4 boys was there, and a few of them were brave enough to talk to me. Talking with them was a lot of fun. Then we had to go to an actual Rotary meeting, though I didn't know why NeungNoo and I had to be there. I considered myself lucky that Sinwia was there, too, so I spent the entire time playing in the back with him. We had fun. I'll really miss him. Around 11:00 p.m., we were both ready to go home, and he was getting really bored and tired. Finally, P'Nuan bowed out of the meeting early and took us home.

This would be my last night at home. Did I sleep well? Definitely not! Nothing to do with homesickness or anticipation or anything about me leaving; we had a storm that night. I love storms and falling asleep to the sound of rain, so that wasn't the issue. I had to go to the bathroom. While walking back to my room from the bathroom, I heard paws prancing around. Curiosity got the better of me, and I walked past my room to look but didn't see anything. On the way back, I stumbled upon a four-legged creature that was trying to walk with me but was between my feet. I had never seen the dog come up to the second floor, so I just assumed that he wasn't allowed up there. I didn't want to just shut him out of my room, and he was, obviously, terrified of the storm and wouldn't go back downstairs, so I let him lie on the floor, beneath my bed. That was fine for about two minutes, until he jumped up onto my bed and curled up in the nook made by my stomach and legs. He wouldn't get off, and I figured P'Pin would wash the bedspread after I left, anyway. I didn't have to sleep there another night, either, so I let him stay for a little while. Then I couldn't sleep well because I could just envision Sinwia barging excitedly into my room to wake me up in the morning, only to find the dog in my bed. Luckily, the storm subsided around 3:00 a.m. I let him out and got a few hours of sleep. I guess I'll miss the poodle, too.

When I first arrived, they had two dogs, Joey and Gogo. They would spend a lot of time at the other house, and Baa Thao and I would often feed them while we were taking walks in the evening through the vacant streets. It was during these walks that Baa Thao taught me how to read, and this is how she and I became so close. One day, Gogo went missing. Everyone was looking for her for about a week, but there was no sign of her. A while later, we were fortunate to have found her at the home of a local dentist. Apparently, they found her wandering the streets and decided to take her in and then grew attached. She was a good dog, so I'm sure the attachment developed quickly. In the end, my parents decided to let the family keep her; after all, we still had Joey. It was really a nice thing to do, but I felt awful for NeungNoo. I'm not a huge animal person, but I still love my dog, and I would be really upset if I returned from exchange and learned that my parents had given her away.

Unfortunately, the occasion that I have dreaded for so long had come. It was time for me to say goodbye. Well, goodbyes stink, especially when you're tired. I was staying composed until I said goodbye to Baa Thao, then I cried. Actually, it was a perfect goodbye. I cried only a little, and my entire family walked to the front of the house and stood there smiling and waving to me as we drove away.

July 4, 2007 (Thailand time)

Wow—time went by fast. I can't believe that I'm sitting on an airplane, returning to America, on her birthday, no less. I'm not really sure what to write. I know it's been a month, but I can't remember anything of importance that I need to include.

I am now sitting in the airport in South Korea. An announcement just came across the public address system saying that they were going to be doing another security check right before boarding the airplane. It is added security for all planes entering the U.S. I was beginning to question the wisdom of flying internationally on this date, but it is what it is. After all, I had changed my return date so that I could spend as much time in Thailand as possible.

My journey home was eventful, actually. I had a short flight from Bangkok to Seoul, South Korea. While departing the plane in Seoul and making my way to the gate of my connecting flight, I noticed that a young woman was, albeit inconspicuously, following me. I found a seat at my gate and began to settle in for a few hours of waiting when, sure enough, she sat down right beside me. I noticed her failed attempt to discretely glance at my ticket, so I asked if she spoke Thai, noticing her petite Asian figure. She replied that she spoke some Thai but was actually from Laos; judging from her actions, she couldn't speak English, either. It was apparent that she was lost. I asked to see her ticket and then went to the service counter and inquired of her departure gate and pointed her in the right direction. I was glad that I could help.

For a second time I was nestling into a comfortable position, my CD player and journal in hand, anticipating a boring two-hour layover. Not 20 minutes later, I heard a bunch of excited chatter and laughter behind me. Because I was hearing people speak English, I curiously turned to see who was so excited and why.

Veronica! I was so shocked and excited when I saw her in a group of about five others, all wearing Rotary blazers. She came over and gave me a huge hug, after which I schlepped all of my stuff over to where they were, and then she introduced me to the other exchange students, all returning to America from Taiwan. It was fun sharing stories and talking about going home; the two hours just flew by. It was a shame that none of us were seated together for the 13-hour flight, but I was able to get some sleep and watch a few movies.

24

COMING HOME

July 4, 2007 (USA time)

WE have arrived at the O'Hare Airport International Terminal, waiting to go through customs. We actually arrived earlier than when we departed, due to crossing the international dateline. For a while, we seemed to be at a standstill until, finally, the line started to move. The officials hardly looked at anything of mine, but, then again, I was wearing my Rotary blazer so proudly.

My parents had seen Veronica's parents at the terminal, so they knew that Veronica and I were on the same flight. For about an hour, we had a short reunion with our parents. We talked, hugged, took pictures, and exchanged pins and business cards. It was a fun time, but at the same time, sad, but the Youth Exchange Conference in Grand Rapids, held July 12th through July 15th, was only a few weeks away. I would be seeing everyone from Central States then.

We said our last goodbyes and started driving east. We were not headed to our home in Ottawa, Illinois, but to my Aunt Gail's cottage, located on Virginia's eastern shore. We didn't drive very far before stopping for lunch at Taco Bell. My $1.30 Crunchwrap Supreme tasted better than any gourmet meal that I could have envisioned; I had been dreaming about it for months.

Aunt Gail is my dad's sister. Her small cottage is located on Smith Beach, near the town of Cape Charles and just west of the town of Eastville. It has been a family tradition for years to get together for a family reunion during the Fourth of July. I had intentionally timed my return from Thailand so that I could enjoy a quick visit with family before heading for Grand Rapids.

I had a good time visiting with my aunts, uncles, grandparents, and cousins for an extended weekend. Then I was off to Michigan for the final event in my experience and the official end of my exchange year. On the way, we stopped at the college that I would be attending in the fall. My dad wanted to ask about the foreign language requirement, considering that I was now fluent in Thai, and he had a few other questions, as well. We were given another campus tour and stopped by to visit the dormitory room that would soon be mine.

July 12, 2007

Today we arrived at Calvin College in Grand Rapids, Michigan. After we registered, we walked to the car to unload our luggage. It had started to rain. Not the warm tropical rain of Thailand, but a cold, bone-chilling drizzle, typical of central Michigan. As I was shivering, I commented about how much I wanted to go home. Mom said, "Well, you'll be home in just a few days." I replied, "No, I mean home to Thailand." It was then that my parents first realized just how much I missed being in Thailand.

I left to put my stuff in my room and to see if any of the rebound students were here yet. My parents wanted to walk around, and we made plans to meet later for dinner. Soon, they met a group of rebounds, and Jennifer was among them. Dad commented to Mom, "She really *did* come home." A short time later, they saw Jennifer's dad. They chatted about what a great year the exchange was and a bit about how great the exchange program was in general. After some small talk, my dad asked if Jennifer was looking forward to college. Her dad said, "Well, yes, but Jennifer has been accepted at Webster University in Bangkok. She's going back to Thailand." Dad just said, "Oh, wow," but was actually thinking, "Way to go, Jennifer. You're really *not* coming home."

The days of the Grand Rapids youth conference flew by. It was such fun seeing the exchange students that I hadn't seen since the trip to southern Thailand, meeting the Thai inbounds, and, especially, speaking Thai. It was so special to be a rebound. I don't think many of us slept much that weekend. We had only a few meetings to attend because this event was more to prepare outbound students for the coming year.

The rebounds participated in a talent show, which had some really good performances. We also took part in a ceremony, during which we were introduced and allowed to walk out on stage and speak briefly about our experience. We shook the hands of some of the important people in Rotary who made our experiences possible. We exchanged pins and had our pictures taken more times than I can count. This is where the rebounds get to show off a bit, demonstrating just how much stuff can be attached to a Rotary blazer.

The country meeting was my favorite. Gathered together in one room were the Thai inbounds, the coming year's outbounds, and us rebounds. It was in this meeting last year that I had learned to *wai*. We had the opportunity to tell some of the many stories of our exchange experience and answer questions that the current outbound students had concerning Thailand. At one point in this meeting, we got on the subject of being called fat by Thai natives and how they seemed to be so obsessed with beauty. Thais are always thinking about how beautiful they are or are not. It was just after we had been discussing the cross-dressers; many of the young "women" gracing the streets of Bangkok are not female. Some of the cross-dressers are remarkably attractive. Many foreigners do not know that they are boys. I could distinguish by looking for an Adam's apple and muscular thighs, more typical of boys. Jeff told a story about when he and a group of Thai friends were walking in Bangkok, and one of the girls was commenting about how she wished that she were more attractive. As the group passed one of the cross-dressers, she exclaimed, "I wish I was beautiful like him!"

There was a lot of down time for the rebounds, but that was okay because we just wanted to hang out together. The session about reverse culture shock was very informative. I had been back for about two weeks and had not yet experienced much of it, but I had been traveling constantly, visiting grandparents and other members of my extended family and attending my family reunion. Little did I know that it would be a shocking experience to return to life here in America. I did not yet realize just how badly I would miss what I left behind in Thailand. I became so close to so many people. I may never see Sinwia and Nadia grow up, may never again hear Paw singing karaoke or watch Baa Thao cleaning the vegetables and talking to her about nothing at all. Leaving this was by far the most difficult aspect of my experience. During my whole exchange year, I was never unbearably homesick because, in the back of my mind, I knew that I had a plane ticket home, dated and waiting.

In the coming weeks, I would experience serious reverse culture shock. A psychologist spoke to us about this phenomenon during one of the sessions at Grand Rapids. During his talk, he asked if anyone had ever seen the arrow in the FedEx logo. Then, he showed us the logo and, sure enough, there was an arrow, right between the E and the X. He outlined it so that everyone would see where it was, shown in the negative space of the logo. Then, he showed the logo again, this time without the outline, and said, "Now, you cannot *not* see it." Everyone laughed, but it was true. He went on to state that most rebound exchange students would immediately notice things about their "new" surroundings that were not apparent to them before they went on youth exchange. How true!

All in all, Grand Rapids was a lot of fun but, at the same time, sad. It was nice meeting all of the people and especially nice seeing all of my friends again. My experience in Thailand had really changed my life. Now, when I open my eyes, I view the world differently. This experience enabled me to really develop into the young adult that I have become. I had such a wonderful exchange year that I didn't want it to end. The schedule for the youth exchange conference had changed little from the previous year; yet, it was far different for me. My two perspectives, as an outbound versus that of a rebound, made the two experiences quite different. This time there was no need to worry about travel plans, what to pack, and what to learn about the host country. Now was a time to savor the last few hours of the most wonderful year of my life.

While driving back to Illinois from Grand Rapids, I remembered the year earlier when I was an outbound, being so envious of all the rebounds. I was such an idiot; I would give anything to be an outbound again.

25

THE NEXT PHASE OF MY LIFE

—❦—

July 16, 2007

LAST night we arrived at our home in Ottawa, Illinois, and, for the first time in almost a year, I slept in my own bed. We were all tired from the traveling during the past several weeks. My dog was glad to see me. My Christmas tree was still up in my room, and my presents still under it; we had Christmas in July! I would spend the next few weeks getting ready for college. Because so many people in Ottawa knew about and were excited about my exchange year, I had many requests for speaking engagements. I think there were about a dozen requests, including four Rotary clubs, a Kiwanis club, our church, my dad's workplace, and several elementary schools. Even though I was really missing being in Thailand, I was busying myself with getting ready for the move to college, but there were times when the homesickness got the best of me. The weeks went by quickly.

Cara, who was to be my college roommate, wrote me on Facebook: "Ummm, I'm kinda confused. It says on my college information sheet that you are from Illinois, but on your Facebook it says Thailand. Are you like in Thailand now or were you in Thailand? Are you an exchange student or a transfer student? Are you 20? Are you going to be a freshman?" I think that we are going to get along just fine. I'm anxious to talk with her, now that I'm back in the USA.

When I look back at my exchange experience, I recall a mix of emotions. I have a warm spot in my heart and, at the same time, tears in my eyes. I learned so much by simply being exposed to a very different world. The confidence I now exude has better prepared me for the future. As I have matured during the past year, it became evident to me that not all of my exchange student friends tried to make the most of their experiences. Some acted as though they were on a year-long vacation. To some, each "D" rule seemed to be viewed as a challenge to see how often it could be broken. Those students did not work to learn the language or culture and seemed to not care that their actions and behavior disappointed their host families and Rotary clubs. The Thai people are wonderful, and some of the exchange students never became involved enough to learn that. Thais are also very proud people, both of themselves and their race. I completely understand why they refer to Westerners as *farang*s. I was also mindful that I was viewed as a young ambassador from America and that my conduct must be appropriate at all times. Those who looked for every opportunity to party or go out to clubs did not realize just how much they were limiting the value of their exchange. I made the most of it and have no regrets.

I recall that during the application process, Bill, my YEO, was wonderful to work with. He and Dad worked very hard to perfect my application. I remember that Dad became so frustrated at having to return to the doctor's office four times, only because the forms were not signed in blue ink. All of the Marseilles Rotarians were very good to me. They took me to the Auto Show in Chicago, to a Rotary Youth Leadership weekend camping event, and extended an open invitation to all of their Rotary meetings and events. They would often write comments on my blog while I was overseas. They are wonderful.

I think I will never have a year that will be as power-packed as this past year has been. I started off by intending to do my best to learn the Thai language and culture, not knowing that so much more would happen to me. I have grown and matured in so many ways. I have gained confidence in myself and in my skills and abilities. I am a more responsible person and am better prepared to enter college. I am confident that I have sharpened my ability to adapt to any situation. I didn't think that I would like returning to life as I knew it prior to my exchange year. It is difficult for anyone to understand that I was not nearly as homesick in Thailand as I am now, in America.

Of the many lessons learned during the year, I put three of them above all others. While my focus at the beginning was to learn a new language and a different culture, I now reflect from a different viewpoint.

1. Accept others for who they are and be sensitive to others to gain their acceptance.
2. Try new things, no matter how strange or different, and encourage others to try things that are new to them.
3. Be mindful that this is truly a cultural exchange; be sure to share as well as learn.

It is strange that when I am alone, reflecting on my experience, the happy feelings return. When I speak Thai or dream in Thai, it makes me feel really good and happy inside. It is when I try to talk about my experience that the sad feelings return.

September 4, 2007

So, now I am a freshman at Washington & Jefferson College. W&J is a small, liberal arts college located in southwestern Pennsylvania. The town of Washington, with a population of a little more than 16,000, is about 20 miles southwest of the city of Pittsburgh. My parents and I had made several excursions around the country after my sophomore and junior years of high school, visiting many colleges. I was in the final stages of the selection process when life became a whirlwind for a year. W&J was very considerate, allowing my acceptance to be deferred for a year so that I could go on youth exchange. Although the college is a nine-hour drive from my home in Ottawa, it can't be that bad, considering that I had just returned from, literally, the other side of the world. I was still unsure about my concentration of study. I had considered International Business

Studies but would eventually choose to double major in Business Administration and Psychology. My choice for a foreign language was Chinese, which I would later find to be extremely easy, probably due to having already learned an Asian language.

After only a few days here, I have already made lots of new friends. It is easy to meet people on a small campus. One friend, after learning that I had been on Rotary Youth Exchange, asked, "How did it feel being a foreigner for a whole year?" I answered that it wasn't that bad, that I did my best to learn their language and culture and to adjust to the country as quickly as possible. As I vocalized those words, I once again felt the homesickness returning. I quickly turned away. I didn't want her to see the tears welling up in my eyes.

The truth is that I have returned to an America that seems so different from the America that I left just a year ago. I have not yet learned how to fit in here. I actually feel more like a foreigner now than I did in Thailand. The psychologist at Grand Rapids was definitely right. I am seeing the arrow in FedEx. Oh, how I miss Thailand. I miss my family. I miss my friends. I want to go home so badly. I feel that I will be forever *farang*.

Nevertheless, I will adapt to this new and different world. I know that I can. After all, I've had plenty of practice.

Ah! Look at the time. Just 10 minutes to get to class. *Sa-wat-dee, ka.*

About the Author

ASHLEY Krepps, from Ottawa, Illinois, traveled to Nakhon Phanom, Thailand in August, 2006, as part of the Rotary Youth Exchange program. She returned home in July, 2007. This book is her journal from her time in Thailand. After returning to America, she started her college career at Washington & Jefferson College. She graduated in May, 2011, with degrees in Business Administration and Psychology. Ashley is now living in Columbia, Maryland. Visit her Web site at www.foreverfarang.com.